THE
TEMPLE
OF
HIGH MAGIC

"*The Temple of High Magic* was described in 'Wiccan Rede, Beltane 2007' as an 'impressive book written by a lady who has earned respect as an expert in the field of esotericism and mystery traditions in the Netherlands.' This book, now available in English, will impress English-speaking readers by its compactness and clarity. Dealing with a large range of subjects regarding the Western Mysteries, Ina has also included Pathworkings/guided visualizations and rituals making this not only a compendium but also a practical workbook. Highly recommended for everyone who is interested in (modern) Mystery religions."

MORGANA, COFOUNDER OF *SILVER CIRCLE MAGAZINE* AND COORDINATOR OF THE 2009 PAGAN FEDERATION INTERNATIONAL

"This book will undoubtedly be regarded as the defining text for a solid basis in ceremonial magic. It offers a thorough explanation of what it really takes to open and enrich yourself with inner work. It is loaded with background information, methods, and techniques you can immediately use to practice. Ina Cüsters-van Bergen explains how you can reach a new and much higher level. She gives the answer of how to structure your magical practice so that you get the full benefit of your efforts. I fully endorse this book and the teaching it offers."

GARDENSTONE, AUTHOR OF *GERMANISCHE MAGIE* [GERMANIC MAGIC]

THE
TEMPLE
OF
HIGH MAGIC

Hermetic Initiations in the
Western Mystery Tradition

INA CÜSTERS-VAN BERGEN

Destiny Books
Rochester, Vermont • Toronto, Canada

Destiny Books
One Park Street
Rochester, Vermont 05767
www.DestinyBooks.com

Destiny Books is a division of Inner Traditions International

Orignally published in Dutch under the title *De weg naar de oude mysteriën* by Uitgeverij
    Akasha, Eeserveen, The Netherlands / Ina Cüsters-van Bergen, Rotterdam, The
    Netherlands
First U.S. edition published in 2010 by Destiny Books

Library of Congress Cataloging-in-Publication Data

Cüsters-van Bergen, Ina.
  The temple of high magic : hermetic initiations in the western mystery tradition /
Ina Cüsters-van Bergen. — 1st U.S. ed.
    p. cm.
  Includes bibliographical references and index.
  Summary: "A practical guide to pathworking and other esoteric techniques from the
ancient mystery schools predating Christianity"—Provided by publisher.
  ISBN 978-1-59477-308-2
  1. Magic. 2. Occultism. I. Title.
  BF1611.C87 2010
  135'.4—dc22

                                                                          2009037889

Printed and bound in the United States by Lake Book Manufacturing

10 9 8 7 6 5 4 3 2 1

Text design and layout by Virginia Scott Bowman
This book was typeset in Garamond Premiere Pro with Trajan Pro, Gill Sans, and Swiss
used as display typefaces

To send correspondence to the author of this book, mail a first-class letter to the author c/o
Inner Traditions • Bear & Company, One Park Street, Rochester, VT 05767, and we will
forward the communication.

I want to dedicate this work to the Rose, the symbol of the sacred tradition of the West and its human helpers:

Dion Fortune,
the Lady with the Roses. She has left a treasure of books, and she has been a source of inspiration during my own magical education. She was the teacher of my teachers.

Ernest Butler,
the White Rose who worked further to spread the sacred knowledge, and who made it accessible to those who searched for it.

Dolores Ashcroft-Nowicki,
who taught me the beauty of the tradition. She laid down the Rose of Sharon at the foundation of my training. She is the Mother of my Heart.

Further, I want to thank my inner Contacts, who are a source of constant inspiration on my road.

I want to thank the people who were willing to support me— my husband, Paul; my friends on the road, Elodie Hunting and Jack van Eijk; Annie Draaijer for making the beautiful picture for the front cover; Jan Gilham for proofreading; and Anneke Huijser for coaching me.

Everything in this book is true
On its own level of reality

For more information and courses concerning the Western Mystery Tradition, you can contact The Hermetic Order of the Temple of Starlight, where Ina Cüsters-van Bergen is the Director of Studies.

www.templeofstarlight.eu
info@templeofstarlight.eu

CONTENTS

FOREWORD

The road to spiritual wisdom through the Western Mystery Tradition is an old one and it is a long one, hallowed by time and proven by the footsteps of all who have trodden it before us. Yet it is also a very modern one, for it perpetually renews itself in each generation, as one line of adepti passes on the practical applications to the next, and there will always be different levels of interpretation and forms of emphasis applicable to the circumstances of aspirants in an ever-changing world.

Thus it was when I first came upon the work of Dion Fortune, who inspired me to follow in her footsteps and to study in her school, the Society of the Inner Light, just as she in turn had studied at the feet of her teachers, whose line extended back into and beyond the Hermetic Order of the Golden Dawn and into lesser known reaches of esoteric Masonry represented by Theodore Moriarty. Thus it was when I teamed up with the grand old adept Ernest Butler and encouraged him to write the basic material for what was to become another major esoteric school, the Servants of the Light, with worldwide ramifications under the tutelage of Dolores Ashcroft-Nowicki.

Now, in a further turn of the spiral path, I have the pleasure of witnessing the work of Ina Cüsters-van Bergen, which develops linearly from all that has gone before. She presents for the twenty-first century the age-old principles of the Western esoteric tradition, based upon the Tree of Life and the practicalities of its various Triangles of Art, from cosmic principles through ethical responsibility to the basic symbols and rituals of empowerment in the outer world. May her work prove a guide to your aspiration and a lantern to your feet.

There is a blessing on all who serve.

GARETH KNIGHT

Gareth Knight has spent a lifetime unearthing and teaching the principles of magic as a spiritual discipline and method of self-realization. He was trained in the esoteric school founded by Dion Fortune and has been actively involved in the Western magical tradition since the early 1960s. He is the author of thirty books, including *Tarot and Magic, A Practical Guide to Qabalistic Symbolism,* and *Magic and the Power of the Goddess.*

INTRODUCTION

THE IMPORTANCE OF THE WESTERN MYSTERY
TRADITION IN OUR MODERN TIME

Our modern society is developing a growing global character. The economies of the different parts of the world have become more and more interdependent, and people of different cultures are living in the same streets and attending the same schools. The worldview of our modern society leans heavily on science. Science offers a mechanistic view of reality and does not meet the needs of the soul. The economical worldview we are surrounded by is actually monotheistic; it knows only one god, and he is called Money. This god thinks only in terms of debit and credit and has no regard for morality and ethics.

One of the reasons for the secularization of our society is that people are very conscious about the danger of surrendering to a church. Also, monotheistic religions have difficulty respecting each other's gods. Political figures and media personalities are hardly role models when it comes to developing a sound moral identity.

Within a society that is so far secularized, the matrix of goodness is not an automatic part of education and upbringing. It is this matrix of goodness that allows us to interact harmoniously with each other, within ethical and moral codes, and to respect each other's disparate views on divinity. The Western Mystery Tradition provides access to spiritual models and practices that go back deep into the history of humanity. These can be translated into our modern society and have proven their worth based on the examples they have offered throughout the ages.

The classical world provides many examples of how a multicultural society can live together harmoniously by using mythological systems. This classical mythology forms an interconnected system of ethics that is not based on sin and the Fall. Rather, it is rooted within the human measures of vices and virtues, which have determined human society since the dawn of history, and allows for individual choices based on individual wisdom.

AN UNKNOWN TRADITION

While bookshops are stocked full with esoteric literature from all the countries of the world, the Western Mystery Tradition is still relatively unknown. This is, of course, peculiar, especially as this spiritual tradition forms the red thread* of the Western gnostic traditions and of the hermetic tradition.

It was only a matter of time before the Western Mystery Tradition would be rediscovered by modern society. The fact that a book such as *The Da Vinci Code* became so popular is a sign of the awakening longing for this knowledge. As soon as a part of the veil is lifted, the Western Mystery Tradition causes strong emotions to surface. It is a treasure house of esoteric knowledge, guarded by occult orders. Stories are told of the classical societies still protecting hidden keys to old mystical knowledge. This knowledge is accessible to everyone, if they know where to find the key. The problem is not that we do not have a Western esoteric tradition, but that this tradition has so many aspects that, for a beginner, it is difficult to get a grip on the material.

The Western Mystery Tradition is part of the landscape of spiritual

---

*The "red thread" is an important symbol in ancient mythology. It symbolizes the experience of life itself and especially the physical and spiritual bloodline to the wisdom of the ancestors. It is very prominent in Minoean mythology in which the daughter of King Minos gives Theseus the red thread when he enters into the labyrinth. The labyrinth is not only an ancient maze but also a metaphor for life itself.

movements. It is a road toward spiritual development based mainly on pre-Christian religions, combining the esoteric wisdom of classical hermetical scriptures, pre-Christian texts, classical mythology, translated text from cultures that have disappeared, and the Kabbalah. The road moves like a red thread through Western culture, always resonating in the background. The Western Mystery Tradition is an old tradition that has been adapted by every generation to fit into the spirit of the current time. This is a sign of a living tradition. The Western Mystery Tradition is an interesting mix of Pagan, Christian, and Jewish ideas. During the last century, the tradition has also been influenced by Eastern mysticism and by ideas from the sciences.

This spiritual tradition has been passed for centuries by word of mouth from person to person, in secret orders. Initiations are also very important to passing down this knowledge. Even in this century, in which the New Age movement is an ambassador for openness, secrecy is still the core of the tradition, as the Mysteries cannot be explained through pure reason. The Mystery unfolds in the form of a meaningful message in silence. Initiates immediately understand this, as they know from experience that it is not possible to translate their journey into words or text.

The basics of the Western Mystery Tradition are formed by a philosophy that assumes a pattern exists in the creation of the universe, an all-connecting unity of material and the unseen forces of nature. From here, cosmic laws are discovered, and the relationship between spirit and matter is studied. At the same time, the philosophy studies the practical applications of these laws by means of spiritual techniques such as meditation, divination, alchemy, and spiritual magic.

GOAL AND STRUCTURE OF THIS BOOK

Through this book, I want to show you the beauty of high magic and of spiritual alchemy. Considering the gigantic scope of the subject, I cannot treat the different parts in depth. Because of this limitation, I focus on the mind-set the trainee should adopt while approaching each subject. It is a good habit within the Mystery schools to teach a subject by looking at it from different perspectives, so I include some of the theoretical and philosophical background for each topic, as well as their connections to each other. Then I provide practical exercises in the form of guided meditations, contemplations, and rituals. Within the Mystery tradition, practical exercises are always the most important part. It is by these methods that gnosis develops within the student.

Exercising the basic techniques is essential to a successful development in the Mysteries. Spiritual magic is an art, and you can only gain mastery over the arts when you exercise your talents. From the beginning, theory and practice are taught together. Every layer builds further on the previous one, which is the reason why it is important to work through this book in the right sequence.

In chapters 1 and 2, I provide an overview of the history of this tradition, where it comes from, and how it has developed.

In chapter 3, I explain the basic philosophy of the Western Mystery Tradition. This penetrates all thinking within the tradition, and is practiced in every magical act.

In chapters 4, 5, and 6, I explain how this philosophy is the basis of symbols and exercises used in temple rituals. With this we bridge the gap between the temple meditations and rituals and the ensouled reality that surrounds us.

Chapter 7 explains the basic exercises. In this section I present a few fundamental exercises for individuals and groups. These basic techniques will be used from this point on, preceding all exercises to generate energy to enhance the results of the subsequent exercises.

From chapter 8 on I introduce you to the Magical Kabbalah, starting with the divine triangle. I teach you about the Sephiroth, the divine emanations. I have emphasized the practical side of the method, so that you learn to how to apply the theoretical model.

In chapter 9 we look at the Sephiroth, which form and feed our ethical consciousness. The Ethical Triangle, which is the matrix for harmony, health, and goodness, is presented here.

In chapter 10, I teach you the magical triangle, the Sephiroth, which cause manifestation of the divine energies.

In chapter 11, I explain to you the importance and the place of the earth in the magical world. Without roots in the earth, all knowledge is just a theoretical model. The Western Mystery Tradition is rooted in the earth.

Chapter 12 is the conclusion. In this chapter I will show you further horizons for development.

In this book I hope to give you an overview of the richness of the road of spiritual development through applied magic. I hope that, by writing as much as possible from a practical viewpoint, I can give you an impression of the splendor that spiritual magic can add to your life.

1

THE WESTERN MYSTERY TRADITION

Until about 1937, knowledge about the Western Mystery Tradition, and about spiritual magic, was not freely available. Then, Israel Regardie published the material of the Order of the Golden Dawn. When these internal documents became available to the outside world, the connection between mythology, Kabbalah, and spiritual magic reached a broader public. The Order of the Golden Dawn was a magical order, an initiating magical school. This school gathered together an enormous curriculum of material that is still used by modern magical schools. Much of this material became widespread without people knowing that it came from spiritual magic. The Rider-Waite Tarot, which is still a standard for modern variations on the tarot, was developed by initiates of the Golden Dawn.

MAGIC OF ALL SORTS AND COLORS

Magic is the red thread of the Western Mystery Tradition; however, the word still raises eyebrows. Among the different types of magic is sorcery.

Initiates in the Mysteries call this low magic. We make an important distinction between so-called low magic and high ceremonial magic and spiritual alchemy. These last two systems together are called spiritual magic. The Western Mystery Tradition does not take a lot of interest in sorcery, but concentrates mainly on spiritual magic.

It's important that I explain a few terms:

> *Low magic* is the word for sorcery. It is the type of magic people refer to most commonly.
>
> *High magic* is the term for magical techniques that are used to serve in spiritual development. These techniques are, for example, meditation, contemplation, prayer, and ritual.
>
> *Spiritual alchemy* refers to the most exalted form of high magic, which comes very close to mysticism. Spiritual magic is a combination of high magic and spiritual alchemy.
>
> *Ritual magic* is also called ceremonial magic. This is the name for the *form* in which high magic is practiced: through a very precisely choreographed ceremony. The rituals are atmospherically similar to, and in structure comparable with, a Christian High Mass. All the words, all the movements, all the regalia used, carefully follow written instructions.

WHAT EXACTLY IS MAGICAL POWER?

The goal of spiritual magic is to create unity between the magician and divinity. Spiritual magic, a system of esoteric development, is also called yoga of the West. Contrary to the immediate association that most people make with witchcraft, sorcery, and Harry Potter's Hogwarts, spiritual magic has not much overlap with sorcery.

High magic and spiritual alchemy are concerned with the study of the nature of magical power. Magical power manifests from harnessing divine creative energy, and working with this energy produces different results depending on the method and the technique that you use.

This divine energy is called qi or prana in Eastern systems, and the Judeo-Christian tradition calls it manna, while the Western Mystery Tradition calls it Magical power. Through the fantastic imagination of Hollywood, these words have generated totally different associations in the general public.

Hollywood aside, practicing spiritual magic is not a flight from reality. Spiritual magic renders normal, everyday experiences more meaningful and brings an extra dimension to mundane life. It adds a spiritual depth to your existence. You gain access to a sacred reality, which reveals itself to you slowly.

WHAT ARE MYSTERIES?

THE SCIENCE OF THE SACRED

Magic fuels all the religions: Christianity, Judaism, Buddhism, Hinduism, and Islam are all rooted in magical principles. Spiritual magic studies the natural laws of sacredness. Within every religion you find a curriculum of magical acts that lifts normal tools up to the level of sacred regalia. Every religion has an interconnected system of mythological stories and actions that relate the central message of the religion. This central message is empowered by ceremonial actions.

Within every religious tradition is an interconnected system of spiritual exercises that trains initiates to generate transcendental experiences. Spiritual magic studies these systems from different traditions, compares them, tries to find out what causes techniques to be fruitful, and what the underlying mechanism is.

THE WISDOM OF THE ANCIENTS

After practitioners of spiritual magic have researched and compared the mechanisms of the different traditions, they apply what they've learned to the practice of rituals and meditation exercises. Out of this practice arose the important rediscovery of the traditions of pre-Christian religions, which did not survive in a Christian society. These old religions are based on mythological stories, which we have inherited, and on the timeless aspect of spiritual magic. Low magic—sorcery—was mainly practiced by the common people, whereas the rituals of the temples were practiced by the priesthood and the higher classes of the ancient cultures.

Inevitably, wisdom from the temples leaked through to the common people. Since classical times it was a well-known phenomenon that common people used aspects of this wisdom to ease the difficulties of everyday life (or: if you had a row with your neighbor, to increase his problems!). As in our present time, healers use certain psalms and passages of the Bible, and this was also common practice in classical times.

These applications of temple wisdom by the shamans of the people form the basics of sorcery.

The Western Mystery Tradition does not encourage a regular use of sorcery. When you lose too much energy from your spiritual development in practicing sorcery, you cannot make the jump to the higher Mysteries. Your focus on low magic causes you to lose perspective and grasp of the higher levels. Sorcery can be useful in isolated cases to lift a big stone on the path of spiritual development out of the way, but it is not a goal in itself.

WHAT EXACTLY ARE MYSTERIES?

I am asked this question frequently when I try to explain the core of the Western Mystery Tradition in more concrete terms; "Mystery" sounds so mysterious!

I try to explain that the reason why the Mystery tradition is so named is because it *is* mysterious. The Mysteries did not develop their reputation of being mysterious without reason. Rather than giving a "textbook" definition of the word, I will instead describe different aspects of the phenomenon that is "Mysteries."

A spiritual realization is an important result of mysticism. Through the Eastern religions, we know that certain spiritual realizations can break through when you have your thinking under control. This is the goal of the training through Zen koans.

A Mystery unfolds when the mind penetrates into deeper layers of consciousness. The rational mind is stopped by using a paradox. This sort of paradox is not created by linguistics, but by internal images that rise through the use of symbols. The Mystery can only be solved by using other layers of consciousness. Thinking, studying, and rationalizing will not bring you into the experience of a Mystery. The language that is used to express the Mystery is symbolic language. Symbols are interconnected in a deliberate way, and this creates a so-called arcanum. The plural of arcanum is arcana. You probably already know the word from the tarot—the great arcana and the small arcana.

An arcanum is a series of symbols that are interconnected consciously.

When the arcanum reveals its inner meaning, the magical, mental, psychic, and moral consciousness of a person is disclosed. When this happens, the person feels a rush of spiritual energy going through his or her system. At the same time, a person will experience a series of peak experiences.

A series of arcana together form a Mystery. These Mysteries cannot be understood on an intellectual level. By means of paradoxes, which block thinking, the spirit is stimulated to open up the part of the consciousness that gives access to a divine-ensouled reality. A Mystery that unfolds will always be accompanied by a strong flow of magical power, which comes freely. Suddenly another part of reality will open itself to you. Mysteries are multilayered, and they will open up over the years in progressively deeper levels.

Without words, in silence, meaningfully, and with a depth and a beauty that is indescribable, a breakthrough happens within your mind. It is commonly called a peak experience. The result is a change in your consciousness, which gives you a totally new view on your life and your circumstances. You also access a series of new realizations, which can be applied to all kinds of different areas in your life. This extra energy causes an explosion of feelings in your heart chakra, and the sense of an awakening of the soul. It is an extremely strong experience; your life seems divine and ensouled. The breakthrough permanently changes your perspective. At the same time you need to process these new insights and apply them in your daily life.

Mysteries were, in classical times, often hidden in mythological stories. They were performed as Mystery dramas for the people. Within the temples the Mystery plays were enacted on a deeper level. Our modern theater originates from the Mystery play. Also, well-known rituals such as the Eucharist Mass and Rites of Passage—such as baptism and marriage—come from the ancient Mystery Tradition.

FANTASY AND I-MAGI-NATION

Spiritual magic uses the instrument of fantasy. The mundane world is connected with the inner kingdoms by means of the i-magi-nation. In this way you create the possibility of experiencing the extraordinary—divinity—in the everyday world. Gradually you develop a new means of experiencing reality. You can train yourself to use intuition, as well as to develop antennae for psychic activity. You gradually start to develop a sixth sense for psychic waves, which always announce events that will express themselves in the world at a later time.

THE KABBALAH

Within modern Mystery schools, the Kabbalistic Tree of Life forms the red thread of the tradition. The Kabbalistic Tree has a unique quality. First of all, it forms the magical and mystical foundation stone within the Jewish esoteric tradition. On top of this, it has the quality of incorporating other esoteric and mythological systems within itself without losing its uniqueness. The Kabbalistic Tree of Life is a map for the inner worlds and shows how they are connected.

The Kabbalistic Tree of Life has the capacity to take in philosophical models that describe the structure of the universe, explain them, unite them, and expand upon them. Because of these characteristics, it is possible to compare different esoteric traditions. Judaism, Christianity, Witchcraft, the Orphic tradition, the Minoan tradition, the Egyptian tradition, the Mesopotamian tradition, the Zoroastric Avesta, the Mithras tradition, the Grail tradition, the Celtic tradition, astrology, alchemy, the angelic lore, and others all fit into the model of the Tree of Life and assume their places without conflict, next to each other, in this model of the divine universe. In addition, the Kabbalistic Tree of Life offers a systematic route of indepth training that makes it possible to penetrate the deeper hidden layers of these systems. The road takes you to the highest mystical inner worlds.

In the renaissance, magicians discovered that the Kabbalistic Tree of Life could be effortlessly integrated with Western occult laws, and in this way the Tree developed into an effective model for an integrated system of spiritual development. The Tree offers a systematic route of training with an unequaled depth. The road takes you to the highest mystical inner worlds.

Thus the Kabbalistic Tree of Life has earned its place within the Western Mystery Tradition.

MEET YOUR HOLY GUARDIAN ANGEL

The Western Mystery Tradition offers models on how to deepen wisdom and spirituality and how each of us can exercise this in our individual lives. The Western Mystery Tradition develops gnosis in its practitioners; knowledge and insight that come forth from our own experiences within an ensouled divine reality. Gnosis is based on inner experience, and not on fate. In order to get to this point, you need to detach yourself from your ego. Your personality becomes a working tool. Your connection with yourself changes into a connection with your Self. You transform and change perspective. Instead of working with your personality, your individuality becomes the central core. Now you can make a conscious contact with the divine spark. This is called the meeting with the holy guardian angel.

The Mystery schools teach a practical system of exercises, by which gnosis can be acquired and deepened. You will experience the divine source underlying material reality that surrounds every one of us. The initiate sees material reality as an expression of divine force fields and thinks of it as the tides in the Cosmic Ocean of consciousness.

2
BACK TO THE ROOTS

WHY THIS BOOK?

When it was proposed that I should write a book about spiritual magic, I first thought about what I would like to accomplish with such a book. There has been a great deal published about the Magical Kabbalah. Although I often work with the Kabbalistic Tree of Life, I would not call myself a Kabbalist; I am a magister. Books about the Magical Kabbalah give extensive tables of correspondences. I notice that many people get blocked because of this, because they do not understand how they can apply the corresponding symbols in their practice. Because of this, the Magical Kabbalah appears to them to be mainly an intellectual challenge. This is a misunderstanding. The Magical Kabbalah is a rich world full of inner experiences. The tables of correspondences are nothing more than the names of roads on a map. The beauty of the road is experienced when the journey is made in actual fact. In this book, the tables of correspondences are in the appendices.

THEORY AND PRAXIS

When working with the Mystery Tradition, it is a pitfall to only regard the Kabbalistic Tree as a theoretical model. The theoretical model aspect is important to explain the nature of reality, but ultimately the model is just a simplification of a true, existant reality. The Tree is more than just a symbol—it is a memory castle wherein the reality, which it symbolizes, is locked. I want to dissuade readers from viewing the Tree from only a theoretical standpoint, but rather to view it as symbolic of a living reality.

From this standpoint, I coach ceremonial magicians to become initiates. Magicians are very practical people—doers—not people who sit in their easy chairs and absorb knowledge on a theoretical level, then discuss it intelligently at parties. Discussions are, of course, part of the fun, but winning an intellectual duel does not make one a successful magician. An initiate is somebody who is able to let his or her soul fly. Initiates are capable of transferring this experience to others, so that new students start on this journey for themselves.

Throughout the book, I switch between theory and praxis to give you, as a reader, the opportunity to apply, on a personal level, the spiritual magic you've learned. The guided visualizations and rituals provide you with an inside view of the practice of spiritual magic. And in doing them you avoid the pitfall of theoretical hairsplitting.

THE MAGICAL WORLDVIEW

Spiritual magic is a road to enlightenment. It is a complete and in-depth esoteric tradition. The magician observes and studies the mechanisms that form the basic structure behind the materialization of reality. A magician assumes that consciousness has different "wavelengths." These wavelengths of consciousness behave like radio frequencies. These "broadcasting companies" are the expression of the intelligences that we call the gods: they are the biblical Elohim. These gods, or expressions of consciousness, determine the events on our planet. They exist in us and outside us.

They determine the life of people on a personal level, on a group level, on the level of nations, and on the level of the spirit of the time.

WHAT DOES A MAGICIAN DO?

The training of a magician starts with gaining insight into a reality that is very different in structure than that which our society accepts. You train yourself to experience this different reality by means of spiritual exercises. These exercises include meditation, prayer, contemplation, and shamanistic and ritual techniques. In addition to this, you learn to recognize the effects of your own actions and beliefs on yourself and on your environment and to gain control over them. In order to do this, the development of self-knowledge is of crucial importance.

You can compare your spiritual development with psychology, which studies human behavior. The psychologist is an observer. At the same time he is a part of the system that he observes. This same principle is also true for the magician. He studies the psychic atmosphere, and at the same time he is a part of it, and subject to it. On top of this, he then tries to influence it by working with the natural laws that are active at this level.

WHAT DOES MAGICAL TRAINING LOOK LIKE?

The training of a novice starts with developing self-knowledge. When you have developed a more or less realistic view of who you are, and what your role is in the events of which you are a part, then you can study the tides of consciousness around you.

Slowly you develop a worldview wherein the psyche and the needs of humans play a part, amid other psychic forces. Magicians look at the universe as an interconnected network of consciousness. The universe is seen as an interrelated organism that sends waves of forces and of thoughts through its entire structure. These waves spread as small vibrations and penetrate all the different particles.

The Universe as a Network

You can compare the nature of universal consciousness with the effects of a stone thrown into a pool of water. When a stone hits the water's surface, concentric circles of waves form, surrounding the point of impact. These ripples move to the shores of the pool. When the shores are reached, the energy bounces back toward the center of the pool. We are all a part of the shores of this pool. We are touched by the waves of the universe, and we react to them.

The magician trains himself to observe these movements. The sensitivity of the magician to these waves increases during the training. Because of this, a magician will regularly come to crossroads in his spiritual development. First you register the waves, then you start to work on your reaction to this movement. When you have understood certain basic principles, spiritual tests will follow. These tests develop in a totally natural way on the road of magical development. The test is to determine whether the ground whereon one is standing is solid enough on magical, ethical, and spiritual levels. When the magician passes the test, a new area of consciousness opens up for him. In this way a magician slowly penetrates into the knowledge of the laws of the universe of consciousness.

Techniques

A magician trains to develop his skills of observation by means of spiritual techniques. In this book I will introduce you to several of these techniques, and to the philosophical background of each, without having the illusion of being complete. The road is so incredibly rich that a summary of the possibilities that magic offers would require the proportions of a large encyclopedia. In fact; every chapter can easily be the summary of what could be a book in its own right.

I will likely cover techniques and subjects that you have learned about in a different venue, such as the world of the gods, the angelic lore, and the tarot. In these cases you will learn that the magical interpretation always takes you a few steps further into the material. Now you learn to use these tools as parts of a whole. The interconnecting structure makes all the different parts clearer and more accessible.

In other places you might find techniques that are not common knowledge, such as working with thoughtforms, complex rituals, and astral doorways.

Tests

During the process of magical development you are constantly tested. The tests start immediately at the beginning of this path. From the moment you decide to work with magic, you will likely notice increased upheaval in your environment. The natural way things happen in your life will start to change. When you begin to practice magic, your view of reality will slowly transform. You will get a feeling for deeper layers of consciousness, and you will start to consider those wavelengths in your choices. This will change your viewpoint drastically. Experiencing reality from a magical viewpoint is a gradual process. A solid training will slowly introduce you to this way of observation so that you can integrate it into your normal life.

PATHWORKING

WHAT IS PATHWORKING?

Throughout this book you will find special kinds of guided visualizations. These are so-called pathworkings. The name is based on the paths that are drawn on the Kabbalistic Tree of Life. Pathworking brings you into resonance with a specific wavelength of consciousness on the Tree of Life.

A pathworking exercise is different from a normal guided visualization. The images of pathworking are chosen very carefully because they generate specific effects. This clarifies the second part of the word *pathworking*. The exercise works on the deeper levels of consciousness and will generate work for you. Pathworking gently shakes up your subconscious mind. This causes you to change, and as a result, things in your environment will change: the paths work and generate work for you.

You can read your pathworking like a story. You can also record the story on a recorder. Afterward you can enter into a meditative state and experience the pathworking. You can also read the pathworking for a group entering into meditation.

A more advanced method is to read the story and to store the important scenes and events in your memory. Then you enter into meditation, and by means of concentration you build the scenes before your inner eye. You keep following the story line. This last method works very well if you are used to concentrating on images during your meditations. Guided visualizations and working with the paths train your third eye.

Sometimes the term *third eye* causes confusion. Training the third eye develops the power of your imagination. This helps you to see the inner images consciously, which we all have the potential to do. You can increase your ability to see them more sharply and to construct images yourself. Working with the third eye sharpens inner sight.

During pathworking you not only use your third eye, but all your extra senses. In your fantasy you see, smell, touch, hear, and taste. Also, when you repeat a pathworking exercise, the images become more detailed. You will get more benefit out of the images by repeating the meditations.

The pathworking material in this book is not chosen at random. They are stories with images that are very carefully chosen. The images have been used in our culture for centuries—accidentally and deliberately—in fairy tales and folk stories, in myths, and in everyday conversation. These images have specific effects on the inner world.

Pathworking can be compared to listening to a beautiful piece of music or looking at a beautiful movie. At the moment that you project yourself inside the story, your emotions and feelings will interact with the story. These movements of the inner world have the goal of stimulating certain processes of consciousness. That is the difference between guided fantasies and pathworking.

In most of the magic literature, these two concepts are mixed up. Many writers call every mythical story experienced from a meditative state of mind pathworking. Working on the paths, however, is an advanced form of meditation, and its goal is to generate specific effects. It is a technique that should be practiced systematically to foster a stable development. This form of meditation is specific to spiritual magic and affects the daily life of people. This meditation method is practiced with the symbols that are classically connected to the Sephiroth and the paths of the Kabbalistic Tree of Life.

THE GATEWAY TO THE UNIVERSE— PATHWORKING

Relax and enter into a meditative mood. Before your inner eye you visualize a beautiful landscape of a wood in which you walk. Look around you. In your imagination you see a winding path through the wood that brings you into the lower regions. Hear in your thoughts the sound of singing birds around you. The weather is comfortable, and you walk here on a day in late summer.

Make yourself ready for a long walk. You wear a rucksack filled with food and drink for a long journey. The landscape is green, and you smell the spicy smell of summer. While you walk, you catch the smell of the flowers that surround you. The warmth is deep and dry. While you walk you feel the threads of a spider's web touching your face. The sun gives the landscape a golden glow, and your mood is light and appreciative. You hear the sound of insects buzzing around you.

Walk downward along the forest path, following the winding way over the dusty trail. The path brings you to a part of the wood that is in a deep depression. The sun is sinking, and you enter into a twilight zone. You notice that you are tired from the long walk and decide to take a short break. You put your rucksack against a tree. You eat and drink something. Once you lay yourself down in the long grass, you feel a lovely tiredness coming over you. When you look at the tops of the trees, you see to your amazement the feathers of birds whirling downward. Very slowly they float down on the wind. In your ear you hear the whispering voice of the wind and catch the words:

> *Sink deep, sink deeper, sink deep into yourself*
> *Sink down in the primordial sleep of the earth.*
> *Travel with me on my voice,*
> *Sink into the timeless stories,*
> *Which float eternally from the source of Persephone.*

From a distance you see a light coming toward you. When it comes nearer, you see that it is a torch. The light is carried by a woman wearing Greek clothes. She waves and gestures to you to come with her. She walks deeper into the woods and brings you to a small lake, located before the entrance of a cave. In the meantime, the sun sinks and it is slowly getting darker. You see stars appearing in the night sky. Next to the entrance of the cave, you see two sycamore trees. The woman takes you into the cave, and with her torch she lights the wooden branches lying ready in the fireplace.

She sits down on a tripod. Next to her seat are two baskets. She spreads the contents of a bag, which she wears on a leather belt around her waist, out onto her lap. She gestures you to pay attention and to look into the dark water, to the scenes that form in the dark pool in front of the cave. The woman opens the baskets and when she does this, two dancing cobras rise from them. The woman takes a handful of herbs and throws them into the flames. You smell the scent of laurel leaves. The woman draws a scarf over her head; in this way she captures the smoke of the laurel leaves and inhales it. She breathes in deeply and lowers her arms. The cobras curl themselves around her arms and crawl upward. Around her head forms an image of moving light, which makes you think of a crown of moving snakes. While the sun sinks slowly, the two sycamore trees cast long shadows. Like long arms they stretch out over the landscape. The woman enters into a trance and recites in a monotone sound:

> Helios, Helios, Helios!
> I swallow you and transform you through my body.
> Travel through my body of night.
> Transform yourself in the deep.
> Be born again from my body of day.
> I am the snake holder:
> I connect Serpens Cauda with Serpens Caput.
> I open the ways, I open your mouth
> With the instrument that causes birth to the Gods.

While she recites this prayer, the sun goes down and seems to disappear in the cave behind the Pythia. At the moment that this happens, three roads become visible.

The Pythia speaks: "The first road is the road of the wisdom of nature. Clothed in beauty, she follows her own laws. This is the road toward the goddess of love. This road is intuitive and moves slowly upward in the tempo of the group mind of humanity.

"The second road is the road toward mastership over events. It is the road of the study of the thoughts of God. It is the road of the magician: he who studies the road and walks out before the crowd. He turns back before the end point is reached, and then tells those who follow that this road exists. He shows them the way. This road leads to the god of Wisdom. This road is steeper than the first one, and thus also quicker.

"The third road is the road of the middle. This is the road of the mystic. It is the road to the highest and leads over the path of the sacrificed god. It is the road to enlightenment. This road is extremely steep and takes you over bare rocks. It is the shortest way to get to the top. It is at the same time the most difficult of the three roads.

"These three roads are like my image. Snakes curl themselves around my body and cross over my waist. Each road carries the experiences of the other two within itself. At the end all roads become one again. They all lead to the same goal. Every seeker gradually becomes a magician. Every magician changes slowly into a mystic. You can choose which road you take to travel to the top of the mountain. When you have chosen one of the paths, there is no way back. Then you need to follow it, to the point where you get to the crossroads: the point where the snakes meet again."

The image of the Pythia lights up in the fire and then—very suddenly—all the flames extinguish. The scene has disappeared. Wondering, you look around you, and only see darkness. You rub your eyes, and slowly you come to your senses again under the tree in the wood. You conclude that you had a vision. Around you, mosquitoes dance on the rays of the sun, and you decide to eat your bread, and to drink something before you return to where you came from. You open your rucksack and take out the food. You want to take a bite from your bread, but at exactly this moment a big black bird comes down from above at an enormous speed. It takes your bread in its claws and flies off with it. Wondrous and hungry, you run after the big raven, in a hopeless attempt to get your bread back. You run after the bird and pass a sign. You run upward, up to the steep road. The bird takes its place on a branch of the tree, irritatingly high.

You come to your senses and think that it is of no use to go after the bread—the bird has touched it. You turn around, deciding to walk back to the place where your rucksack is. Then the raven starts to crow at you, as if he wants to tell you something. You walk back: the landscape does not change. When you walk the landscape appears to remain at the same point. You turn around and walk upward.

That is no problem at all. Without effort you walk the path. Then you try again: you turn around to go back to the starting point of your journey. Again the crazy phenomenon takes place: the landscape remains at the same point and you cannot walk back. Suddenly you realize that you passed the crossroads when you ran after your bread.

The raven sits in the tree and crows. Under the tree you see a marking stone. You wipe away the moss on the stone and read what is carved into it. There it says in clear letters:

Road to Mastership over Events
The Road of the Magician.

The letters of the marking stone get bigger; they become so big that they fill your entire view. Then they slowly become transparent. Behind the letters forms a landscape of your life: the place in your life where you are right now. In this way, the letters become engraved in the landscape of your daily life. Your life becomes the path of the magician. See how the letters slowly melt together with the environment where you are right now. And then come slowly back to the here and now.

THE HISTORY AND EVOLUTION OF THE MYSTERY TRADITION

THE ROOTS OF OUR CULTURE

Spiritual magic is really a lost tradition. I find it alarming to discover that the best way to explain spiritual magic is by using the terminology of Eastern philosophy: magic as "yoga of the West," magical force in terms of qi, the magical system as a whole in terms of kundalini. The words to describe the Western spiritual exercises have become loaded with negative connotations. Magic is regarded as creepy, as a pseudoreligion. Modern people who are interested in spirituality regard it as normal to do exercises from shamanic traditions from all over the world. When I tell them that we in the West have our own shamanic tradition, with unique exercises, they act surprised. For this reason I think that it is a good idea to make a short summary of the history of magic. Then it becomes clear where spiritual magic stands in the landscape of cultural development, and it is clear where the breaking points developed as well.

THE ATLANTIS MYTHOLOGY

The Greek philosopher Plato has left us two texts that have caused considerable discussion and speculation throughout history. They led to scientific and pseudoscientific investigations in the most unlikely directions. In the two texts, *Critias* and *Timaeus,* Plato tells a story that he heard from his own teacher, whose name was Solon. Solon heard the story from an Egyptian High Priest who worked in the temple dedicated to the goddess Neith.

This High Priest tells about the existence of a great civilization that went down in a gigantic natural disaster. The story of Atlantis is an important myth for Westerners, because it contains many themes and viewpoints directly or indirectly connected with the legacy of images of our cultural heritage. The question of whether Atlantis existed is of secondary importance for the tradition, because this myth can—like so many other myths—be read at different levels of meaning. The myth tells us about the Great Flood, about the survival of a few who escaped from the disaster by means of a boat they had built in advance.

Plato mentions the Greek names for the couple: Deukalion and Pyrrha. The entire story reminds us of the biblical story of Noah's Ark, about the flood myth from the *Gilgamesh Epic,* and of the creation mythology of Egypt, where a bird landed on the first mountain in the land after the Flood, which came forth from the Primordial Waters, called the Nun.

The goddess Neith, who is mentioned in Plato's story, is an entity who belongs to the oldest gods. The Greeks called these gods Titans. The primordial gods already existed in the times preceding the well-known pantheons. You meet them every time that primordial forces initiate a new development. The goddess Neith of Egypt represents the same energy as the Greek Athena, the Roman Minerva, the Sumerian Anatu, and the snake goddess of Crete.

Plato tells about an Egyptian priest who shared a very old myth with Solon. Plato explains to us that the Greek story of Phaeton, who flew too close to the sun, is not about a human hero. The story tells about an event that took place in our solar system. The persons mentioned in the story represent the heavenly bodies of planets and asteroids that move around the sun. One of these became unstable and left its orbit. It caused a world-wide cataclysm and a series of natural disasters on Earth. In the process a civilization—which was highly developed—was destroyed. Plato describes in his texts the location of the drowned continent, the structure of the main city, and the organization of the state.

Because of the disaster that destroyed this ancient civilization, cultural centers that were located in the valleys and in the coastal areas were also destroyed. The ones who survived the disaster were the people who lived in higher areas: shepherds. In other words, Plato tells that the higher classes who carry the culture, and who lived in the main cities, did not survive the cataclysm. The survivors were mainly uneducated people, nomads who lived in the high mountains. The result is that an enormous body of knowledge from that time did not survive the disaster. The Flood was so all-destroying that the level of culture fell back to the nomadic level of surviving.

The Egyptian priest tells Solon that the priests of Atlantis foresaw this disaster and took precautions. Before the disaster took place, they had created colonies away from Atlantis to make the chances of survival greater. In this way the likelihood that a part of the old knowledge would survive the disaster would increase. One of these colonies was Sais, the city devoted to the goddess Neith. In the time of Solon this city would already have existed for eight thousand years.

POWER, WISDOM, AND LOVE

The cultural breakdown of the continent took place during several phases, and every phase was accompanied with a wave of colonization.

In this way, the megalith builders spread over the earth. They are the founders of the shamanic traditions. Within occultism they are regarded as the bearers of the ray of power. They are the people who work with the magic of the natural forces.

They were followed by a wave of colonization from the ray of wisdom. They are the adepts and founders of numerous monasteries and temples, mainly situated in the East. These people developed the philosophical context of the Western Mystery Tradition.

Representatives of the ray of love formed the last outflow of colonists. These groups arrived just before the final destruction of the continent, and they arrived mainly in the Middle East. Their teachings were the foundation of the Egyptian Mystery Tradition, the Babylonian tradition, and the Jewish tradition. These teachings are also the source of the Minoan civilization, from which the Greek tradition developed. Later Christianity also developed from this ray. All of these traditions formed the building blocks of Western philosophy.

THE PRIEST KINGS

When you study the old Egyptian sources, it is peculiar that the oldest texts—the pyramid texts—have the highest spiritual level. These texts not only describe the funeral rituals of the old pharaohs, they also present a vision of the nature of the universe, which indicates knowledge of the highest spiritual levels.

In these old times, Pharaoh was a priest-king. He combined two functions within his person. The entire land was ruled according to spiritual laws. This knowledge was carefully transmitted through genetic lines. These so-called bloodlines guaranteed that the next generation had the physical constitution to receive inspiration for spirituality directly from the oldest gods.

In time the functions of priest and king became separated, but kings were for a long time initiated according to the old traditions. This initiation methodology is described extensively in the so-called *Book of the Dead*. To read this information you need to have access to the right keys.

After this initiation, Pharaoh was the living god Horus on earth. He was transformed. He was no longer a normal person, but changed into a channel used by the gods to rule the country. You can see this very clearly in the statue of Pharaoh Kephren. The god Horus in his falcon shape touches the pharaoh. At this point of contact, the divine influence classically enters the body of the human host.

Pharaoh has become Horus himself and is divine from now on. The influence of the old gods becomes more difficult to receive, when the ancient bloodlines become thinner, and the initiates become less penetrable for these cosmic energies.

THE FOLLOWERS OF HORUS

Slowly the priest-kings disappear, and the function of priest and king become separate. In this way the Semshu-Hor develop: the followers of Horus. The old occult knowledge of Atlantis becomes available for a greater group of persons. The quality of the knowledge becomes thinner. The role of a pharaoh gradually becomes political, although the initiation still exists at the time of the Roman emperors after Christ.

This secularization process is felt by the ancients, and with it a sense of desperation. In the old texts you still find descriptions of how the ancient kings were looking for scriptures from the generations before

them. When these ancient scriptures were found, they were thankfully researched for knowledge that had already been lost.

There exists a fairy tale of Prince Khaemwaset, the fourth son of Pharaoh Ramses II, who was already in his age doing archeological work. He looked in underground tombs and made restorations to the pyramids, which were already old, and to the temples in Memphis. Some of these monuments were then more than a thousand years old. He looked for old scriptures. Finally he found papyruses that had been in the hands of a magician. The papyruses described the building processes of the pyramids. According to this story, the pyramids were built to a plan that predated the Flood.

Pointing in the same direction is the story of the Tower of Babel. This tells of the disappearance of the general language that was used by the ancients to make contact with the primordial gods. When you look to the Mystery Tradition going back in time, you see that the knowledge more and more democratizes, and spreads over the entire population. At the same time, the quality of the knowledge decreases.

With the democratization of spiritual knowledge, the misuse increases. The consequence is that some important Mysteries became desecrated. The true power of the oracles decreased, and in its place, the priesthood developed statues of gods that have internal chambers in which the priests hid and from which they would speak to the people. By means of this mechanism, the priests spoke on behalf of the gods to the kings of earth. Priests developed into intermediaries, becoming bridges between the gods and the world. Kings visited the temples to get divine advice. A beautiful example is still to be seen in the crocodile temple of Kom Ombo in Egypt, where a series of passages leads to the Holy of Holies. Here the High Priest could take a hidden position in a secret room.

TANTRIC INITIATION RITES

Another example of desecrated Mysteries is the sexual Mysteries. Probably they were practiced in classical times to pass on certain esoteric powers. These powers were important in the development of the priesthood. You find texts that state how the initiate became the "bull of his mother," meaning that the son impregnates the mother, a ritual that in the time of Ramses II was already described as very old and barbaric.

The goal of the ritual is to introduce the Horus energy in an initiate, which makes him into a "self-created god," born without a physical father and of a virgin mother. The tension between the sexes is gradually built up and *instead of* being released through physical channels, it is transformed through spiritual channels. The goal was to gain control over the sexual drive, and to transform these energies into magical power and spiritual experiences.

Dion Fortune describes in her books *The Sea Priestess* and *Moon Magic* a modern version of this type of ritual. Already in the classical world these rituals had become degraded to so-called sacred prostitution.

(The translation of this name already shows us that the real meaning of these rituals was lost. A better translation would be "sacred marriage.") Mary Magdalena had probably been a high initiate in this tradition.

Because the Mysteries at this time were already slowly being desecrated, you see that in those days young women needed to "offer their services" to the goddess Venus before they could get married. This desecration is probably the cause of a countermovement where celibacy becomes the norm for the priesthood.

FOLK MAGIC AND BARBARIC NAMES

As I mentioned earlier, spiritual magic techniques would leak from the temples and be used and abused by local magicians. In this way the so-called barbaric names develop. These are titles for what originally were names of gods. Also, consecrations, incantations, and invocations were transformed into a verbal mishmash because they were not understood or were wrongly heard. These incantations were recited before attempting magical work. A well-known example of this is "hocus pocus," a phrase that is immediately associated with magic. These words are degenerations of the Latin *Hoc est enim corpus meum,* the words that are used in the Latin Mass to consecrate bread and wine. Their meaning is, "This is my body."

THE GREAT INITIATION

The Great Initiation is a high-level ritual undertaken by a High Priest to reach the highest spiritual levels possible while alive. Unfortunately, this privilege was sometimes conveyed in ancient times because of political pressure and for political reasons, before the necessary process of purification of the personality of the ruler in question had taken place. An example of this was the Roman emperor Nero. Because of his lack of preparation, Nero became stuck in the phase in which the candidate for initiation is confronted by his own inner demons. Nero was not capable of transforming them. Under the influence of this demonic energy, he became alienated from reality. In other words: he went mad.

The Greek scientist and High Priest Plutarchus writes in his work *De Defectum Oraculum* about the fact that the oracles in his time were increasingly failing. He states that "unbalanced mysticism" is the reason for this: referring to those who tried to harvest the fruit from the Tree of the Mysteries before the Tree had developed any roots.

This message is also true in our "New Age." The old wisdom is presented as a product to be marketed, and consumers do not get any further than the most superficial layer. Disappointed about the quality of the offered knowledge and the teachers, some people start to search for the source of spiritual knowledge without a teacher. These seekers go without a guide, without a map of the road to the inner world and only armed with a few books. They search with egos that are not corrected and with the opinion that they can do this on their own.

The plight of the "New Age" seeker reflects the process that occurred in antiquity, when the high spiritual knowledge that was developed in Atlantis was leaked from the temples, spreading through the commoners and all the while becoming more and more watered down. Many of the applications became misunderstood. The god Horus is symbolic of this process—he was lame in one foot because he was lacking parts of the knowledge.

THE LIBRARY OF NINEVEH

In an attempt to keep the spiritual and scientific knowledge pure and to preserve it for the next generations, the ancients raised libraries. In 1800 CE excavations in Iraq and Syria revealed the old Assyrian culture. At that time, this culture was no more than a vague memory. The old capital Nineveh had totally disappeared, not one brick rediscovered. In 1849 the lost palace of King Sennacherib was unearthed, and right after this the ancient library of King Ashurbanipal, with more than 22,000 clay tablets in it, was found. Ashurbanipal lived from 699 until 626 BCE. He was king and High Priest at the same time. He collected the first scriptures, descriptions of omens, dictionaries, holy laws, epic poems, and folktales. The library contained holy astrological texts. Among these clay tablets were ten thousand documents written in cuneiform script, describing the organization of the state, the laws, and the religion of the old Assyrian kingdom. The library even contained clay tablets from ancient Akkad. The scriptures from this library often replenish scriptures of the Old Testament and Egyptian texts, and they confirm one another. Among these tablets is a work called *Enumah Elish,* which is an older version of the story of Genesis.

The Babylonian Flood myth is described on the eleventh clay tablet of the Gilgamesh Epic.

In the *Gilgamesh Epic* we find a very old story about the Flood. The version of the *Gilgamesh Epic* found in Nineveh dates from about the year 2000 BCE and points toward even older versions of the same story. There is also a king list with the names of Sumerian kings who lived before the

Flood. They describe the Sumerians as the people who rebuilt civilization after the Flood.

THE LIBRARY OF ALEXANDRIA

The library of Alexandria was very famous in the ancient world. Alexandria is a city located at the outflow of the Nile Delta, on the Mediterranean Sea. Alexander the Great raised the city when he conquered Egypt. Alexandria was a meeting place for the intellectuals of that time, and it became a melting pot for all kinds of people who immigrated to the city. In this way it became the center of the ancient world and attracted scientists and sages from distant regions who came to share their knowledge with their colleagues. Thanks to this exchange of knowledge, the library of Alexandria developed.

Scriptures from all over the world were copied carefully and stored in the library. The library developed in restless times—the world was in movement. After Alexander the Great had conquered many countries and established his regime in them, his conquest of Rome followed, and after the year zero Christianity started to spread.

The Mysteries slowly became discredited. The result was that more and more temples were taken over by the Christians. Pictures and representations of the gods of old were damaged and hacked away from the stones. The "Houses of Life" (temples) were deconsecrated and used for profane purposes. Some of them were rebuilt into churches, whereas others became houses for families. The temples that gradually disappeared under the desert sand are the ones that are the best preserved.

In this turbulence of clashing interests, the library of Alexandria was set on fire several times. The death stroke came in 415 CE when Hypatia was the head of the library. History tells us that the early Christians caused this fire, dragging Hypatia through the streets and into the burning library, where she died.

The library must have been immense, because there is a story that Marcus Aurelius alone gave a gift of 200,000 papyrus rolls to Cleopatra. The library of Alexandria contained more than 700,000 book rolls, among which would have been the king's lists of Manheto, the Books of Thoth, and the Emerald Tablet. A treasure of ancient texts was set on fire.

With the coming of Christianity, Pagan traditions were forced to go underground. Christian churches selected what parts of magic were useful in Christian rituals, and they declared everything they could not use to be heretical. Excellent techniques from the Mystery Tradition, which had been proven to be powerfully effective for thousands of years, were thrown into the rubbish box, together with all kinds of dark practices that could not bear the light of day.

THE DARK MEDIEVAL TIMES

During the Middle Ages, Christianity slowly took possession of the Pagan world. In the European countries—where shamanic traditions and influences from the Middle East always coexisted peacefully—a "purification process" was imposed on the non-Christian traditions. Christians, who in earlier times were thrown to the lions in the Coliseum by Roman Pagans, took revenge in later times in the form of the Inquisition.

Christianity is not against magic itself, it is against all theories and viewpoints that differ from Christianity. As I mentioned before, the church adopted much ritual knowledge from the Mysteries and declared what it did not approve of as heretical, falling into the category of "magic."

There were also all kinds of political reasons for the church to not acknowledge the pagan origin of many of its rituals. The church did not want certain knowledge to fall into any other hands. Through this subterfuge, slowly the definition of magical rituals changed, and the word *magic* became more and more loaded with suspicion. The result was that basic structures were still studied and practiced, but the word *magic* was avoided.

Certain ideas about magic were approached in a positive way in the twelfth and thirteenth centuries. In the *Malleus Maleficarum,* magic and witchcraft are separated. Certain texts circulated wherein magic, astrology, and alchemy were mixed. Important magicians of those times were very concerned, because some demonic practices became integrated into magical systems. For this reason magical texts became discredited, and scriptures that contained useful information were unfairly undermined.

In the late Middle Ages, certain forms of ritual magic resurfaced. Except for the "binding of demons" (a type of ritual performed by ancient magicians to make demonic forces harmless), they also invoked heavenly energies like angels. New techniques were developed such as astrological magic, and texts circulated in which Hermes was mentioned as the source of knowledge.

The medieval magical literature contained sources from antiquity and combined it with local shamanic practices. The church itself also contributed to the mixture. Magical literature was transferred to universities, churches, and monasteries.

Despite this resurgence, there was not much opportunity to practice group magic. Orders like the Knights Templar were suppressed with force when they became too powerful. Magical texts were often simple notes, as were the personal notes of the magister.

FROM ASTARTE TO ASTORETH

The ritual magical texts from the Middle Ages were mainly based on Christian texts. The names of the earlier Pagan gods were slightly changed and demonized. An example of this practice is the name of the goddess Astarte. In the *Goetia,* her name is changed into the demon Astoreth. In this way the texts—which were already corrupted by copying mistakes—now became demonized, and these names were added to the "barbaric names."

Other texts were—as in the ancient times—directed toward mystical enlightenment. They were concerned with the attraction of spiritual forces by means of ritual, on the mechanics behind prayer, and the attainment of moral purity. Ritual texts from these times evoked both angels and demons. These rituals can take a longer period of time to accomplish; for example, there are rituals that require several months to complete. During these long rituals, first a magical landscape (in thoughtforms) is gradually built up in the inner mind of the magician. When the landscape has become solid on the inner levels, the magician then starts to interact with it, resulting in visions and ecstatic religious experiences.

The magician in the Middle Ages was a learned scientist. He was handicapped in his investigation because every book was under strict censure by the church. On the other hand, the multiscientists* developed in the Middle Ages, and they were not afraid to apply magic in their investigations. Science as we know it today did not yet exist. Theirs was a "philosophy of nature," in which *magica naturalis* and alchemy developed.

The Renaissance subverted medieval censorship by the church, and original texts from ancient Greek philosophers such as Plato became reaccessible. Plato was an initiate of the ancient Mysteries, as is very clear from his writings. Before the Renaissance, scientists were not even aware of the existence of these texts, and they could not read the old languages.

All these factors meant that during the Middle Ages, there was little room for the Mysteries. The old magical techniques were mixed and corrupted with all kinds of bizarre practices. The result is that a lot of the grimoires from medieval times are barely usable. They are interesting to study as a curiosity, but there is too much risk in trying to use them. Many of the techniques need correcting, and the practitioner must truly know what he or she is doing.

THE PLACE OF THE MAGICIAN IN ANCIENT SOCIETIES

The magicians from the Renaissance were colorful personages, and you find them in countless unexpected places. Some worked at the courts of kings, others worked as medical doctors during the plague epidemics, such as Nostradamus, who was in fact a multiscientist. He learned the Kabbalah from his Jewish father; he became famous because of his capacities as a seer. Dr. John Dee worked at the court of Queen Elizabeth I as an astrologer and a mathematician. Merlin probably was not a real person, but it was the name for a function in Celtic Society.

---

*In ancient times a scientist was not specialized in only one area but rather practiced several disciplines at once.

The knowledge about magic was kept safe by the "secret brother-hoods," such as the Freemasons and Rosicrucians. Rosicrucianism developed in Germany; an old scripture surfaced called the *Fama Fraternitatis of the Honorable Order of the Rosecross*. Freemasonry probably developed from the craft guilds, which were involved in building cathedrals. The old documents—called the Charges—connect the Order with the builders of both the Tower of Babel and the Temple of Solomon.

During the Renaissance, a separation between religion and science developed, and magic was crushed between the millstones. The scientists of the Renaissance regarded magic as religious, sure that it was *not* a science. They dusted their hands and declared it to be a problem for the theologians, who also rejected magic, considering it to be an antireligious movement. Keep in mind that at this time no movement was deemed religious if it was not Christian.

In this way, magic became an outcast of society: by theologians it was called demonic, by science it was called irrational. Politically it was a useful, strategic move to declare the religious practices of people in the colonies magic. To gain power over the inhabitants, their religious practices were called pseudoreligion and were conquered with brutal force. Christian politics had science and theology on its side in its oppressive campaign against Paganism.

In 1463, Marsilio Ficino translated the *Corpus Hermeticum* for Cosimo di Medici. This translation generated a renewed interest in the Mysteries. The magician during the Middle Ages only had access to Christian texts. By this time there was no living person remaining who had actually practiced the Mysteries, and the translation of the texts without the inner experience from which they were written was an extraordinarily difficult task.

In our day, we have access to good translations of the ancient works, a solid background in history, and freedom of thought. In the Middle Ages, magicians had to work with limited resources, with knowledge that they collected in little pieces, learned from the Arabs. It is no wonder that the grimoires are such a mishmash of useful and useless concepts. The Christian church had in fact established a dictatorship for centuries.

With the Renaissance, the power of the churches over society was broken, the sciences started to bloom, and the Mystery Tradition began the immensely difficult challenge of filling in the gaps in a tradition that had not been practiced for over a thousand years.

The adepts of the Renaissance partially succeeded in reintegrating the old Hellenistic and Egyptian philosophies into the practice, as far as the culture and the poor translations allowed it. Still working from a Christian background, practitioners related to the old gods as angels. As long as these gods and goddesses were safely placed behind the sign of "mythology" and were kept outside the structure of the official religion, adepts were able to work with the old religious stories.

Through the Fall of Constantinople in 1453, the hermetic texts came to Europe, and after the Jews had been driven out of Spain in 1492, the Kabbalah became accessible to the magicians. Slowly the remnants of this tradition could be developed into a structured practice with the help of these texts.

THE GOLDEN DAWN AND ITS OFFSPRING

At the end of the eighteenth century, Madame Helena Blavatsky introduced the Eastern Mysteries to the West, and theosophical societies sprang up everywhere. Eastern magical techniques and philosophies spread into the Western world, and this made the West hungry and curious for more. There was a renewed interest in the West's search for its cultural roots. The Western philosophy is oriented differently than the Eastern ones. Our climate asks for a more practical spirituality. Western people are often doers, and rituals seem to penetrate the Western mind more easily than meditation. In addition, it is easier to work with symbols that already permeate the entire culture.

When laws against the practice of magical techniques disappeared, it became possible to openly practice the Pagan roots of the old tradition. People researched the old sources—Greek sources, Babylonian and Chaldean texts—from within their own cultural context. Additionally, the translations of the old Egyptian Mystery texts slowly became available again.

In 1887, Dr. William Wynn Westcott was given a manuscript containing rituals of a group who called themselves the Golden Dawn. The content of these papers was based on hermetic knowledge. Westcott translated the manuscripts, and his work brought the Mystery tradition to the surface from age-old dust. A new Golden Dawn had begun. This was the beginning of a Mystery school that is still authoritative today. Together with the theosophical movement of Helena Blavatsky and the anthroposophy of Rudolf Steiner, the teachings of the Golden Dawn were very important for the esoteric movement in the twentieth century.

The teachings of the Golden Dawn were published by Israel Regardie after the order itself had closed its doors. By doing this he violated his oath of secrecy. If he had not done this, however, a unique curriculum would have been lost. The magical Order of the Golden Dawn combined in its teachings the esoteric knowledge of the Rosicrucians and the Freemasons. The founders of the Golden Dawn were dissatisfied because, within these organizations, the esoteric content drifted slowly to the background in favor of the social network that became more important. The Golden Dawn founders made spiritual knowledge their main goal, and combined the knowledge they already had with extensive research into the original sources of magic. They visited libraries, translated medieval grimoires, visited archeological sites, and used newly translated texts from antiquity in their rituals. The adepts from the Golden Dawn mainly came from the upper classes of English society, who had the money and the time and the energy to devote to this investigation.

In the relatively short period of its existence, the order had created so many adepts that conflicts were unavoidable, and the school started to fall apart about 1903. The adepts from the Golden Dawn started orders of their own, which you could call the daughters of the original Golden Dawn.

In their new magical schools, the adepts also developed a high level of quality in their training system, which had famous students—the torchbearers of the tradition. This was all in the best interest of the Western Mystery Tradition. Their curriculum still determines the content of the teaching of modern magical schools. But it is good to realize that here also time goes on and new things develop. Since then, as more material from antiquity has become available, the Golden Dawn rituals are slowly adapted. The experience with ritual has grown. The exercises are refined. The knowledge of pre-Christian societies has increased and with that the understanding of ancient systems. In addition, we have access to the Eastern systems that are still practiced and taught, and we can compare techniques. The magical systems of modern schools continue to grow and broaden and deepen themselves.

3

THE GREAT WORK OF
THE MYSTERIES

*Let us wash ourselves in holy water. We are brought
before the Hierophant. From a stone book he reads us
things that we are not allowed to reveal. . . .*

*Then, at last, the temple fills with the serene light of
wonder. We see the pure Elysian Fields. Not through a
philosophical interpretation, but factual and in reality.
The Hierophant becomes the creator and revealer of
these matters. The Sun is just his torchbearer, the Moon
his servant, and Hermes is his mystical Messenger. The
last words sound: Konx Om Pax. The ritual has been
consummated and we are seers forever.*

PORPHYRIA, GREEK INITIATE FROM
THE MYSTERIES OF ELEUSIS

Gnothi Seauton was written above the Temple of Delphi. It means "Know
Thyself." Knowledge of the Self is central to the Mysteries and is essential

if you want to take the road of spiritual magic. It is a road of development on which practice and theory walk hand in hand. It is a road without an end. You will never stop learning.

In this book I will explain a few basic principles. In addition to this foundation, continued growth requires study and regular practice. Everyone can learn to practice spiritual magic. The results depend on the energy you yourself put into it. You do not need to have special psychic abilities beforehand. They will gradually develop in most students during the training. The training systematically opens onto the deeper levels within a Contacted* Mystery school.

You can compare magical training with learning how to play an instrument. In the case of spiritual magic, the instrument is your own soul. First of all, you need to practice reading music and learn to play simple melodies. When you practice often, you will see your talent developing. An experienced teacher can help you avoid certain pitfalls.

When you decide to step into the world of the Mysteries, your world will gradually start to change. This is explained to everyone who enrolls in a Contacted school. The teachers of the Inner Planes do not accept anything without testing it. They will take you to the depth of your strength.

Fairly quickly after you have been accepted within a Mystery school, changes will start to appear in your life. The most difficult phase is the first year. You need to learn to adjust to the principle of change, and to the energy that makes these changes happen. Changes come unexpectedly; they will surprise you! What mainly happens during the first year is that you start to question everything that belongs in your life at that time. Everything that is not necessary will disappear. It is the beginning of the spiritual purification process that you are undergoing. The purification is an essential part of the process, and it will transform you gradually into a channel of light: that is your birthright.

Purification never stops. As you walk further along the path, you will always have to deal with this. In every phase the questions change,

---

*A Mystery school is "Contacted" when it is in contact with the higher beings, forces, archetypes, and guardians.

together with the theme. In every phase you will need to seek an answer to questions related to a theme that is in your life and has surfaced into the light. These inquiries are examinations of the Inner Planes. They can work like stumbling blocks. It can be that certain obstacles within your life cannot be transformed by you, and then the growth stops for a while until you have gained control over the theme. Then, at a later date, the test will repeat itself.

You can also be the person who passes the first tests with your feet firmly on the path. Your environment supports you—or at least does not discourage you—and the Mysteries have become a part of your life. Gradually you reach the level of initiation into the lower Mysteries. The question repeats itself: are you willing to be tested? In other words, the tests never end; they are part of the deal.

CROSSROADS

On this path you will also reach crossroads. These crossroads test you on how you apply your growing magical powers. When that has become clear, you can break through the barrier. These are choices that come forth from your ethical and moral steadiness, and you build character— loyalty, courage, ego, and other qualities—in the process. The tests that you meet on the road are dependent on your character, the talents that you are developing, as you progress on this path. They will be individually different. The Masters of the Light understand that we humans are not perfect. That is the reason why we are here, and that is why they guide us. But when we make major mistakes and misuse our forces, then they will act upon that, and the doors of the Mystery schools close themselves against us. The energies of the initiations can be reduced and, in an exceptional case, have even been withdrawn by the Master.

For those who are destined to become channels of the teachers themselves, this purification is more rigorous and goes even deeper. It is essential that blockages become cleared away.

VIRTUES AND VICES

The Kabbalistic texts speak about virtues and vices; in other words, sins. The old-fashioned word *sin* has gained a very negative meaning. Sin in our perspective has to do with being guilty of something. But that is too limited a view. The word *sin* factually indicates that an energy channel is blocked or weakened. The light is not capable of penetrating deeply enough, because the right solutions have not yet been learned, or the grip on certain characteristics has not been developed strongly enough.

When someone has no experience in a new field of life, they make mistakes because of naivety. Maturity and experience to handle new situations has not been developed yet: suddenly pressure builds up on an area that is still weak, because there has not yet been need for it to be strong. The energy stream that is generated by the magical exercises slowly starts to build up a "pressure" on the entire system, and the weak points become clear automatically. Then it is your task to look very carefully at these weak areas and to make them stronger. In some cases it is possible to create a "deviation" around the weak point.

Compare this with water flowing in a river, or with the system of blood vessels in your body, or with the traffic in a city. When there is not a festival taking place in a city, then the roads have the capacity to absorb the normal amount of traffic in the periphery and in the center of the city. Suddenly someone decides to organize an event, and a stream of traffic that is unknown for this place comes toward the city. The result is a traffic jam, because the incoming and outgoing routes do not have the capacity for this amount of traffic. Should this city organize this type of event more often, then the extra traffic would be calculated into the planning so that moments of intense traffic can be processed. The result is that the normal capacity for traffic has increased.

The traffic scenario is analogous to your practice of spiritual magic—your entire system needs to adapt to a higher amount of energy than you are used to.

ENERGY CHANNELS

Now let me compare the stream of psychic energies in the mind with the bloodstream in blood vessels. When your vessels get blocked, the blockage obstructs the stream of nutrients and oxygen in different parts of the body. This can remain unnoticed for a little while, until the body needs to work under a higher pressure. The pressure in the vessels increases, and this pressure can disloge the blockage, usually a clot, and the clot is released into the bloodstream where it becomes stuck in a smaller blood vessel. Now the bloodstream itself is blocked. Physically this can cause a stroke or a heart attack. When we compare this with psychic energy, a person's capacity to process information is not capable of handling the impulses, and unwanted dissociations can appear. These are sometimes mistaken for "psychic experiences."

It can be that the psychic energy is pushing against weaknesses in the character, where the person cannot control the input of impulses. Compare this with rivers. Engineers know how much water flow a river has during the different seasons. Based on this information, they calculate how high the dikes must be to contain the water. These calculations determine where houses can be built near the river. But then the weather becomes extreme, and great quantities of water soak the environment. The water rises to an unexpected height. The dikes break and the houses on both sides of the river are flooded. The parallel with magical forces is that, by increasing psychic energy, "dikes" can break in the energy system, which can cause damage to somebody's psyche or in someone's environment. The damage can, in some cases, be irreversible.

This does not mean that magical energy is evil, in the same way that the water is not evil. It just streams in the wrong place and causes damage and problems. In the case of magic, there are people who handle things sensibly, and there are fools. Not everyone who holds a scalpel in his hand is a surgeon. In the same way, not everybody who holds the Wand of Power is an initiate. I make a strong dividing line between so-called sorcery and magic. Most of the websites that pretend to talk about magic in fact offer sorcery. Love spells, money spells, talismans that are offered to gain "power" are, in the most innocent case, not effective. In discussion forums the lame often help the blind.

LIVING IN THE DREAMTIME

Real magic is a spiritual system that works in a way that is comparable with kundalini yoga. The process needs to be guided. It is different from psychotherapeutic systems in that it works with the deep layers of the subconscious mind, and it works from direct experience. The main difference between magic and psychology is that practicing magic is a spiritual process rather than a therapy. Jung is often very popular with writers of spiritual subjects because he gave names to the phenomena of the subconscious mind. This gives them a scientific description. Jung created the word *archetype* to describe the primordial patterns in the human spirit. By defining these patterns, you create a distance that can prevent a direct experience. Within magic, we do not work with archetypes: we communicate directly with the gods.

Here, though, you come directly to the causal layers of consciousness. Jung's work created signals pointing in the right direction, signals that indicate the road between everyday experience and magical reality. When we do the Mystery work, we will enter into this imaginal, numinous reality. In Egypt, they called this the "First Time," or *Zep Tepi*. It is the old Egyptian name for what the aboriginals call the "dreamtime." In the Bible, this state of consciousness is called "Genesis." It is a timeless mythical reality that has a causal effect on all events in the material world.

WALKING BETWEEN THE WORLDS

Most of the people who start practicing magic have some slight problems in the beginning, because they experience living in two worlds. Looking to spiritual forces from a psychologist's point of view can be a temporary solution for this problem. Once the student has both feet firmly planted on the path of the Mysteries, an integration will slowly develop. The two types of realities will gradually switch places without having consequences for the way someone performs in normal life. The magical world becomes dominant, while the material world is experienced as an illusion: this is in line with the teaching of the Eastern traditions.

The goal of the Mysteries is to gradually make a connection with the divine world. This causes deep transformations in the human soul. The divine nature of the All is experienced, carried by virtues, love, and wisdom. In this way, the magic abilities are immense, great powers.

Within this system, low magic is used to clear away blockages, to get access to the knowledge that leads to an encounter with the self, or to learn to understand yourself better. Daily life, with all its possibilities and difficulties, is seen as the mirror of the Self. In your daily life you can practice Gnothi Seauton—Know Thyself—which was written above the entrances of the temples of the Oracle in ancient days.

Daily life is a constant stream of energy, of change. You yourself are the center of your own solar system. Around you, you create your lessons, because you—as the sun—light up the planets. The planets are the different aspects of the divinity of yourself. In your life, the life force flows easily and without problems, and the sunlight reaches the surface of the planets.

At other times, resistance develops (clouds and weather circumstances), and the sun is not able to reach the fertile soil. This causes problems for the life force. Then difficulties arise for which solutions need to be found. The people and the events in your environment mirror your own inner world.

An energy stream that is blocked starts hurting. Do you dare to look at what is happening, or do you take flight and run as quickly as you can in another direction? You can work at stable solutions within your life, and the energy will become accessible. You can also search for escape and live in denial, manifesting in a lethargy of superficial amusement, alcohol, and drugs or become a consumer of the newest gadgets and other forms of distraction. Remember that the long-term, stable solution comes from changing something about yourself.

THE GREAT WORK

Every day offers a challenge to gain better control over your mind and your emotions and to improve your relationships. Finally, you arrive at the point where you can tell somebody else that you understand his or her problem. People arrive at the gate of a Mystery school and ask what it can do for them. In fact the question should be rephrased: how can I serve the Great Work? The term comes from spiritual alchemy. It indicates the process by which a person transforms him or herself from lead to the gold of the spirit.

THE DEFINITION OF MAGIC

The Temple of Magic has been so overgrown with the
lush growth of uninformed and superstitious thought
throughout the ages that, in the Western world at least, its
true appearance and nature has been lost.

W. E. BUTLER, *MAGIC, ITS RITUAL,*
POWER AND PURPOSE

You have probably become aware that magic in this book is approached in a different way than you are used to. No spells and sorcery. In this book I lead you from the hocus pocus back to the *Hoc est enim corpus meum*. The original magic was practiced within the Mystery schools as a method to create experiences of enlightenment. The longer you train yourself in this way, the more the power of your magic increases. Magic is practiced within initiation traditions.

The modern word *magic* comes from a Persian priesthood. Their priests were famous for their knowledge of the holy traditions. In ancient Greece the *magiké* was worked by an adept called the *mágoi*. To our modern eyes, the ancient magician would be a mixture of a shaman and a priest.

Dion Fortune and Ernest Butler define magic in this way:

> *Magic is the art to cause changes in consciousness with*
> *the will*

The first peculiarity is the use of the word *art*. An art is a skill that is acquired by practice. An art grows wings by means of inspiration, which takes it to greater heights. It is remarkable that, in this definition, there is no trace of the use of magic to cause effects in physical reality. This is because, within magic, we assume that the material reality surrounding a person is a reflection of the consciousness of someone. At the moment that you start to create changes there, the material world will change around you, because you changed your relationship with it.

50

Can you use magic to get a computer? The answer to this question is that it is much simpler and quicker to get an extra job and earn the money to buy this computer than to study magic until you are experienced enough to do this. Studying magic to earn more money is a method that is unnecessarily complicated.

Practicing magic means that you develop a different relationship with the realities that surround you, and one of these realities is the material world. You can use magic to change your relationship with money. If you have problems regulating the stream of money in your life, because you have a hole in your pocket, then you should consider getting control over this impulse. In the Western consumer-driven society, we are conditioned to see material circumstances as solutions for happiness in life, other solutions which are much more logical are overlooked. What is wealth? I am incredibly wealthy because I have houses all over the world. This does not mean that I own these houses. They belong to my friends, who are pleased when I come to visit them.

By means of this example, I want to make clear to you that magic is mainly a spiritual art that is directed to transform the reality around you, and to see the aspects of your life from a different perspective. In this way, your personal possibilities broaden, and you release energy to stimulate growth in your life toward your personal goals.

THE ENSOULED DIVINE REALITY

Within the Western Mystery schools, we assume that everything around us—both material reality and the different frequencies of consciousness—has a divine nature. We assume that reality is ensouled and living, and that everything that exists has a form of consciousness. A stone is in a coma, a plant sleeps, an animal dreams, a human is awake. With this perspective, you can create a relationship with everything around you. Magic assumes that there exists a web of interconnecting relations between all phenomena. By playing the right strings on this web, you can create effects that reverberate in the universe of manifesting consciousness.

Because of this relation with the ensouled divine reality, the magister holds the keys in his or her hands to let the soul fly upward to the causation level. Here, you get access to the complete orchestra of divine forces and hierarchies.

Western spiritual magic is a tradition in which all religions meet without conflict. They are seen as diverse ways to connect with the same underlying divine reality. Whether a monotheistic system such as Christianity, or a polytheistic system such as the Egyptian pantheon, both are concerned with one primordial source: divinity. The word *divinity* is defined as uniting both sexes within itself, Elohim, or in other words "S-He."

THE EFFECT OF MIND ON MATTER

How do mind and matter relate in the worldview of the initiate and within the practice of the Mystery tradition?

The so-called low magic practitioner trains to use magical forces to effect material reality. The difference between spiritual and low magic can be explained by this metaphor: imagine the divine forces as long ropes of energy hanging from the sky. At the bottom, weights are attached. The ropes are a metaphor for the waves of consciousness going up and down: from Below to Above, from Above to Below. The weights are the material crystallizations—in other words, material reality. The outcomes of these streams of energy are visible in one's life in the form of chances, situations, pure matter—your daily life.

When you work at changing your reality with low magic, the ropes of consciousness are like a pendulum, and you are pulling the weight at the end of the rope far to the side by using the force of your muscles. Once the weight is pulled back as far as it can go, you release. Yes, you have created movement as the pendulum swings, but you must quickly get out of the way, because when it swings back it will likely hit you from behind.

BACKFIRE

This phenomenon is called backfire. It is regarded as the repercussion of magical force applied in the wrong way. Then the sorcery turns threefold back upon you. The first slap you will get is spiritual, the second is mental/emotional, and the third is material. When you are too fixated on causing these types of effects, your spiritual development will not grow beyond a certain point.

Spiritual magic is directed toward growth of the sacred Self and is seldom occupied with manipulating matter. Willpower and concentration on a target are mostly enough to stay on the upward flowing spiritual stream. In the rare event that you notice being blocked by circumstances, the initiated magician will make a connection with the causal level: Tep Zepi. Here he or she studies the wheels of the machinery and changes the unwanted movement of one of the pendulums by oiling the machinery or redirecting the forces over another wheel of the mechanism. This action causes almost no force—it might cause a little bit of movement in the pendulums, but does not bring the entire mechanism out of balance. By an unwanted movement I mean events that create blockages on the road, preventing personal growth.

In other words, when you use magic on a causal level, changes take less energy to establish and cause less upheaval. As a result, the personality becomes more stable.

HOW DOES THIS MECHANISM WORK IN PRACTICE?

The subconscious mind works with images, symbols, and associations, not by means of reason. Each of the five senses sends sensations to the brain: sight, touch, taste, smell, and hearing. In the subconscious mind they are connected to certain emotions.

If your favorite food is chicken, then the smell of a chicken turning on a spit at your butcher's shop will cause a chain of physical reactions. Your stomach starts to rumble, your mouth waters, and you will promise yourself to put chicken on the menu in the near future. This mechanism is stronger when you are hungry. The entire body prepares itself for food. When I create a guided visualization, and I suggest the same sensations of eating chicken, then you will also start to react physically. I create the images and the sensations: the smell, the saliva in your mouth, the beautiful color of grilled meat, the smell of the herbs, the feeling in your mouth when you actually put your teeth into the meat, the taste of the fat. The images cause the same physical reaction as the smell of the actual food, because they are a part of the same association chain.

During your training in spiritual magic, you will slowly build similar association chains. At a slow tempo, step by step, the images, incenses and oils, symbols, music, spoken text, tastes, and movements are charged with a spiritual meaning. The spirit is trained to concentrate around these association chains. We do not work with emptying the mind, which is often the case within Eastern systems. We let the mind circulate like a little weight on a prayer mill. It turns around the core with the energy that is raised by the interconnected symbols. In this way the mind concentrates, and the rational mind is blocked. The buildup of concentration is easy to learn in this way, because the mind is kept busy. It prevents you from getting bored, and so the mind will start to wander less quickly.

THE CORRESPONDENCES

The spirit is conditioned, or trained, by recognizing the meanings of consciously created association chains. The images are connected to natural phenomena that cause an instinctive reaction in one's psyche. In this way, a series of associations is learned. When the association chain holds, the images will automatically generate the emotion that belongs to the chain. This is the reason why magic does not work instantly, and why there is often much preparation needed, involving sometimes boring and repetitive work.

The next thing that needs to happen is to create a gateway for the content of the subconscious to enter the conscious mind by going into a light trance. The trance is generated through a ritual or by autohypnosis. In this state the subconscious becomes suggestible to the chosen thoughtforms.

In this way, the student works with the four magical weapons, all the sacred symbols, sigils, lights, robes, and invocations. Piece by piece they are anchored in the subconscious mind and are interconnected by means of association chains. The tables of correspondences are created for this goal. The correspondences of each series bring you into contact with a particular frequency of consciousness.

THE CREATION OF SACRED TOOLS

Along with the process of learning the tables of correspondences by experience comes the creation of materials for the temple. To do this, you do not need to be an artist. What's important is the time and energy that you put into the creation of these objects, which is a meditative process in itself. During the time you work on these tools, understand why you are creating them, what qualities they represent. Focus your thoughts on the purpose of the objects and what psychic qualities they represent. Think about all the forces that underly them, which will be disclosed by means of this weapon. In this way, the temple tools absorb an energy layer that is more than the objects themselves. By doing this work directly on the physical level, you develop a relationship with the tool(s) from within your mind. The effort that you invest in giving the objects their beauty will repay you in the emotions, the ideas, and the images with which you, at a later date, use them within the temple.

Finally, you do not need a temple, or magical weapons, or robes. None of this is essential in the end. When I am on a holiday I can, on my own, lying on the beach, experience an entire ritual with forty officers in a complete furnished temple. The ritual does not need to be worked step by step. The visualizations take the shape of whirling energies, working through me. A dialog develops between the symbols I put forward consciously and the reaction from the Inner Planes. But to come to this point you need to train yourself for many years.

SYMBOLS

The main thing is to create a bridge of language between your conscious mind and your subconscious mind. The language of the subconscious mind is symbology. One of the most important parts of the work of an aspiring magician is building up a vocabulary of symbols, and the opening and closing of the subconscious mind in a systematic way. You cannot allow any "leaks" to develop. This is the reason why the training goes slowly: to prevent you from developing problems caused by the content of the subconscious leaking into everyday life. Your tempo of inner development must be balanced. When you want to go too fast, you get problems with dissociation. People think then that they are psychic when the world of fantasy streams over into everyday reality. That is why the credo of every magician must be:

Make haste slowly.

Of course this is difficult when the beauty of magic captures you. I have met so many people who started to read at high speed every book they could afford to buy on the subject. Who had the feeling that they had discovered this path too late in their lives, and who now decided to make up for lost time.

ENCHANTMENT

When magic enchants you with her beauty, it seems that there is nothing more important than mastering the art as soon as possible. Magic then can become a jealous lover, who tends to overshadow everything else that was of importance in your life. Then it is important to reduce your speed a bit, and just go as quickly as is healthy in your life. Magic comes into your life at this time because now you are ripe to receive the teaching: not sooner, and not later!

Think about the length of the genuine education by a real shaman or a yogi, how many years of training it takes to gain a good level of mastery. Such an education easily takes between fifteen and twenty years. An education in magic can take this long as well, if you have the intention of reaching adepthood. At the same time, it is of no use to hurry toward a final goal. It is much better to enjoy the path itself and to profit from the fruits that will come to you during this spiritual training. This prevents you from succumbing to the pitfalls that are hidden to the left and right of the road. Within the field of magic you have the choice to practice different traditions. My advice is first to walk the main road, which has been traversed by people before you. In this way, you get a good grounding in this spiritual path. At a later date, you may start to apply this knowledge to the tradition that is closest to your heart.

THE EMERALD TABLET
OF HERMES TRISMEGISTUS

THE EMERALD TABLET

To give you an image of how spiritual magic works, and what the work is based on, I will use the Emerald Tablet of Hermes Trismegistus.

According to tradition, the Emerald Tablet is made out of one piece of emerald. The message on the tablet is prophetic and contains many hidden keys. The tablet was translated in Alexandria around 330 BCE, and would have been a part of important documents preserved in this city's library. The tablet forms the core of some of the ancient sciences: astrology, alchemy, and magic. Translated copies of the tablet surfaced in Arabic countries from 600 CE, and from there the first texts migrated through Spain into Europe.

The Emerald Tablet describes the premises you need to work with spiritual realities. The Emerald Tablet is *not* a religious document. It describes the laws of spiritual forces. It also describes the peculiarities of the "One Thing." This One Thing is essential within magic, because it forms the basis, the most spiritual and unmanifested form of matter: *Prima Materia*.

PRIMA MATERIA

Prima materia was also called dew by the alchemists. In the Egyptian tradition, this principle is embodied by the goddess Tefnut. Her name means "moisture." *Tef* is the Egyptian word for spitting, and *Nut* is the name of the goddess who embodies the starry heavens. At the same time, she embodies the Cosmic Ocean. On the Kabbalistic Tree of Life, primal matter belongs to the Sephirah Binah. Physicists encounter this principle in quantum physics: particles and waves can switch into each other's shape. Here, in this area of investigation, magic and physical sciences meet on common ground—much to the fright of scientists, and hilarity among magicians.

The laws described on the Emerald Tablet are formulated by Hermes Trismegistus. This is a Greek name for a god who surfaces under different names in more than one pantheon. From his name stems the term *Hermetic tradition*. Hermes is the Greek name for the Egyptian god Thoth. Trismegistus means "three times great." Other appearances of Hermes Trismegistus are Enoch, Idris, and Tubal Qayin (also known as Cain from the Bible). Apart from the profession of blacksmith—which is of course a very logical link for the god of alchemy—Thoth is also connected to the development of writing and of science. Above all, he is the god of the Word. By speaking the Word, the universe developed. By speaking the Word, the waters were divided. Thoth predates the Flood, and thus he belongs to the oldest gods.

The laws described on the Emerald Tablet form the basis of all kinds of magical invocations. By making contact with this One Thing, divine forces are called down and anchored in physical objects. This is the basis for consecrations in which statues of gods and other ritual objects were charged, and temples and churches were consecrated. Initiations are given according to these principles. Also, practical applications such as the creation of talismans and purification of spaces are based on these laws.

The texts of the Emerald Tablet* must be approached from a meditative attitude, which fosters the forming of association chains, which in turn provides a further understanding of the text. The text must be read on all the levels of consciousness. The tablet is divided into seven rubrics.

Here you find the text of the Emerald Tablet and the seven rubrics, which I will explain further in the next paragraphs.

The Emerald Tablet and the Seven Rubrics

In Truth, without deceit and in endless purity.

That which is Below corresponds with that which is Above
And that which is Above corresponds with that which is Below
To create the miracles of the One Thing.
And exactly as all things come forth from this One Thing

---

*An extensive description of the rubrics is in the book *The Emerald Tablet: Alchemy for Personal Transformation*, by Dennis William Hauck.

—through the meditation of One Mind—
So come all things forth from this One Thing, by transformation.

Its father is the Sun, its mother the Moon.
The Wind carries it in its belly, its nurse is the Earth.
It is the source of the All, the consecration of the universe.
Its intrinsic power is perfected, when it changes into Earth.

Divide the Earth from the Fire, the Subtle from the Gross
Carefully and with great intelligence.
It raises up from Earth towards the Heaven and descends back
*   to the Earth.*
Thereby it combines in itself the forces
Of the Above and the Below.

In this way you will gain the Glory of the entire Universe.
All darkness will lift up for you.
This is the greatest of all powers,
Because it exalts every subtle thing and penetrates every solid
*   thing.*

In this way the Universe was created.
From here derive all wondrous applications,
because this is the Pattern.

This is why I am called the Three Times Greatest Hermes
I possess all three parts of the Wisdom of the entire Universe
Herewith I have explained fully the Operation of the Sun.

THE INTRODUCTION RUBRIC

In Truth, without deceit and in endless purity.

This rubric tells us that these texts are not only written in truth, but they should also be approached in a specific state of consciousness. The words *pure* and *truth* point to the ancient Egyptian goddess Maat.

When, in the ancient text, a wife is connected to Thoth, there are sources who tell us that her name is Seshat, but others mention Maat. Maat was the goddess of the absolute and perfect truth. She was seen as the scales. Our image of Lady Justice derives from Maat. It is a truth that is unbendable, naked, unveiled. The texts point toward this absolute truth. To enter into this state of consciousness, you also need—apart from this unveiled honesty—an absolute freedom of consciousness. This rubric tells us that the truth here is the source. This is something you can experience when you have achieved a freedom of the soul to think and act independently from any conditionings. It requires a freedom of moral and ethical codes, a state of being centered in the essence and the core of the Self, a state of absolute freedom of dualities.

Imagine if everybody you know told you the unveiled truth about what they think of you. I think that most people would not be able to bear this scrupulous truth, let alone appreciate it. You can also imagine that it is probably even more unbearable to be confronted with the eternal and absolute truth of the universe. That is the meaning of the goddess Maat. This sentence also inspires one to "Know Thyself," a vital attitude when approaching the Mysteries. It means that you are willing to let yourself be weighed in the light of the absolute truth. But most important when working with the Emerald Tablet is that you enter into a meditative state of consciousness where you try to reach that perfect equilibrium within yourself.

THE ORIENTATION RUBRIC

That which is Below corresponds with that which is
*   Above*
And that which is Above corresponds with that which is
*   Below*
To create the miracles of the One Thing.
And exactly like all things come forth from this One
*   Thing*
—through the meditation of One Mind—

> *So come all things forth from this One Thing, by*
> *transformation.*

In these sentences, the living relationship between heaven and earth is described. The entire universe is built from consciousness. Between the Above and the Below runs a cosmic axis of energy exchange, and this is called the Spine of God. It reaches from endless high to endless deep. Above, the causal forces are located. When the One Mind thinks, clouds of consciousness are formed, and they condense and crystallize in patterns. In this way the matrixes of the archetypes are formed. They are the images of the dreamtime; they are the oldest gods and archangels. They are the archetypal forces that form the matrix for the natural laws of the psyche. This process is what is meant by the meditation of One Mind. This is how Prima Materia is created. Primeval matter was called *Tefnut* in ancient Egypt, and also "alchemical dew." This is the One Thing that is the root of everything. From this Prima Materia, from the thoughts of this One Mind, everything is created. From the moment that you can connect yourself with this One Mind, when you can become one with divinity, then you take the position whereby you can cause, with your powers of thought, an impression on Prima Materia. The Prima Materia crystallizes according to one of the forms of the One Mind who overshadows the dew. In this way, Prima Materia gains consciousness.

As in a hologram, the thought of the One Mind crystallizes from Above to Below. The thoughtform crystallizes through all the layers by means of transformation, until it becomes material reality. At the moment you are capable of unifying yourself with this point of being—balanced in endless purity and truth—then you are at the point of One Mind and in unity with Above. At that moment you are, yourself, in the middle of the spine of God: the channel of transformation.

The Inner Planes of the Mystery tradition represent the macrocosmic level of reality, the "Above" of the Emerald Tablet. Spirituality does not—contrary to what often is assumed—have its roots in fantasy. The roots are in the causal forces of the collective subconscious, which are Above and Below these microcosmic and macrocosmic levels. This is a frequency of consciousness that is broadcasted throughout the universe. It is available to those who are capable of receiving the images of the Dreamtime. If you can unify with the One Mind, you can change your reality by creating different patterns in primal matter. This is the reason why we, in spiritual magic, connect ourselves time and again with the creation myths.

The Orientation Rubric also describes, by implication, the doctrine of correspondence. Every situation mirrors a cause that is found on the level above. At the same time, this rubric indicates that all the events in our life—the Below—are the natural outcome of hidden laws of the universe. The tablet indicates that the cause of the events is to be found in the spiritual causal world, and not in the Below.

THE ENIGMATIC RUBRIC

Its father is the Sun, its mother the Moon.
The Wind carries it in its belly, its nurse is the Earth.
It is the Source of the All, the consecration of the
Universe.
Its intrinsic power is perfect, when it changes into Earth.

In this rubric, the true nature of primal matter is explained. It is the source of everything, the text says. It is the building block of existence. It is called the cause—the source—of the All. The All is another word for the manifested universe. Primal matter is also called the consecration of the universe. A consecration is something that makes a material object holy and divine. Primal matter *is* the consecration of the universe: it is the robe of God.

Also in this rubric are mentioned the four classical Elements from which Prima Materia derives: the sun is mentioned for Fire, the moon for Water, the wind is Air, and lastly the Element Earth is mentioned. I will explain these Four Elements later, when I talk about the magical circle. For now it is important that these Four Elements come forth from the causal level of the Above (the Element of the One Mind), and that these Four Elements indicate four levels of reality from Above to Below.

The father of the One Thing is the sun: the sun represents light and life. The sun gives us vitality and life force. It is a symbol that is often used to indicate higher consciousness.

The mother of the One Thing is the moon. The moon reflects the light of the sun. The symbol of the moon is used to describe the subconscious, the state of meditation, and the reflection of the self. As water reflects its environment, so in this way your meditation reflects the meditation of the One Mind.

"The Wind carries it in its belly"; this tells us several things. First of all the wind is symbolic of the Breath of God, the Word. Traditionally, air contains nectar. Nectar is a word to indicate the presence of magical force. Nectar, also called ambrosia, is the drink of the gods. This you breathe in with every breath. The wind is symbolic of the touch of the Word, and by breathing you are soaked in this unseen nectar that makes life radiate. When the higher consciousness marries the meditation of the One Mind, then the wind comes into being—the Breath of God. By the wind, the word of God is created. The sun and the moon marry, and the wind is the fruit of that marriage. That is the splendor of the life force itself: the Word.

All this is fed by the earth. The earth itself—the physical world of matter—is called the nurse. The earth was seen as equally holy and causational as all the other Elements. Without earth these principles are not capable of generating life. Through your existence on earth you are the nurse of the One Thing.

At this point it is interesting to reread the text of the Emerald Tablet. The words that describe the Mysteries of Eleusis contain all the Four Elements and the Element of the Dreamtime: the Elysian Fields.

THE PYRAMID RUBRIC

Divide the Earth from the Fire, the Subtle from the
   Gross
Carefully and with great intelligence.
It raises up from Earth towards the Heaven and
   descends back to the Earth.

Thereby it combines in itself the forces
Of the Above and the Below.

Here the work starts with the forces of Above to Below. The word *Above* in magic does not indicate the image that we normally define as heaven. Above is the area of the One Mind, the consciousness wherein everything is one. This is the consciousness where divine will and divine thought rule. This rubric describes how you can connect with this principle. At the moment when you can make a division, you can ascend to Above and descend to Below. Above is the world of the One, Below is the world of the Four Elements, and this creates a pyramid. By moving between the levels of consciousness, you will start to combine these extremes. What is important to understand about the last rubric of the Emerald Tablet is that every side of the pyramid forms a triangle.

This rubric teaches you that, first of all, you need to learn to discriminate between these different Elements. Secondly, you need to learn to divide between important and unimportant information: the subtle from Above and the gross from Below. In mythology, you will meet this theme every time the help of the little animals is called in to solve a problem. The ant is used regularly as a totem animal for this goal. In the Minoan Mysteries, it is the ant that helps Daidalos to take the red thread of Ariadne through the core of the labyrinth. In the Greek Mysteries, the ant helps Psyche when she has to pass tests to come into the favor of Aphrodite. The ant helps her to sort out the seeds. In the Egyptian Mysteries, we see Horus appearing as a mouse.

This rubric tells us that this sorting process must be done very thoroughly—with great intelligence. You need to go from Above to Below, and from Below to Above. What is revealed here is that there is an immense body of riches, and keys are hidden in the correspondences. These you need to investigate very thoroughly, following the lines between the causal world and the material world. Think again about the example that I gave of the ropes that connect the pendulums and the wheels. These ropes are the metaphors for all the energies, transformations, and appearances that are to be found between materialization and causation.

THE RUBRIC OF THE STONE

> *In this way you will gain the Glory of the entire*
>   *Universe.*
> *All darkness will lift up for you.*
> *This is the greatest of all powers,*
> *Because it exalts every subtle thing and penetrates every*
>   *solid thing.*

This is the rubric that describes the consecration of the pyramid, and in this way the Stone of the Wise is created. The Stone of the Wise is capable of transforming every metal into gold. The creation of the Stone of the Wise was, for the alchemists, the end stage of alchemy, the stone that changes everything to gold. A great amount of speculation and investigation was put into methods to change metal into gold. Kings have spent enormous amounts of money to support this alchemical phenomenon.

The Stone of the Wise is not physical; it is a metaphor for another reality. The Stone of the Wise is gained at the moment that you, with your consciousness of the One Mind, can unify all four of the Elements from Above to Below. The metals in alchemy are connected with the planetary forces, and together with the sun, they form the Azoth: depicted by a seven-pointed star. The cosmic temple of the alchemists was furnished with this key symbol. When you project the Four Elements around you, and you regard Above and Below as separate directions within the temple, then you—as the central sun—are in the middle, and you are able to penetrate everything with your light. The "entire Universe" tells the tale of Hermes Trismegistus to us. There will no longer be darkness for you, everything is explained and enlightened.

This is the consciousness of the Glory of the Universe: the experience of the unity of the all. These are the Elysian Fields. This consciousness of the Glory of the Universe penetrates everything from Above to Below. This image is incredibly ancient.

In the Egyptian Underworld texts, the traveler is described as one who journeys into the Otherworld and who faces the scales of the goddess Maat. Forty-two judges ask the traveler questions related to the choices he has made during his or her life. The number forty-two is meaningful in this context. It is the product of six times seven: seven is a key number in the Mysteries. Seven times seven is the number that symbolizes you standing at the door that gives access to heaven. In six times seven, one series of seven questions is lacking. And that is the part that the traveler needs to fill in with his or her own wisdom, and with the purified heart—the Alchemical Gold—when his or her heart is weighed on the Scales of Truth.

THE RUBRIC OF THE PATTERN

In this way the Universe was created.
From here derive all wondrous applications,
because this is the Pattern.

This rubric tells us that the laws described in the previous rubrics form a pattern that is the core of the entire universe. Finding the applications for this pattern is of major importance in the emotional, mental, and spiritual world. The Mystery schools applied this pattern to everything you can think of, including the entire culture and design of the landscape, the buildings, mythology, and storage of historical information. If you want to access the knowledge of the Mystery schools and the application of spiritual magic, then you need to study how this ancient pattern was used in classical times, and how, even in this day and age, it still forms the core of both the great religions and the primitive shamanistic practices.

THE RUBRIC OF THE TRINITY

This is why I am called the Three Times Greatest Hermes
I possess all three parts of the Wisdom of the entire Universe
Herewith I have explained fully the Operation of the Sun.

In this piece of the text, the emphasis is on the number three. Three times great is Hermes, and he possesses all three parts of the Wisdom. In classical times, the triangle was often used as a metaphor for divinity. The year was divided into three seasons in Greece and Egypt. In Mesopotamia, the oldest sources mention two seasons, at a later date three. Temples were often dedicated to a trinity of gods: father, mother, and child.

The triangle is the simplest geometrical figure that has a form. The triangle is placed on the Kabbalistic Tree in the Sephirah Binah, together with Prima Materia from which all consciousness derives. The Trinity is an image that is used in the Christian church for the divine form: The Father, the Son, and the Holy Spirit. That the Holy Spirit is a female energy is less known.

The pyramid—the Stone of the Wisdom of Hermes—has one foundation containing the Four Elements and one spirit that penetrates everything. And from the connections between these two levels of consciousness, four divine triangles derive. When you meditate through this numerological puzzle you will come to surprising conclusions.

Hermes has described three levels of consciousness in our reality—the spiritual world, the mental world, and the world of the imagination—and how these levels of consciousness are active in matter. The "Three Times Greatest" indicates three different periods in the history of humanity. The first period is the time before the Flood, in which the gods communicated directly with humanity. This is the mythological First Time. It is the period of the oldest gods, which are known in Mesopotamian mythology as the Seven Sages from before the Flood. The second period is the period of the Mystery tradition, where the organization of primitive societies took place, and where writing was developed. The third period starts with the Greek, who learned to think along logical lines.

You should not regard Hermes as the separate incarnation of one god in a human body. He is an impulse on a long line of a wavelength of consciousness in humanity, which takes place throughout millennia. This stream of consciousness is widely spread and is active in great groups of people in a diversity of professions. It enlightens people who are sensitive to this wavelength. It is an expression of consciousness that inspires humanity as a whole to grow toward a higher level of development. This type of impulse is the essential nature of all the gods.

The "Operation of the Sun" is a way to describe the process that leads to the enlightenment of the Self, the process that is called in alchemy and magic the "Great Work."

THE BOOK OF THOTH—PATHWORKING

Prepare yourself for a meditation. Take special care of your body posture. In the Western Mystery Tradition, we meditate in the Egyptian god-form position. This is the body posture in which pharaohs are pictured while seated. The spine should be straight, both feet placed next to each other on the ground. You need to have a chair that is proportioned for your height: your knees must make an angle of ninety degrees. Take care that your head is straight, and your chin is lowered in the direction of your chest. Start to breath rhythmically. You breathe in during four counts. When your lungs are filled with air, you stop for two seconds, without blocking your throat. Then you breathe out for four seconds. When your lungs are empty, you again take a break of two seconds. This is the rhythm that you are going to establish for all the meditations and the workings on the path. Take a few minutes to establish this pattern of breathing and then forget about it. Assume that your breathing will automatically continue in this slow tempo. If you do not have much experience meditating, the four-two-four-two rhythm might be too slow for you in the beginning. Accept this and practice relaxing your body, because this will also slow down your breathing. Then gradually work toward this rhythm.

———————◆———————

When you are sitting comfortably, relaxed, and your breath slowly moves up and down, you imagine standing before a double wooden door. It is a very old one, like those you sometimes see in castles, with iron hinges and a rusty lock. The upper edge is curved, and it is surrounded by an arch of weathered yellow-colored stones. It is the door of an old building. Imagine this door in as much detail as you can, and then knock on it. The door opens, and you clearly hear the sound of the old iron hinges. It is opened by a figure dressed in a black robe with a hood. Around his waist he wears a cord, on his feet sandals. At his breast he wears an ankh. The face of this figure remains hidden in the shadows of his hood. You hear a male voice ask you what you are searching for here, because you are at the Gate between Time. You answer that you are looking for information that will help you at the beginning of your road of the Mysteries.

The guide shakes his head, he takes up a torch from a bracket on the wall, and he gestures you to follow him. The corridor smells of old stone and it feels a bit damp. The guide closes the door, and then the two of you walk downward into a dark cor-

ridor. Your footsteps sound hollow in this subterranean space. The way curves to the left and to the right, and soon you have lost your sense of orientation. The only thing you know is that you walk downward. Your guide is silent and leads you with assurance. Then, finally, after walking for a while, you come to a second pair of doors. On both doors you see the picture of the holy Ibis, the bird of Thoth.

The guide turns around and says, "This is the door to the library of Alexandria on the astral levels. Here ancient scriptures are stored. Some of them still have physical copies on earth and are stored in libraries, in stone jars under the earth, and in the graves of deceased ancestors. Others only remain in the spirit of those who experienced these truths in the memory of the One Spirit, he who saw these images and took them into himself. You are an exceptional person, because the Inner Planes allow you to explore this information. When you pass these two doors, you come into the reality of this history. Think that what you experience in the inner worlds becomes a part of your consciousness, and thus an irreversible part of the reality that you live."

The guide takes the ankh that hangs around his neck on a chain, and uses it to open the doors. At the moment that your guide unlocks the doors, an inscription on the doors becomes visible. This is burned into the wood with a glowing red flame that appears to come from nowhere. You see to your amazement a text appearing on the door:

> *Everything in this book is true*
> *On its own level of reality.*

At the same time, the outer appearance of the guide changes. He transforms into a youthful well-built young man with bronzed skin. You can see that he has been exposed to a lot of sunlight. The robe changes into an Egyptian costume: a loincloth around his hips, which is woven of very fine white linen. Around his upper arms he wears heavy golden bracelets. His eyes are outlined with black kohl. You do not see any hair on his body. He wears a striped headdress—a blue and gold striped nem-eys, which indicates that this is a person of a high rank. In his hand he holds a wand, around which a snake is coiled. The doors swing open, and suddenly you feel hot air streaming inward. The corridor is lit by blinding white sunlight. The air smells of sweet herbs. Before you, you see a burning hot desert. The sand swirls inward. The guide gestures you to follow him, and you walk along a primitive road between dusty palm trees. At both sides of the road you see low houses built from mud brick. You see that the people use palm leaves for the roofs.

A few chariots pass you by, drawn by horses. The guide tells you that you are on your way to the palace of Ramses the Great. His son has a message especially for you. Now you enter the palace building. The guide greets the guards as if they know each other very well. In the palace you are welcomed, and are led to the rooms of the prince. The guide tells you that the person you are going to meet is the son of Ramses the Great, Prince Khaemwaset. As the oldest son of Pharaoh, he has access to all the scriptures in the empire, and to all the old sacred buildings. He can investigate the Mysteries, which are already ancient even in his time. The special thing about this prince is that he is a very talented and learned writer, as well as a magician at the court of Ramses. He regularly teaches old Egyptian magic. Students from all times throughout history are invited to attend his lectures. Khaemwaset is a very learned man in the area of old scriptures. He has worked with the legendary Book of Thoth. He has investigated it, and today he will teach about it.

Then the double doors swing open and the prince enters, together with his court. He takes his place on the central throne in the reception hall, and gestures that everyone be seated. You look around you and see that a group of people has gathered together who come from all cultures and times. Magicians and students sit on the cushions that are spread throughout the hall. Everyone has brought writing

materials from their own time. You do not have anything with you, not knowing that you needed to bring anything. Next to you, someone takes a piece of parchment and a goose feather out of his robes. Another has a wooden stylus to engrave letters into a clay tablet. A bit further away, somebody opens a laptop computer. Khaemwaset raises his hand, and immediately the whispering around you stops and it is quiet.

Khaemwaset speaks: "Today I am going to tell you about the discovery of the Book of Thoth. Thoth has of course left us many scriptures, which are all very worthwhile. This book is probably the most important one of all. I heard about this book when I visited one of the Houses of Life, and read in the inscriptions about the existence of this book. It is probably the mightiest magical writing, because with this book a human can enchant heaven and earth. You can learn to understand the language of all the birds and the animals.

"The inscription told me that this book was buried in the necropolis of Memphis. I decided to look for the book. Finally I found it in the tomb of one of my ancestors,

prince and magister Nanefer Kaptah. I knew that Nanefer Kaptah was a seeker after spiritual truths. I entered into his tomb and made a sacrifice to his Ka. I shared a meal with him in his mastaba. When I put the gifts down on the offering table, sprinkled water around, and called his name to greet him, both the prince and his wife appeared to share a meal with me.

"When I asked about the Book of Thoth, it immediately appeared between the two of them. I asked Nanefer Kaptah whether I could take the book with me, because it probably contained the knowledge that I needed. Both the prince and his wife protested forcefully, because the book has caused them unending difficulties. Nanefer Kaptah said that he also had studied the inscriptions and texts of the walls of the temples. During his quest for wisdom he met a priest in one of the chapels, who started to laugh at him very loudly. Nanefer Kaptah asked why this priest laughed so loud.

"The priest answered; 'I do not laugh at you. I laugh at the fact that you want to decipher these texts. There is one text that is really important: the Book that Thoth wrote himself. That is the book that will bring you to the gods. When you read just two pages of this book, you will enchant the heavens, the earth, the abyss, the mountains, and the sea. You will know what the birds say in the air, and learn to understand the language of the creeping animals. You will see the fishes in the deepest parts of the ocean, because you have access to a magical power that will call them up from the deep. When you read the second page, you will arrive in the worlds of the spirits, and you will regain your own shape, which you have on earth. You will see the sun shine in the air, together with the gods and the full moon.'"

All the students hang on the words of Khaemwaset. A wave of excitement goes through the study room. A book that gives this much power is exactly what everybody is waiting for! Khaemwaset looks round the room. He raises his hand and immediately it is quiet again.

"Yes," Khaemwaset says. "I reacted in exactly the same way. I stood there in that tomb and had this very book within my reach. That book was lying before me, ready to take with me, in the mastaba between the Ka of Nanefer Kaptah and his

wife, protected by seven boxes. There was no clearer proof that Nanefer Kaptah had actually found the book.

"Nanefer Kaptah told his story. He too became totally excited when he heard this story. He had but one wish left, and that was to get access to this incredible book full of magical knowledge. After he had royally rewarded the priest for the gift of knowledge of the existence of this book, the priest told him where he could find it.

"The priest told Nanefer Kaptah, 'This book lies in the middle of the river at Coptos. It is enclosed in an iron box. In the iron box you will find a bronze box. In the bronze box there is a box of sycamore wood. Then comes a box of ivory and then one of ebony wood. In the ivory and ebony wooden box is a silver box, and therein a golden box. This box contains the book. The golden box that contains the book is surrounded with snakes, scorpions, and all kinds of creeping animals. A snake that has eternal life has encircled itself around this box to protect it.'

"When the priest told all this to Nanefer Kaptah, he became ecstatic and was swept off his feet by the words of the priest."

Khaemwaset continues the story: "The face of Nanefer Kaptah became very sad. 'I did not tell you the rest of the story yet,' he said. 'An object of power such as this also asks for the capacity to control its power. The temptation to use this kind of power before this control has been mastered is enormous, and the results are disastrous.' Nanefer Kaptah decided to go to Coptos. He decided that he must have this book. His wife tried to talk to him because she realized that he was on his way to sorrow, but he refused to listen to her. He went to the king and told him everything the priest had told him. Pharaoh gave his royal boat to Nanefer Kaptah, and everything that belonged to it, to travel with his wife and his little boy to Coptos. He had decided to fetch the book from there. The priests and the High Priest of Isis in Coptos came to greet them. They entered into the temple of Isis and Horus. Nanefer Kaptah brought an ox, a goose, some wine, and sacrificed food and drink to Isis of Coptos to ask her blessings on his adventure. Together with his wife, he was given a beautiful house to stay in, and he celebrated there for four days together with the priests of Isis of Coptos and their wives.

"On the morning of the fifth day, he called a priest to him, and this one created a magical cabin for him that was filled with magical helpers and tools. He enchanted the vessel. The priest lowered the royal ship into the water and filled it with sand. The priest said good-bye to him, and he sailed toward heaven. Nanefer Kaptah was waiting at the river in Coptos for the results of this journey. The priest said: 'Ushabtis work for me at the place where the book is.' The magical helpers worked day and night, and when they found the book after three days, the priest threw the sand out of the magical cabin and made a sandbank in the river. Then Nanefer Kaptah and the priest saw that the box that contained the book was surrounded with snakes, scorpions, and all kinds of creeping insects.

"The priest enchanted the snakes and the scorpions so that they were unable to move. He went to the eternal snake, fought with it and was able to kill it. But it became alive again and took on a new shape. He fought it again and killed it for a second time. And again the snake reassumed its shape. He slashed it into two parts and put sand between the pieces, so that the snake could not heal itself. Then Nanefer Kaptah opened the iron box, then the bronze box. Then he opened the box of sycamore wood. He opened the ivory box and the ebony box. He found the silver box and the golden box. Then he found the book. He took the book from the box and started to recite the Hekau—the magical words—and he enchanted the heavens and the earth, the abyss, the mountains, and the sea. He understood the birds of the air and the fish of the deep and what the animals of the hills said. He read another page of the Hekau, and he saw the sun appearing in the air, with all the gods, the full moon, and the stars in all their shapes. He saw the fish from the deep, because there appeared a divine force that took them up from the water. Then he read the spell he had spoken over the Ushabtis, and he said to them. 'Work for me and bring me back to the place where I come from.'

"They worked day and night, and thus it happened that Nanefer Kaptah returned to the place where his wife was waiting for him at the river in Coptos. She did not drink nor eat, nor had she done anything on earth. She sat there as someone who had died. She told him that she too wanted to see this book, for which she had had to stand up against so many difficulties.

"He gave her the book, and when she started to read the page with the Hekau, she also enchanted the heavens and the earth, the abyss, the mountains, and the seas. She also knew what the birds of the air and the fishes of the deep were saying, and the animals of all the hills. She read a second page, and she saw the sun shining in the air, together with all the gods, the full moon, and the stars in all their shapes. She saw the fishes from the deep, because there appeared a divine power that pulled them upward from the waters. Because she could not write, she asked Nanefer Kaptah for help. Nanefer Kaptah ordered a new piece of papyrus and wrote on it everything that was in the book that was lying before him. He drenched the papyrus in beer and washed all the letters off so that their powers would be a part of the liquid, and then he drank it, so that he would know everything that was written down.

The students in the study room write and nod with their heads. Everyone knows that the Hekau contain a tremendous power. When you drink the Hekau of a book with such powers, they become a part of yourself, and then you become as mighty as the great god Thoth, who wrote them down.

Khaemwaset continues the story of Nanefer Kaptah: "I am still in his mastaba, and I listened to how my forefather told his story. I loved the story; I did not see any reason for sadness. The voice of Nanefer Kaptah sounded like a broken man when he spoke further. He told how they returned to Coptos and organized a party to honor Isis and Horus of Coptos. They went to the harbor and sailed north. When they were on their way, Thoth discovered what Nanefer Kaptah had done with the book. Thoth immediately consulted Ra and told him, 'I know now for sure that my book and my revelations are within Nanefer Kaptah, the son of Pharaoh. He has pushed me from my place and taken it for his own. He has robbed my box with scriptures and killed the guards.'

"Ra answered, 'He is yours: take revenge on him and his family.' Thoth sends down a ray from the heavens with the command: 'Let Nanefer Kaptah not return safely to Memphis with his family.' And half an hour later, the little boy fell out of the royal ship and drowned. Everyone on the ship screamed. Nanefer Kaptah ran from the cabin and read a spell. By divine power, the body of the child came up out of the water. He read another spell, and this one caused the boy to speak about what happened to him. The boy told about what Thoth had said to Ra. The boy was dead, and they had to embalm him. They buried him in his coffin in the cemetery of Coptos as a rich and noble person.

"The disasters were not finished yet. They wanted to travel back to Thebes as soon as possible to inform Pharaoh about what happened. So they went to the harbor and sailed away from Coptos. When they arrived at the place where the little boy fell overboard, the wife of Nanefer Kaptah bent too far out of the boat and fell into the river. Nanefer Kaptah read a spell and brought up her body out of the river by means of divine force. He let her tell him what happened to her and he heard what Thoth had told Ra. He brought her back to Coptos, embalmed her in the manner of an honored person, and laid her in a tomb beside her child.

"Then Nanefer Kaptah went back into the heavens and sailed over the Heavenly Waters. He came to the spot where his wife and son had fallen into the river. He spoke to his heart: 'Is it my obligation to go back to Coptos and lay at their side? What do I tell Pharaoh when I return in Memphis? I cannot tell him that they are both dead and that I am still alive.' Nanefer Kaptah let himself be tied to the book and dropped out of the boat.

"The royal boat went along without anybody knowing where he was. It traveled to Memphis and there Pharaoh was told what had happened. Pharaoh mourned, and the soldiers, the High Priests, and the priests of Ptah mourned. Then the king saw Nanefer Kaptah and he was lifted out of the water. He still had the book. Pharaoh decided to hide the book. This happened when Nanefer Kaptah was buried."

The classroom of students is entirely silent. Everyone is impressed by the story. Khaemwaset continues with the remark: "It is important for all to understand that certain kinds of Wisdom are not fit for everyone, because they are not ready to receive this teaching. Arrogance and power can cause them to gain access to certain materials and levels of consciousness. When they are not yet ready to understand what they experience, and because of this cannot integrate it in the right way into their lives, the consequence is that they destroy themselves, as well as the ones surrounding them who suffer from it. This is caused by their shortsightedness, their *greed, and egotism. These qualities can be so subtle that even people who have posi-tions of power—such as royalty—can act against the law. Also, they can become guilty of unjust thoughts that appear to be just and true.*

"Finally, Thoth himself has the authority about all this. Although Nanefer Kap-tah had been warned, he neglected this warning and caused pressure. Aspirants must practice patience and humility while they purify their hearts. Then they will meet an authenticated teacher who will guide them in the right direction, and who will show them the Mysteries at the right time and the right place."

Then from behind Khaemwaset there rises a gigantic energy. It is as if it emerges from the prince. For a flash of a moment you think you see a gigantic jackal, then you decide that it is an optical illusion. Khaemwaset rises and speaks: "Apuat, can you take the students back to where they come from?" Your guide rises and bows. The entire room stands up. People collect their things, and your guide takes you out of the palace. A little bit further, the Ibis doors of the Temple of Thoth appear. Apuat opens them with his ankh, and together you walk back into the winding cor-ridor, ascending this time. The climb makes you short of breath.

Finally you see a light in the distance, which shines through the wooden doors that form the gateway through time. When you arrive there you notice that, some-where along the road, your guide has clothed himself in his black robes again. It is much colder here. He opens the gate for you and you thank him. Then you stand before your body, which is sitting deeply relaxed in a chair. Stand before your body and sit back into it. Very slowly you feel how your consciousness reconnects with your body. Come back to the here and now in your own time. When you are ready, you stretch yourself in order to ground yourself firmly. After this exercise you eat and drink a little bit.

BASED ON AN EGYPTIAN FAIRY TALE

4

THE TEMPLE OF
THE COSMOS

*Do you not know, Asclepius, that Egypt is an image of the
Heaven, or to express it even more precisely: that in Egypt
all the mechanisms of the forces which rule and are active
in the Heaven have been transformed unto the Earth? No,
you can better say that the entire cosmos inhabits this land
as its temple.*

HERMES TRISMEGISTUS

In the text above, Hermes expresses precisely how in antiquity spirituality, culture, and the land were all interconnected. This entire chapter
will be devoted to these sentences, which express exactly how, within the
Mystery tradition, the law "as Above, so Below" was applied to the smallest details. The robes, the decorations of the temple, the placing of altars,
the expression of the central myth in the temple, the rituals: everything is
drenched with this interconnectedness.

THE ROBE OF THE MAGICIAN

Accordingly, Moses selected his brother, choosing him
out of all men, because of his superior virtue, to be High
Priest, his sons he appointed priests. He washed them
all over with the most pure and vivifying water of the
fountain and then he gave them their sacred vestments,
giving to his brother the robe which reached down to his
feet, and the mantle which covered the shoulders, as a sort
of breast-plate, being an embroidered robe, adorned with
all kinds of figures, and a representation of the universe.
PHILO OF ALEXANDRIA, *THE LIFE OF MOSES, II*

When we try to imagine a magician, automatically an image of a fig-ure wearing a pointed hat and dressed in a long robe covered with stars appears. This image has been carefully cultivated by Hollywood, and comes to us from fairy tales. However, this image is not complete, nor is it correctly understood. The function of the robe is, first of all, to indi-cate that you are leaving everyday reality and that you are stepping into mythical time. Your dress is dependent on the myth with which you are working, and you dress in costumes that belong to the myth's culture. When you work with the Greek Mysteries, you wear Greek robes. When you do your work in the Mesopotamian tradition, then you clothe your-self in the manner of the priesthood of that time. When you are working with magical astrology, then you dress yourself in a robe that reflects the starry heavens.

In the field of magic you will see very plain robes and also very elabo-rate robes. Every robe is in accordance with the ritual that is planned. You may work with the different practices of the Mystery tradition, and each one has its own background in clothing. A basic robe is the simple one that monks wear, which has a hood and a cord around the waist.

I was already dressed in the straight black robe and the
silver headdress of a Moon priestess: now I assumed the

astral robes, imagining myself clad as befitted my grade. I felt the weight of the Uraeus serpent arch itself over my brow: I felt the pressure of the silver kestos on my hips. In my hand was the Astral Ankh as well as the terrestrial one. With this I drew the Moon signs of the Moon and I invoked with the great Names of power. The Power came down. Every piece of ritual furniture, every symbol on the walls was edged with light.

DION FORTUNE, *MOON MAGIC*

Just as in the case of the robes of the High Priest of Philo of Alexandria, the basic robe is a representation of the entire universe. The meaning of the robe is visualized every time and is consciously repeated in the robing prayers. In many temples, practitioners are in the habit of naming the function of the clothing in the form of a prayer. The robing prayers are recited first of all to focus the attention on the ritual. By means of the robing prayers, the shift to trance consciousness is made.

When each part of the ritual clothing is put on, the appropriate lines of the robing prayer are repeated in silence. During the dressing, a first transformation is made between the world of everyday life and the magical reality of the Inner Planes. In this way, dressing yourself in the robes becomes the first step in the shift to what is called the magical personality. This is a part of the self that is kept apart and is *solely* used during magical work.

What does a basic robe look like? The basic colors of the robe are black or white. Black is used as a color because this is symbolic of the soil of the earth. Also, this color indicates that you are trying to transform all of the colors of the light around you, and to absorb them to make them a part of your inner core, in the same way that black as a color also absorbs all colors of light. White is the second basic color for a robe. It is used as an under-robe, because white symbolizes the purity of the soul—the soul that has purified itself by means of the work in the Inner Planes, and that radiates this to its environment. When the white robe serves as an under-robe, then the black robe is to protect the sacredness of the work from those eyes that cannot appreciate it. The basic form of the robe is symbolic as well. It has the shape of the Hebrew letter Tau, our letter T. This letter is located on the Kabbalistic Tree on the path you use to walk from the earth plane to the first layers of the astral world: the thirty-second path.

The robe of the magician—with all its attributes—speaks to the imagination of the people who are performing the rituals as well as to the outside world. It is a tool that carries with it the potential pitfall of enchantment through glamour. But it also belongs to the tools in the temple that can lift the entire atmosphere by its beauty. The reciting of the robing prayers has the function of emphasizing the goals of the ritual. You can understand why a sexy Gothic dress is not appropriate ritual clothing: a ritual is not an episode of the Addams Family. It goes without saying that all upside-down crosses and pentagrams are also totally out of place in a ceremony of spiritual magic.

The hood of the robe is functional in that it serves to prevent you from becoming distracted by any light in the environment while performing the pathworkings. When the hood is used in ritual, it just covers the eyes. The shape of the hood is the shape of the Hebrew letter Yod ׳.

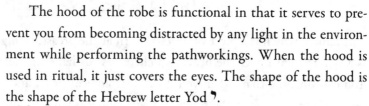

This can be beautifully observed in many versions of the tarot card, the Hermit. The Yod is the basic letter of the Hebrew Aleph-Beth. All the other letters are variations on the Yod. The Yod is the divine spark that comes down from the highest heavens, and when these Yods descend, they form the Word of God. This causes the universe to come into existence. Here you see the Yod and the so-called Tetragrammaton. The letters Yod, Heh, Vav, and Heh (a second time) together form the image of Adam Kadmon, the Heavenly Man. Yod is the head of Adam Kadmon. The first Heh are his arms and shoulders, the Vav is the spine, and the second Heh forms the legs. The Yod symbolizes the divine nature of the soul.

THE CORD

The cord is used to tie the robe around the waist. The colors of the cord vary per group, and are used to indicate the degree of the person. It forms a circle around the body. This is symbolic for the *ouroboros,* the snake biting itself in the tail. It is a circle that is symbolic of the unity of divinity.

THE SANDALS

The practitioner's footwear should be sandals that are used only in the temple. These symbolize the path that is walked. When you wear these, you are walking the sacred road. The sandals provide the connection between yourself and the earth. If the floor of the temple is the earth itself, then the sandals are in fact the winged sandals of Hermes, which bring you from the road on earth into the astral world.

THE LAMEN

The lamen, which is a piece of jewelry worn at the breast, is important. It is a symbol worn over the heart, which serves to shape the heart energy. You can imagine that, when you do an astrological ritual and you represent a planetary power, the symbol of this planet is worn as a lamen.

THE MAGICAL RING

The magical ring is worn on the forefinger of the dominant hand. The ring is made of gold or silver and contains a gemstone or semiprecious stone. The stones in these rings are of one piece and are quite large. Stones that are used for magical work—and especially a stone used in a ring—are chosen very carefully and are purified and consecrated before being used in ritual. The energetic charge of the rituals is stored in these rings. The accumulated magical energy transforms the ring into a highly charged object.

There are other objects that can function as ritual clothing that are added for special occasions. Though black and white are the basic colors of the robe, you may want to wear different colors for other occasions. You can very easily make a series of tabards to wear over your basic robe. Instead of a hood, you can also wear all kinds of headdresses from different cultures.

COSTUMES

In addition to the basic robes, there are also robes that are worn on special occasions. Look back to the picture of Khaemwaset and see how he is dressed. This is the ceremonial costume of the Sempriest, to be used during Egyptian rituals. These robes are used when working with mythology. Magical rituals that make use of ritual drama have a very strong effect on the imagination and can free high quantities of energy. The participants dress in the robes that represent the gods that they personify.

THE CLOTHING OF THE HEAVENLY MAN—
PATHWORKING

To give you an idea of the importance of ritual clothing and the effect it has, I will take you with me on a pathworking journey. First, prepare yourself for a meditation. Take care that you will not be disturbed during the exercise. Avoid wearing clothing that is too tight. Create a nice atmosphere for yourself: light some candles and incense. Make sure that you are comfortable. First relax and stabilize your breathing into the rhythm of four-two-four-two. When you look toward the black of your closed eyes, imagine gazing into the blackness of a starry night. See how an endless space stretches out on all sides. In your mind, look downward, and you will see that your feet are standing on a floor with black and white tiles.

Suddenly you hear a soft voice: someone or something speaks to you. You listen to what this voice has to tell you. You focus on the soft whispering. It takes all your effort, and it seems to come from nowhere. You do not see anyone, but clearly you hear the whispering in your right ear. "Do you see that you are walking on consecrated ground? You are standing on the consecrated floor of a temple. You are walking on the floor of opposites, which are moving between light and darkness, between day and night."

Now the floor appears to be moving. It seems to stretch out in all directions. You are highly impressed by the wideness of the landscape as it expands further in all directions. It becomes bigger as you are aware of your own heartbeat. You see that, slowly, stars start to appear in the space above you and below you. Now you clearly hear the voice of this guide, who is female.

"I will take you with me to a place on the Inner Planes where you will be clothed in divine robes. It is important that you lay down your common clothes. Take off your clothes and cleanse yourself with the waters that come down from heaven."

To your amazement it starts to rain softly. The black and white floor begins to change shape, and stairs materialize in black and white. The water starts to reflect the starry heavens. You decide to undress yourself and bathe in the basin that forms at your feet. As you carefully descend the stairs and step into the water, you now hear the voice reciting very melodiously:

> *Sink down, sink down in your spirit.*
> *Sink down in the purifying oceans of divine love.*
> *I call you, come to the areas where I live.*
> *I live at the place where fate is spun.*
> *The cloths that I weave are made of silk threads.*
> *I am the weaver, I weave nets of Wisdom.*
> *I capture you in my nets and weave you in my web.*
> *From love I weave relationships.*
> *Light and darkness are the woof and the warp.*
> *I weave robes of cosmic foam.*

"Be welcome in the Cosmic Oceans of purification. Drench yourself in joy!" You decide to drench yourself in the basin. When you come out of the waters, it has started snowing. In spite of the white flakes that descend on your skin, you do not feel cold. Together with the white snow, a golden-colored spider descends on a thin thread. The spider hangs before you, and she weaves the snowflakes into a pattern. To your amazement, the snow crystallizes on your skin into a silk robe that is decorated with the most beautiful ice flowers.

"I dress you in the purity of a winter night. This absolute purity is the state of your soul when you cleanse yourself in the primordial source of the universe."

You see your image mirrored in the surface of the water. You feel so pure and clean that you appear to radiate light.

"That is indeed the case," the female voice says—she hears your thought. *"This purity is your birthright. I will weave the light that you radiate into the robes I am going to make for you, for now and for the future. The cleansing waters wherein you are standing at the moment are always available to you, to give you back your purity when you bathe yourself in this liquid. The only thing you need to do to regain it is come to these areas with this intention. The method to come here is by means of prayer, meditation, contemplation, and willpower. You will be helped by your inner guides.*

"The joy and sorrow that you will experience in your life in the House of Crystal will not leave these robes untouched, so you will need to return to refresh them— for a shorter or a longer time. To take care that your core remains pure as long as possible, I will now weave a mantle of concealment for you. This I weave from velvet threads, black in color, which I will spin out of the starry night."

You watch how the spider works: she tears threads out of the night and, where she pulls them out of the surface, little holes form in the velvet black depth.

"Because I weave the mantle of concealment, an activity is generated," the spider tells you. *"Everywhere that I take threads from the night, a void is created. This nothingness will fill itself. The cosmos always returns to its state of balance, and the emptiness will fill itself with fate. And now watch how the emptiness fills itself with star fire. In this way a horoscope is created. Do not fear,*

because fate will strengthen your soul and give it more splendor than ever."

The spider finishes the beautiful black mantle that is woven from the starry night. "Now we need the materials with which to fasten this mantle onto your white robe." The spider starts to work again, and she plucks fire from the stars of the zodiac from the heavens and attaches sparks of stellar fire on a brooch. The jewel radiates, and as you watch it you are struck by realizations without understanding where they come from.

"See here, the jewel of Wisdom," the spider says. "This appears to me an excellent brooch to pin the mantle of concealment onto your left shoulder. Now we need another pin to fix the right side." The spider looks into the night sky and says thoughtfully: "The mantle of concealment will embrace you and protect you with the Understanding of the Great Mother."

And promptly a supernova explodes in the dark night, a bloodred explosion against the deep black background.

"Ah . . ." the spider says. "Of course! The mantle is pinned on the right side with a black rose with a bloodred heart: the symbol of the Great Mother." The spider takes the explosion out of space, and weaves it into a brooch of black obsidian with a kernel of bloodred star ruby. This she uses to pin the mantle at your left shoulder.

"Shoes," the spider whispers. "Someone who works for the Light always walks on sacred soil. Blessed sandals will ensure that the ground on which you walk is always sacred. The novice needs to learn to balance light and darkness into the self. I weave your sandals from the hair of the beautiful woman of the House of Experiences."

You look where the spider goes, and you see that you have become very big because of how you view the cosmos. You have become so big that the world under your feet looks like a ball with a diameter of one meter. From the globe a female figure forms. She is dressed entirely in white. She speaks to you: "Weave your shoes from my hair. I give you wings, and you can create winged sandals for yourself," the woman tells you.

When she has spoken she changes into a white flame that rises and generates a glow that spreads over the entire landscape. The flame rises and causes rainbows to form in the atmosphere. The flame rises higher and changes into a gigantic dove. The bird shakes its wings, and a cloud of white feathers comes whirling downward.

Your intuition tells you this is a magnificent gift from the Bride of the Cosmos. Your sandals become winged, woven out of the feathers of the holy dove.

"That is a gift that you need to be grateful for," the spider says. You shake your head in amazement. You cannot fully understand the reach of this gift, but the meaning will become clearer during your journey. At the same time, the spider has begun weaving your temple slippers out of the feathers of the dove.

"What we need now is a decent cord."

"A cord?" you ask.

"Yes," the spider says. "The cord is the symbol of the unification with the gods. The cord dresses you in the circle of unity. The cord is the cartouche in which you as a living soul—a spark who came from the unity—unite yourself with the source. This intention renews itself every time you bind the cord around your waist. Cords I always weave from the colors of the rainbow with the rays of the light of your aura, as you grow in purity along the path. The novice starts with a ring of white light."

The spider starts to weave a cord from the rays of light that are radiating from your aura, caused by the whiteness of your under-robe.

"You are now dressed in the regalia of the novice. I weave all other pieces of clothing of the Heavenly Man when you have earned them. You need to create the warp of the threads by your aspiration, hope, and prayer. The woof you create by endurance, sound thinking, and sweat. The regalia of the initiate are hidden in the secret spaces you find at the sides of the road of the Ladder of Light."

At the moment the spider says this, the black-and-white–colored tiles change into a staircase that leads into the endless depths of the cosmos. "This stairway spirals upward to areas that you are totally unaware of. It takes you to the deepest depths and the greatest heights of the cosmos. It takes you along abysses of egotistic needs and lack of understanding. It takes you along ecstatic experiences and holy visions. Along the road, you will be helped by the entities of the inner worlds: they will help you to pass through the dangerous places when you choose to listen to their advice. The angels and the gods are delighted when a new seeker starts *to climb the Ladder of Light. They will help you. You will slowly find the regalia of the initiate after you have successfully passed the valleys of the stumbling blocks, and have passed the gaps of desperation. When you are dressed in the robes of the Heavenly Man, and are carried forth by the winged sandals, then you are ready to climb the staircase toward the universe. My work is finished for now. It is time for me to travel back to my own time and place."*

Before your eyes, a red thread now becomes visible. "When you want to find me and have need of my knowledge, you only need to follow this thread." The spider fastens a red thread to your belly button. Very quickly the spider climbs the thread. You follow her with your eyes. As the spider climbs upward, a spider's web of red threads becomes visible. It stretches out over the entire horizon; wherever you look, you see the web. It is in fact strange that you had not noticed this web before. The spider has connected everything together: heaven and earth. The worlds of the gods and the world of humanity are connected with a gigantic umbilical cord through which "bloodred" blood pulsates.

"My web is my garment," the spider says. "My robe is woven from the love of the blood-ties that connect heaven and earth with each other. It connects the animals, the humans, the angels, and the gods. When you need my help, connect yourself with the place where I live. My residence is the crown of stars. Crown yourself with the Corona Borealis. Call me by my name, and I will come to you."

And now the spider has entirely vanished from sight. You are standing alone at the beginning of the staircase that rises upward from the black-and-white—blocked landscape. Everything is ready for you to start your journey. For now, you have learned enough, and the knowledge of the inner worlds needs to sink in and be processed. Create a wardrobe in the portico of this temple and hang your magical robes carefully on coat hangers. Now you should dress yourself once more in your normal clothes and walk back to the place where your body rests. Connect yourself with it, and return back to the here and now.

THE SYMBOLOGY OF THE TEMPLE

THE BODY FOR A GOD ON EARTH

Now that we have examined what the clothing of ritual symbolizes, it is time to explain the symbolism of the ancient temples. A Mystery temple is the body of a god on earth. The temple is constructed according to the same rules of the law "As Above, so Below" that is applied to the robe of the magician. A temple's design is based upon the mythology of its tradition. The temples were built pointed toward cosmic events, such as the heliacal rising of a particular star, or a special time in the cycle of the year.

Slowly, archeologists and astronomers have come to discover exactly how some buildings were positioned so that they pointed toward the stars. Some temples are constructed in such a way that the sun passes exactly above the main corridor. There are temples in which the sun lights up the main altar or the statue of a god on an exact date, such as the summer or winter solstice. The locations of stone circles are chosen based on the same principle. What is important to realize is that all of these sacred structures, constructed in classical times, were built according to the matrix of sacred mandalas. They were located at meaningful places in the land where—according to mythology—important events had taken place.

*Malta, Mnajdra Temple; picture taken from the place of
the lacking head (see map on next page).*

91

A PRAYER IN STONE AND LIGHT

The temple is a prayer in stone and light, just as the robe is a prayer in fabric. The entire building was designed and built in accordance with certain directions of heaven. Many temples chose the East as the central direction, while others were directed to the North. The choice of a central direction is related to the god, the myth, and the natural phenomena of the tradition.

THE BODY OF GOD

Temples were built to serve as houses for gods or goddesses. The temple itself was often given an interior design and the outer look of a human being to create a fit house for the deity. On the island of Malta you can see this very well. These very old sanctuaries, even older than the Egyptian pyramids, have the shape of a goddess with a figure resembling the statue

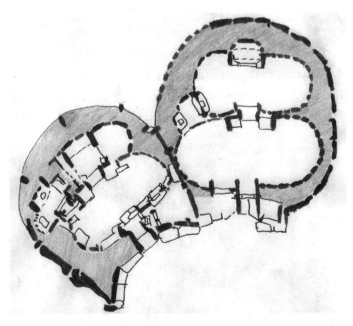

Map of the Temple of Mnajdra on Malta. The temple has the form of two goddesses who—like the goddess statues found on Malta—are very voluptuous.

of the Venus of Willendorf: a small and broad woman with a good deal of body flesh and large breasts.

The temple entrance is located at a position analogous to the goddess's vulva. When you enter into the temple, you enter into her womb. When you leave the temple, you are born again.

This practice of giving sacred buildings the shape of a deity was followed in the Middle Ages by the builders of cathedrals. Every church—Roman, Greek Orthodox, or Russian Orthodox—was built in the shape of a cross. In the East you find the crown of the church. On the level of the heart, you find the main altar while, traditionally, the baptismal font and the organ are located directly opposite the place where, in the body, the Element water is located (the bladder, the womb). The arms of the cross are dedicated to the father and the mother of Christ. If the church is devoted to the holy mother, then you can sometimes find, at the place of the womb, a labyrinth as a symbol for the gateway between life and death. You can find an example of this in Chartres, France, where Catholic churches have adopted this tradition of the Mysteries.

THE FOUR CARDINAL DIRECTIONS

A space used for a temple to perform rituals is first divided into the four cardinal directions: East, South, West, and North. These directions follow the movement of the sun according to the principle "As Above, so Below." The sun rises in the East, moves to the South at noon—the hottest part of the day—sinks in the West, and becomes invisible in the North. In this way, the eastern interior of a temple is dedicated to the symbols expressing the rising sun; the South is devoted to the noonday sun; the West to the sinking Sun, and the North to the night.

The journey of the sun through the wheel of the year is also expressed within the temple. In the East it is spring, in the South it is summer, in the West autumn, and in the North it is winter. On the winter solstice, during the darkest part of the year, a new light is born. The East is the quarter of the rising sun, the rising light. The North is the quarter of Earth and, at the same time, also the quarter of the eternal stars.

THE BASIC STRUCTURE OF THE TEMPLE

Let us take a look at the basic structure of the temple. For an example I have chosen a square, because in this shape most aspects can be optimally observed. In a square, there is an equal amount of space for each cardinal direction. Of course you will meet variations on this plan. But as a plan, it expresses the symbols of the temples from classical times as well as those of today. The plan presented here is based on the Golden Dawn tradition, which itself has been based on Kabbalistic symbols.

In the middle you find an altar that is waist high—exactly as high as the middle of a human being. It has the form of a double cube. The inside of the altar is white, whereas the outside is black.

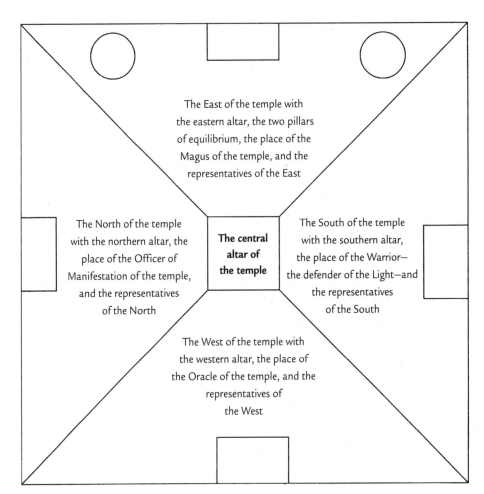

The East of the temple with the eastern altar, the two pillars of equilibrium, the place of the Magus of the temple, and the representatives of the East

The North of the temple with the northern altar, the place of the Officer of Manifestation of the temple, and the representatives of the North

The central altar of the temple

The South of the temple with the southern altar, the place of the Warrior—the defender of the Light—and the representatives of the South

The West of the temple with the western altar, the place of the Oracle of the temple, and the representatives of the West

The altar has this form because it conforms to the principle "As Above, so Below," corresponding to the three-dimensional holy space of the cosmos around us. The colors have been chosen for the same reasons as the colors of the robe. On the central altar the energy of the rituals is collected.

Every cardinal direction is furnished uniquely and is assigned its own color. The colors tend to vary between ritual group and per school. The colors express the quality of the sun in that quarter, and are in relation to the magical landscape that is built within the temple. The furniture of the temple supports the magical circle within which the energy is called during ritual.

I work with the color scheme presented below. It is based on the three axes that form the three dimensions of the manifested universe.

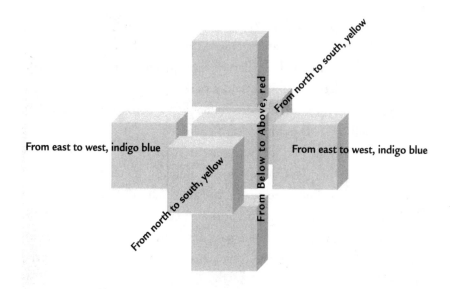

THE RAINBOW IN THE TEMPLE

The first axis is the one running from Below to Above, to which I give the color red. I call it the axis of Rising Fire. It is a column of passion that connects the fire of the core of the earth with Cosmic Fire. The second axis is that from east to west, to which I give the color indigo, because it divides the sweet Waters Above from the salt Waters Below. The third axis is that from north to south, to which I give the color yellow. This axis I connect with the Breath of God. This is the increasing and decreasing light associated with the sound heard throughout nature when the mantra "Yod-Heh-Vav-Heh" is vibrated (see below) through the wheel of the year.

א Aleph, ox, Breath of God

The Breath of God is in Hebrew writing connected with the letter Aleph and to the Element of Air. The magical image is the ox, the animal that warms with his breath the newborn redeemer.

מ Mem, Cosmic Water

Cosmic Water is connected to the letter Mem. These are the heavenly Waters wherefrom the divine manna falls downward.

ש Shin, tooth, fiery life force

The fiery life force is summarized under the letter Shin. This letter is in fact an altar from which three flames rise upward. The magical image belonging to this letter is the tooth of a snake.

These are the three Mother letters of the Hebrew Aleph-Beth. Red, indigo, and yellow are the three primal colors. When you mix these three primal colors in paint (matter) you get the color black, the color of the earth. When you mix these same colors in light, then you get white light, the essence of God. These are put on the altar: dark on the outside, light within. In the inner cube, where the three lines of primal colors meet, the color of the altar and of the human soul naturally develops: the blackness of the concealment through the Garment of Matter, the Light of Purity of the soul.

The next step is the connection of the colors to the cardinal directions: light blue to the East, orange to the South, green to the West, and violet to the North. In this way I have created the entire rainbow in the temple: God is light. The rainbow is the symbol of the connection between a human and God: light in seven different colors. These four colors for the cardinal directions relate to the qualities of the Four Elements in the magical circle.

5

THE MAGICAL CIRCLE

The Central Mandala of the Western Mysteries

Contrary to what people often assume, the magical circle is built within the square space of the temple. All the psychic qualities are divided into the Four Elements (Air, Fire, Water, Earth) and Spirit. They have been connected to the journey of the sun throughout the day and throughout the seasons. When you start to work with the magical circle, you must realize that you in fact make a three-dimensional sphere that also extends beneath the ground. Contrary to what I had previously thought, the magical circle is not a flat circle drawn on the floor. It is an astrally projected sphere in the temple space, centered at eye level.

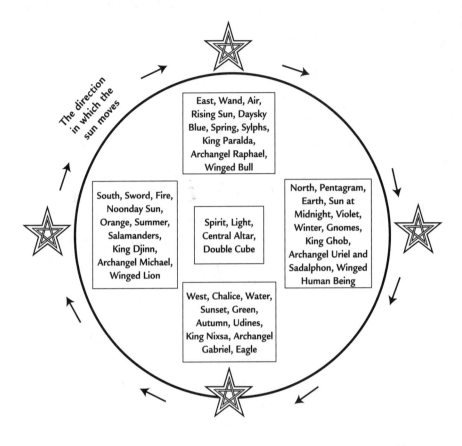

The direction in which the sun moves

East, Wand, Air, Rising Sun, Daysky Blue, Spring, Sylphs, King Paralda, Archangel Raphael, Winged Bull

South, Sword, Fire, Noonday Sun, Orange, Summer, Salamanders, King Djinn, Archangel Michael, Winged Lion

Spirit, Light, Central Altar, Double Cube

North, Pentagram, Earth, Sun at Midnight, Violet, Winter, Gnomes, King Ghob, Archangel Uriel and Sadalphon, Winged Human Being

West, Chalice, Water, Sunset, Green, Autumn, Udines, King Nixsa, Archangel Gabriel, Eagle

THE EAST

AIR ELEMENT: COLOR LIGHT BLUE

When you look at the design of the magical circle, you see that at the top is the representation of the cardinal direction East. This is our starting point. It is in the East that the sun rises in the morning. It is the beginning of a new day, and an atmosphere of freshness hangs over the inner landscape. This is connected to the Element of Air.

Air is the Element that is connected to the psychic quality of clarity. Seen from the air, you may have an overview of the whole. Clear thinking is also a quality related to the Air Element.

Springtime is associated with the cardinal direction East. Just as the sun rises in the East at the beginning of a new day, so the light and warmth increase in spring at the beginning of a new year. For this reason, spring as a season belongs in the East.

The wind belongs to Air. An airy landscape is wide and open with a wind blowing over it and clouds traversing through a clear blue sky. Sound belongs to Air and thus also does music. Rising smoke is, in essence, rising Air, and is thus connected to the East.

Everything that flies belongs in the East. That is why birds belong to the East, as do feathers. Feathers were once used in olden times to write. Writing comes forth from clear thinking, and the word that is spoken by using Air. Thus both the spoken and the written word belong to Air. In this way, all kinds of objects, animals, plants, and qualities are connected to an Element through association.

In connection with the Elements, it is very interesting to see how they have gained their place in our common language. We see our need to *air out* a problem, or that a *fresh wind* needs to *blow* through a specific situation. We may have an *airy mood*. We may describe a certain person as having a *fiery* character. A situation can be *explosive,* and one *spark* can cause it to escalate. An unclear situation we call *misty*. A large group of people we call a *whirling mass*. When somebody studied a subject, we say that he is well *grounded* in the discipline, and a person well known in a community may be described as being *well-rooted*.

OFFICER: THE MAGUS*

The officer is a functionary in a ritual. The Magus is the one who leads the ritual and oversees the whole. It is the place for the High Priest or the High Priestess. He or she is responsible for the whole of the ritual and the effects it causes.

---

*In ancient magical systems, the primary direction is the North. In such systems, the Magus's position is at the North and the Officer of the East takes the role of being the Messenger or the Alchemist.

MAGICAL WEAPON: THE WAND

Every cardinal direction has a so-called magical weapon. The magical weapons are symbols that you may also meet in the minor arcana of tarot cards: the Wand, the Sword, the Chalice, and the Pentagram. These magical weapons return us to the times when we lived as nomadic tribes. They form the minimal survival kit one needed in the wilderness for defense, for hunting, and for eating.

When I teach about the magical weapons to groups, the inevitable question arises as to whether those things are actually needed. Can you do without them? The simple answer is, "Yes, you can." When you are outside on your own, and you desire to perform a ritual, then your own tongue and forefinger are the Wand. Your teeth and fingernails—your claws— are your Sword. Your hands can be folded together to form a Chalice that can hold water. Your arms, which can be used to embrace something, can also become a Chalice. You can flatten your hands and hold them next to each other to present something and, in so doing, create your own Pentagram.

Within different traditions, there is a discussion as to where the magical tools belong in the circle. Some traditions place the Wand in the East, while others place the Sword there. The creators of the Golden Dawn Tarot deck have decided that the Sword is to the East in the quarter of Air, while the Wand is in the Fire quarter. In the tradition where I was educated, we do not agree with this.

In our tradition, the Wand is the weapon of the Magus and is directed to the Eastern quarter, while the Sword, which is a weapon for battle, belongs to the Southern quarter. It may make it a bit more difficult when you have been used to the other associations through the use of the tarot cards.

The Wand is used within the circle to direct psychic energy. It is an extension of your forefinger. You can point at things through the air to give directions over a long distance. You can use your hands to make movements that give instructions to people or emphasize a point. A wagging finger of an angry parent under the nose of a naughty child makes a deep impression. A Wand is used to underline certain happenings in the ritual.

Ritual wands have been known from the most ancient of times. Wands have different lengths. Some are shoulder high and are used during walking, or to give knocking signals on the ground to the group by means of sound. Other wands are as long as the spine in the back, while others have the length from the elbow to the tip of the forefinger. Wands carry a symbolic meaning. They are used around the altar to project energies. The magical circle, for example, can be projected as a ring of fire to protect the work that is done inside it.

Wands can be decorated with a diversity of symbols. At the top of a wand you find the central symbol that indicates the specific power of this instrument. There can be an animal form on the top, or the representation of a god. A wand can be decorated with a magical scripture. There are a lot of different wands, and they can be made from a diversity of materials. Wood is popular, and when you choose that, you can specify the type of wood and adapt it to the specific powers you desire to work with as a magician.

THE INNER PLANES OF THE EAST

THE SYLPHS UNDER GUIDANCE OF KING PARALDA

Every cardinal direction is populated by what are called Elementals. Elementals are the smallest psychic aspects of an Element. The sylphs, also known in the northern countries as *elves,* are Air Elementals. In ancient times, all of the psychic energies were personified, as it is easier to form a relationship with them in this manner. In the same way that the Elementals attained their humanlike form, they also were given geometrical form. Geometry, in actuality, would better fit their true nature. Compare an Elemental with a fractal. Fractals are geometric structures that repeat themselves endlessly. They continue in one direction, without deviation.

Elementals may be considered as natural forces in movement that do not have access to free will. What differentiates Elementals from other natural forces is that Elementals are forces of consciousness and are not mechanical. The Elementals, such as the sylphs, may be viewed as being the smallest building blocks of an Element. The sylphs are the building blocks of Air. Imagine that you have a cloud of sylphs gathered together. All those little building blocks are ruled and directed by the sum of the whole. They coalesce to form one organism, becoming the Elemental King of that Element. You can compare them with the human body, which is built of cells. The cells cluster together in groups, and as organs they acquire specialized functions. When they start to work together they form, for example, a kidney.

The King of the Air Elementals is named Paralda. He may be visualized as a tall elf who has the appearance of air. His skin is bluish, his eyes are blue, and his hair and clothing wave in the winds that surround him.

ARCHANGEL RAPHAEL

On an even higher psychic layer of consciousness, the forces of the Elementals connect and form there a structure of psychic energies: an archangel. Most people these days get images of winged cherubic toddlers when they think of angels, or the little angels they hang on the Christmas tree. Winged toddlers are absolutely not a good image for an angel, let alone an archangel. An archangel is gigantic in size. He has cosmic proportions. He is the sum of all psychic energies of one Element or one aspect of divinity on a cosmic scale.

In a quick review of the history of angels, you will discover that, in ancient times, a small angel was seen as having at a minimum wings that covered the entire horizon. An angel that respected himself was not limited to just two wings, but could easily have seventy-eight wings. These angels were armed to the teeth, and their weapons were hurricanes and thunderstorms, which they used to support their actions. Those ancient angels where not cute little beings; they were forces that were held in awe and respected.

Each of the Four Elements falls under the jurisdiction of an archangel. There are more than four archangels. In magical circles there is some discussion as to the placement of two of the archangels. Within our tradition Raphael, as the archangel of daylight, is assigned to the Quarter of the Rising Light, while Michael, as the defender of the light, is assigned to the South.

Compare Elementals, angels, and archangels to the human body. The Elementals relate to the cells; the angels relate to the different organs; and the archangels coordinate the working of the different organs.

CHAIOTH HA QADESH: THE WINGED BULL

The Chaioth ha Qadesh are the Four Holy Living Creatures. They stand highest in the angelic hierarchy. Most people know them under the names of the four evangelists from the Bible. They are much older. They are the Winged Human, the Winged Lion, the Eagle, and the Winged Bull, and they represent the highest form of the Four Elements.

The Four Holy Living Creatures are capable of living in pure holiness on the highest level of the Creator her- or himself. They are connected with the constellations Taurus, Leo, Scorpio, and Aquarius. They

represent this energy from the moment of creation. John the Evangelist describes them in the following words: "Around the throne there were four animals full of eyes, in the front and in the back. They did not rest, neither by day, nor by night."

We already find the Winged Bull in Assyria. Here you find him as the Lamahu. In the starry heavens you find him as the constellation Taurus. In ancient cultures the Winged Bull played an important role. One example is in Minoan Crete, where the Winged Bull came forth from the cosmic sea as a gift to humanity from the sea god Poseidon. The Winged Bull represents the holiness of the creative processes, which are involved in explosive developing life force and consciousness. He is the representative of all the new consciousness that creates a road and prepares a vessel to be born on earth. He represents the so-called Lords of Form.

The Lords of Form are the psychic forces that direct all the chemical and physical processes. The Lords of Form cause a twofold movement. Under the influence of the Lords of Form, consciousness descends from the source into matter.

The Winged Bull makes it possible for force to function, by creating vessels upon which this can happen. Under the influence of the Winged Bull, consciousness descended into new bodies, the vessels that enabled the growing light to become visible. All ideals, new forms, plans, and projects rise as a seed from the bottom where they have rested, toward the growing light. By their twofold movement, the Lords of Form create friction, without which development is not possible.

THE SOUTH

ELEMENT FIRE, COLOR ORANGE

In the magical circle, the sun travels further to the South, ultimately arriving at the highest point in heaven. The light is at its maximum, as is the heat. The South of the circle is not only associated with the noonday sun, but also with the season of summer. This point in the magical circle is associated with the Element of Fire, which is representative of the life force itself. Fire is symbolic of all the characteristics related to the qualities of vitality and passion. The powers of attraction between the sexes are also associated with Fire.

The Fire quarter is known for its intensity. The fires of passion belong to the South, the fire of love and the fire of battle. Devotion to an ideal and loyalty are qualities belonging to this quarter. It is the quarter of the largest quantity of light, and the quality associated with this quarter is the Defense of the Light. The Dutch poet Lucebert once wrote the sentiment that "Everything of value is vulnerable." That is why the vulnerable need to be protected. And that is the spiritual task of the Warriors of the Light. These are the people who fought throughout the centuries to protect what they regarded as valuable and being threatened. This is the reason why we place the Sword in the South, because of the importance of this task to the Officer of the South. Within your own life, this is an aspect that awakens when you stand to protect the loved ones around you. The Element Fire also tests you, because you need to gain control over this Element.

OFFICER: THE WARRIOR
FOR THE DEFENSE OF THE LIGHT

The Officer of the South is responsible for the safety of everyone in the temple. The Element Fire is stationed on his altar in the form of a burning candle. It is his function and responsibility to care for the physical safety, as well as the astral defense, of the temple.

MAGICAL WEAPON: THE SWORD

We previously met the Wand as the tool best used to direct psychic forces. Here we meet the Sword as a symbol of the forces of fire. The Sword can be present in the circle in the form of a ritual knife—an athame. The athame is used on the altar to carve symbols into objects. Like all instruments, it serves as a focus point for concentration on the qualities it represents. The Sword is created in fire and thus can be seen as a fitting tool on the Fire altar.

Nowadays, it has become quite easy to obtain or to buy a sword. Not too many years ago, acquiring a sword was a test in itself. However, after you have purchased a sword, you still need to earn it. A real magical sword cannot simply be bought: it must be earned through a test of courage. I do not mean to say that you need to go out and start bungee jumping. Magical tools are earned and made sacred through the events encountered in life itself. You earn them by entering into life situations where you have to exalt yourself and come to new solutions by challenging your own deepest fears and restrictions.

THE SALAMANDERS UNDER
THE GUIDANCE OF KING DJINN

Salamanders are the most fundamental particles of the Element of Fire. Don't confuse them with amphibeans; rather, they are the Spirits of Fire. On the cellular level, you can visualize them as residing in the cell's core, and it is their function to perform the burning process. They may be seen as cold-blooded lizards, their association with the Element Fire arising because they spit out poison when defending themselves. The salamander is said to live in the hottest fire, and she lays her eggs in it. King Djinn is the name of the Elemental King who controls these Fire Elementals, and he may be visually represented as an Arabian knight seated on a fiery horse, set against a background of a burning hot desert in the noonday sun.

ARCHANGEL MICHAEL

Archangel Michael belongs to the highest rank of the angels. He is the personification of the Warrior of the Light. In the Bible, we meet him in the story of the War in Heaven. He has been pictured as wielding the Sword with which he brings down Satan, who is shown lying under his feet, and stands poised to kill him. Often Archangel Michael is pictured as a Roman soldier clad in armour. He wears sandals with straps that cross his lower legs. He is described as having "wings the color of emerald green and hair the color of saffron. Each hair has a million faces and a million mouths." Archangel Michael is not just a biblical angel, but was present in Chaldea, where he was worshipped as a god. He is described in Mesopotamian writings, in the Persian Avesta, and is well known in both the Jewish and Islamic traditions.

CHAIOTH HA QADESH:
THE WINGED LION

The Winged Lion is the symbol of the Lords of Flame. He is a formation of consciousness that has been derived from a previous formation of consciousness. You could visualize this as the big bang, as an explosion of energy. This energy transforms into magnetism, which is then capable of forming interconnecting patterns.

The Lords of Flame direct the forces of nature in their most powerful aspects. When you create these images, you need to keep in mind that this is neither a historical description nor a representation of natural laws. It is an explosion of consciousness. The Chaioth ha Qadesh are, in essence, a type of super-archangel, and their task is to direct the force fields on the boundary between matter and energy. They are omnipresent.

THE WEST

ELEMENT WATER, COLOR GREEN

The sun travels further, through the day and through the wheel of the year. The light slowly decreases. We now reach the time of sunset in the cycle of the day, and the season belonging to the circle here is autumn. Autumn is a moist season: mushrooms start to grow, the leaves of the trees color, and in the evening the sunset bathes the entire landscape in a surreal light. The air is misty, and nature prepares itself for the coming winter. Animals go underground, and life gradually withdraws. Spring was a season of expansion; now we are dealing with tides of contraction. The West is associated with the Element of Water and with the beginning of the journey of the sun through the Underworld. When the shadows lengthen in the light of the setting sun, the twilight descends, and a gateway between the worlds is opened. It is the most magical time of the year. The veils between the dimensions are thin, and it is now very easy to contact other realities.

This thinning of the veil explains the qualities of this cardinal direction. The characteristics of consciousness associated with the Element of Water are psychic qualities: the ability to make contact with the worlds of gods and angels. Water reflects when it is still, and thus it can become a perfect mirror. The quality of self-reflection is derived from this abilty to mirror. Meditation is a method used to reflect upon oneself, to reach the quietness within the soul. With stillness the mind produces images that come up from the depths of the self. The Element of Water is opposite to the Element of Air. Air represents the abiltiy to produce clear thoughts, to reason. Water represents intuition and emotional capacity. It brings you into contact with invisible force fields of energies.

OFFICER, THE ORACLE

The Officer of the West is traditionally someone who is very intuitive, because this person brings the Otherworlds into the temple. This person forms a gateway to the inner worlds and in this way is the channel for the magical energy that is directed and molded through the circle by the Magus.

MAGICAL WEAPON, THE CHALICE

The Chalice is the tool to carry water in ritual. The Chalice can contain water, and thus it gives form to this Element. Without a container, water flows away. The abiltiy to be the Chalice is central for the energy of the Western quarter. By this I mean that you are the container, or the carrier, of the psychic energies. Without a container to shape them and give them form, they would not gather, and they would flow away and disappear. The Chalice filled with water forms in actual fact a mini pool in the temple, which can be used for psychic scanning. At the same time the Chalice is also the vessel containing wine for the ritual. The wine is a symbolic substitute for blood, the Fluid of Life. In the Catholic Mass, when communion is prepared, the Chalice is filled with wine. The bread is raised upward. Bread and wine are consecrated. The bread and wine, changed by means of applied magic, are consecrated into the body and blood of Christ. The Chalice also represents the womb of life. In the human body the womb is the Holy Grail, bringing forth all life. In the temple, which represents the Body of God, the West is also the place of the basin for baptism. The quality associated with the Chalice is love.

A magical Chalice is a gift of love. Also, here you are tested. Of course anyone can buy a beautiful cup and use this in the temple. But when do you really earn a magical Chalice? When you succesfully pass the test from the Inner Planes, your Chalice will aquire its magical charge. The Chalice is symbolic of a love in which the self is transcended. When your aunty Mary gives you a beautiful coffee cup for your birthday, this does not necessarily mean that you have earned your magical Chalice. It also does not help to make an appointment with a friend to give each other a magical Chalice. The beings of the Inner Planes know these tricks, and they do not buy them.

Magical tools are directed toward you on the currents of synchronicity from the Inner Planes, in a meaningful moment when you have succesfully passed the test of love. The Elements test you: these are very specific tests, and I will explain them when I talk about the fifth Element, Spirit.

THE INNER PLANES
OF THE WEST

THE UNDINES UNDER GUIDANCE
OF KING NIXSA

King Nixsa is the Elemental King of Water, and he rules the undines, the smallest particles of this Element. King Nixsa is called the Keyholder of the Doors of the Heavenly Flood. He is the force that causes the sources of rivers and fountains to rise. He stands at the source of the Four Rivers of Purification, which spring forth from the paradisal Eden. He rules the essence of moisture. He is the King of the Rising Fluids of Life. You can hear him when he speaks to us with the voice of the floating waters of rivers and brooks.

Undines travel over the entire world. Remember that you yourself are made of 90 percent water. The undines travel through you to their next destination. They penetrate and drench everything. Without them life is not possible. They rise and become clouds and, under the influence of the burning sun, fall down in showers at other places on the earth. They travel deep through the caves of the earth, and lay waiting frozen at the highest mountaintops. Wherever they are, they are in constant movement. When they find a chalice to contain them, for example your physical body, they travel inside you to reunite themselves with other undines, who gather in streams and rivers and float toward the oceans.

ARCHANGEL GABRIEL

The archangel of the Element of Water is Gabriel. As I mentioned earlier, angels and archangels have no gender—Gabriel unites both sexes within himself. Clothed in blue-green robes, he holds a chalice as he rises from the oceans. Or, you see him when he appears in a waterfall. The robe of the archangel is hemmed with the foam of the splashing water when it falls in a mountain lake. His name means "Strong One of God." The archangel is the Messenger of the gods. In his hands he holds a trumpet

113

by which he announces the birth of the redeemer. The trumpet is one of the secrets of Gabriel. It is a horn of abundance, the horn of the fertility of life, which is poured out over the land. In addition, the upside-down trumpet is the phallus of the Corn God. The trumpet of Gabriel is a symbol for the womb, the Chalice of Life. Gabriel is the archangel who told the virgin Mary that she was pregnant. Gabriel is the Messenger who communicates between divinity and humanity.

The two sides of the horn indicate the ambiguous character of the archangel. Gabriel is the announcer of birth and death. It is for this reason that he is also the announcer of the Resurrection. After death is the birth of a new life, and the horn of Gabriel bridges these two realities within the soul. On the tarot card the Judgment, the archangel is pictured as the announcer of the Resurrection.

Judgment

CHAIOTH HA QADESH: THE EAGLE

The Eagle, the Lord of Mind, is a Holy Living Creature, the winged being that belongs to the West. He represents the Element of Water, and he behaves on the level of consciousness as water. Penetrating everything, soaking everything, omnipresent as spirit. Because he penetrates creation as spirit after the diversification of unity, this penetrating consciousness is an individualizing force. The Eagle is the source of individual consciousness and of personality. The Eagle is the highest form of the third fixed sign of the zodiac, Scorpio. In the Eagle we see beautifully expressed how every layer of conscious spirit gives access to the next one by means of transformation. Scorpio changes into the Snake, the Snake transforms into the Eagle. In this way the road is opened for the human being, who walks the Path of Return whereupon all the instinctive features are transformed and transcended into a higher form by means of the power of the mind. The Four Holy Living Creatures are forces that work upon individual beings, and at the same time, they are the impetus behind the evolution of the planet itself. They are cosmic forces.

THE NORTH

ELEMENT EARTH, COLOR VIOLET

With the Element Earth we now arrive at the Northern side of the magical circle. The sun here travels downward to the nadir; it is the time of darkness. In the cycle of the day the time here is midnight. In the cycle of the year we are at the winter solstice. It is the mystical time of the Sun at Midnight. The Sun at Midnight is archaic symbology. It was assumed that the sun traveled through the Underworld during the night, through the lands of death. The sun was transformed by this journey and, after this transformation and purification, was reborn on the next day.

The Sun at Midnight is also a mystical concept representing initiation. An initiate was a "Twice Born," taken symbolically through the Underworld. Also, you can picture the Sun at Midnight as a solar eclipse: a black disc with a flaming corona of light against a surreal, blue-purple sky in which the stars are visible.

The winter solstice is the darkest time of the year, and after this point in time the light increases. In mythology, this is the birth of the light in the form of the redeemer. This is not only Christian symbolism; in the ancient Pagan faiths this was the time when the Son of Light was born into the world.

The quality of the quarter is manifestation, and it is the descent of the divine child in the realm of your consciousness. Manifestation is the ability to give form to what you have prepared by working with the previous Elements. You have formulated ideas and thoughts in the East, you have vitalized them with your passions in the South, you have taken them inside yourself and transformed them in the West. Now the time has come to give them hands and feet in the North, and to make them concrete on earth. The descent of the divine child in your consciousness is the result of a spiritual process that is described in many mystical and magical systems.

The Northern cardinal direction is the most peculiar quarter of the magical circle. This is because it combines the most esoteric and spiritual energy with the most material. This is also characteristic of the Western Mystery tradition. The road to the highest spirituality goes directly through the world of matter. Mystical and ascetic exercises have their own time and place, and the road toward the heavens leads to the initiation at the place of manifestation, the House of Crystal: in other words on earth! This is the reason why I have chosen to place the highest spiritual color in the North.

THE OFFICER OF MANIFESTATION*

Traditionally the Officer of the North is seen as a person with a firm grounding. This is a very practical person who serves as a channel for manifestation, and who is capable of grounding the energies of the ritual.

MAGICAL WEAPON, THE PENTAGRAM

The Pentagram is sometimes also called the pentacle. A pentagram is a five-pointed star. As a ritual tool the Pentagram is a plate on which this star is pictured. At the bottom of the Pentagram is often written the motto of a person or a group in a magical alphabet. It can be a personal motto or the magical name of the person who created the Pentagram. This motto tells about the ideas and the goals that the person wants to realize.

A pentagram is made of a material that can easily be associated with earth, such as wood or clay. You can also create your pentagram by baking salted bread dough. A pentagram made by hand is the product of effort, and this fits in exellently with the qualities of this quarter of the magical circle. The round form is a representation of the surface of the earth herself. Within rituals, the Pentagram has the function of presenting and blessing food. The food that is consecrated during the rituals varies. Mostly it is bread, but you can encounter an endless variety of food sacrifices. Also the consecrated communion is presented on the Pentagram.

---

*Alternatively, the Magus, who we saw earlier as the Officer of the East, can work from the North as a channel to give form to the highest spiritual energies and to direct them into matter.

Very elaborate offering rituals can be found in the ancient Egyptian texts. Here a large offering table is made, whereupon a complete meal is shared with the Otherworld. You see meat and birds, but for example also linen. These are always deliberate offerings with a high symbolic value, as are all practices within the temple. The test of the Pentagram is to give concrete form to your ideals. In the things you undertake during your life, do you reach the goals that you set for yourself?

THE INNER PLANES
OF THE NORTH

THE GNOMES UNDER
THE GUIDANCE OF KING GHOB

The Elementals of the Earth are called gnomes, and they are ruled by King Ghob. The gnomes are a very active energy, and these Elementals are often met in houses. When objects dissapear, or when something draws your attention at the edge of your sight, this is often caused by gnomes. Screws, scissors, coins—all are fun for them. They love to play.

When they meddle in your home, you can start an endless search for hammers and nails, which seem to dissapear as soon as you put them away. You can motivate them to work with you by playing music or sacrificing some chocolate to them. You can speak to them and ask for your things back, and you may soon find what you have lost in the most improbable place you can imagine. When you have a lot of chaotic energy in your home, you can make them a little house, which concentrates their energy there. Around Christmastime you can find little stone houses, which can be lit, for sale in the shops. Gnomes love them.

Gnomes are often connected to the inner earth. They are active in caves and guard the treasures of the Underworld. Of course this is all metaphoric language. The Element of Earth is the metaphor for everything that materializes on the concrete level. The treasures hidden underground are those of your own spirit: the unused talents and capacities that are lying undetected, because they need to ripen in the subconscious part of your mind or develop through life experience. The gnomes are also symbolic of the forces that activate the processes of growth in nature.

The Elemental King, King Ghob represents the soul of the Elemental world. You can visualize him as a gnome who is as big as a human being. He is dressed in a leather jacket, leather boots, and wears a leather belt around his waist. He wears a red blouse and a red pointed hat. He is well built, muscled. He is often pictured with long gray hair and a beard.

THE ARCHANGELS URIEL
AND SANDALPHON

There are two archangels addressed to the cardinal direction of the North. The best known is Uriel. His name means "Fire of God." He is described in the Book of Enoch and is called the "angel who holds guard over thunder and terror." He protects humanity from these energies. The old scriptures say that Uriel is the archangel who brought the Kabbalah to earth, and he holds the key to the mystical interpretations of the Bible. These roles are actually one and the same, because the Kabbalistic Tree of Life gives access to these biblical secrets. The archangel is pictured in the colors of the earth: green, yellow, black, and brown. He carries plates that contain the fruits of the earth, and he has incredibly sharp vision.

Archangel Sandalphon represents the mental aspect of Earth. There was a time when Sandalphon was human and known as Elijah. The Old Testament and the ancient Mysteries tell us that Elijah was a prophet living on the earth. He did not die, like most humans, but was transformed to a higher level, and his spiritual substance was refined. He gave up his humanity for a higher goal. By doing this, he became an example for the spirit of humanity. The redeemers we know from the history of the Mysteries—like Osiris, Dionysius, Inanah, and Jesus—come forth from the form-giving forces of Divine Consciousness. The human redeemers come forth from these forces as well. These great Cosmic Forces are called the Lords of Humanity. It is said of Sandalphon that he is the twin brother of Metatron. On the Ark of the Covenant, Sandalphon is the female cherub at the left side. Sandalphon is also said to be the tallest angel in heaven. His feet stand on the earth, yet he is so tall that he is still able to sing before the throne.

CHAIOTH HA QADESH,
THE WINGED HUMAN

The Winged Human is humanity transformed toward perfection. The *Lords of Humanity* is an expression of the consciousness we as humans have developed when we have reached the perfect unity with divinity. This will be the case when all humans have united themselves with God at the end of this cosmic day.

You will notice that when I describe the Four Holy Living Creatures, I use a time factor that far transcends human proportions. It is said that God can awake and fall asleep, as we do. When he wakes up, the light is born and everything manifests itself. When God sleeps everything returns to nothingness. One day and one night of God are together one cosmic day, and we cannot imagine the length of such a day. As for the Holy Living Creatures, the first three I've described are created during earlier manifestations of the cosmos, during a previous cosmic day.

6

THE SPIRITUAL QUARTER

ELEMENT SPIRIT: COLORS WHITE AND BLACK

The fifth Element of the magical circle is Spirit. The four cardinal directions are the directions of the compass, and the Element of Spirit exalts above them. In the temple, you find the fifth Element in the center. There is no time of the day that can be associated with this Element, nor a time of the year. The Element of Spirit transcends time. It is located in a timeless dimension. This is the time of creation, Zep Tepi, dreamtime: these are all words to express this timeless unity of the eternity wherein divinity IS.

The magical weapon belonging to this Element is the altar. This is a so-called Altar of Sacrifice. The sacrifice that is asked is of the self. The sacrifice belongs to all kinds of things that we experience during our lives—all the love and sorrow, all talents and shortcomings, our fears and hopes. We work day and night with our Four Elements. We handle Air by means of our creative thoughts and our willpower. We work with Fire through our passions and by giving form to our ideals during our earthly lives. We work with Water when we handle our emotions. We work with Earth when we encounter concrete matter and the forces of manifestation.

In the temple, we open toward these Elements. They function as metaphysical doorways to the Inner Planes, and we invoke these forces within ourselves as great archetypal images. We experience the images of the divine worlds that have been used by our ancestors for thousands of years. We worship them as examples of our transformed exalted self, and through trance, ritual, and prayer we burn them deep into our subconscious mind.

The divine archetypes are the example. When we strive toward these facets of perfection within ourselves, we build the Heavenly Man, the end point of our quest. While we metabolize and empower these harmonious images in the deep layers of ourselves—in ritual after ritual—our daily self weighs itself on the scales toward this potential perfection. Sometimes there is joy, and sometimes sorrow when we are not capable of reaching this perfection. Then we use the Four Elements of the temple to heal ourselves.

THE SACRIFICE OF THE SELF

We look into the mirror of the moon with the consciousness of the sun. We open the path between consciousness and subconsciousness, and we work with the content, the divine images. We sacrifice our essential being on the altar. When we are not capable of sharing parts of our personalities with the divine wisdom, then we offer them to the gods. We transform them to a higher quality. That is why this altar is called the Altar of Sacrifice.

Suppressing human qualities is not the intention of the sacrifice. When you sacrifice something, you transform it to a higher quality. Sacrificing is not destroying something; it is sublimating it. When you spend time singing in a choir, and you decide that it is time for you to take acting classes, then you sacrifice the choir on behalf of something you think will develop you further. A sacrifice is sublimation to a higher quality of energy by transformation.

The magical tool of the Element Spirit—the Altar—is the place where the connection with divinity is made. It is the sum of the Four Elements, and something extra. The altar is the place where the energy of divinity is directly experienced.

This is the road that is called the Great Work. It is the goal of alchemy and of spiritual magic. The creation of the Stone of the Wise and the making of Alchemical Gold are metaphors. The work is the exaltation of the soul. When I described the Eagle in the Element of Water, I told you about the transformations belonging to the constellation of Scorpio. The ancients already knew these transformations. The mystical and magical theme of the Temple of Horus in Edfu is the transformation of the soul into the Winged Solar Disc. That was the Egyptian name for the transformation toward Alchemical Gold.

THE BOOK OF NATURE

The Great Work is work. You do not get anything for free. If you grew up as a child in pre-Christian times, your culture would have been soaked with this type of metaphorical thinking. It was so normal that people did not realize that other ways of thinking were even possible. Humans lived and worked with the gods. They lived much closer to nature than we do. Nature was read like a book wherein the gods wrote their messages. For us, this language of imagery and nature has almost become a foreign language. That is the reason why we need to learn to understand these images again, and anchor them in our minds. The fun is that, when you learn the symbolic language, buildings, churches, and paintings suddenly start to tell stories, which are written in the language of imagery. Learning to think in imagery is a significant part of the work.

Another part of the Great Work is transforming energy. When I explained the four cardinal directions in the temple, I was referring to the tests of the Elements. These tests take place during your entire life. They happen on a smaller and on a greater scale. They happen within yourself and within the social context of your family and your work. Every Element presents itself time and again to be sublimated to a higher level. And through this your possibilities broaden. When the stream of energy in your life gets blocked in a certain area, it is useful to self-reflect to see if you are within an Elemental test.

THE TESTS OF THE ELEMENTS

Every Element represents psychic qualities. These qualities have their roots in instinctive reactions. Let me take the Element of Fire as an example. Fire can, by its nature, quickly be expressed as anger. In common language we say that someone enflames easily, or that a person has a short fuse. When somebody is not controlling this temperament adequately, he or she can easily get into trouble, because the instinct for self-preservation will dominate at the expense of the other Elements. The Element Fire must be balanced by the other Elements: understanding, compassion, and mercy from the Water quarter; clear analysis of all the circumstances by the Air quarter; and the intention and capacity to be constructive by the Earth quarter.

If you are such a person who, because of your temperament, quickly runs into problems, then you can, in addition to the development of the powers of the other Elements, also start training to control the Element. In the case of fire, work toward increasing your tolerance for frustration. Do this under controlled circumstances such as exercising in martial arts. This is the work needed to gain control over the Element. But how to transform it? And what is magical about this?

From the moment that you decide to transform an Element, you will be exposing yourself to tests, the effects of which will touch your entire personality. In the case of fire, it asks for the buildup of a greater tolerance to frustration; for example, that you develop some callus on your ego. Because you are no longer hurt so quickly, you will get angry less often. The effect will be that the amount of trouble you cause for yourself because of your anger will lessen, and the energy that is set free can be used for other goals. Situations from your daily life, which raised constant problems because they created emotional hooks in your consciousness, no longer bother you, and the energy that becomes free can be used for spiritual growth.

Controlling the Elements can cause great changes in someone's life. This is work that is never finished, because there is always a new horizon to be reached, and a new barrier to be conquered. The tests of the

Elements take different forms in different phases of your growth and have a relationship to the phase of your life that you are in. Magic can enrich you and help you in this work. It provides instruments and methods that communicate with the subconscious mind.

People often turn to psychotherapy to help themselves through growing phases. Magic works on deeper layers of the soul and can create gigantic movement. It makes changes in consciousness.

STORING CHANGES

Ritual has an enormous impact on the mind. This is the reason why important changes in life and events in society are marked by rituals. By means of a ritual, you store images in your subconscious. Compare this with the resurrection and unveiling of a statue to mark an important historical event. In this way, a ritual anchors a state of consciousness. You connect yourself in the temple on a spiritual level with divine energies. You can find this energy again when you need it by repeating the ritual, which is the path to your inner landscape.

In every phase of your life, you will experience the tests of the Elements. When you have finished a test to a sufficient level, then you can go on with the next phase in your development. These tests are, in spiritual magic, connected to the four weapons. Ordinary life will take you through these transformations; spiritual magic speeds up the process. You want, by means of ritual, to intensify the transformation, and to climb the Ladder of Light more quickly. To do this, you use the magical weapons. You could buy them in a shop, but then you would not pass the first test. You have bought a Wand or a Pentagram, but you do not own them magically. Making your own weapons is a better approach, because by making them yourself you will get involved in a meditative process that opens the inner doors.

The real power comes when you have passed the spiritual test successfully. In this way your magical weapons are charged. They will not be charged otherwise! Your weapons will get a stronger charge when you have taken the tests of the Elemental weapons on higher levels of consciousness.

Charging your magical weapons is a long-term process of growth. You can initiate this process by consecrating the weapons in a ritual. The tests by which you gain control over the powers must still be taken. In the meditation of the Clothing of the Heavenly Man (chapter 4), it is written that the regalia of the initiate are to be found in unexpected places when you climb the Ladder of Light.

THE POWER OF THOUGHT, THE TEST OF THE AIR ELEMENT

The test of the Element of Air gives you access to the Wand of Power. This test is about controlling the power of thought. You start with controlling your own thoughts. How often are you distracted by all kinds of meaningless ideas that have nothing to do at all with your activities at that moment? First, you need to learn to concentrate, to keep your consciousness on your goal. By controlling your mind, you can also cut off unwanted thoughts.

Can you imagine what influence this can have on your mood if you are capable of cutting off depressing thoughts and uncertainties? When you gain awareness of your cognitive processes, you will notice that you also pick up thoughts surrounding other people (and animals). Thoughts are like sparks of consciousness floating around, and you can give them access to your mind or refuse them. Thoughts can be weakened or strengthened by images. Control over your thoughts is connected with the first of the four so-called hermetic axioms. Every Element has its own motto. The four hermetic axioms are:

> *To will*
> *To dare*
> *To know*
> *To be silent*

Willpower belongs, in this context, to the Element of Air. Controlling your mind is the first step toward working with thought power. The key to both is willpower.

THE TEST OF COURAGE,
THE TEST OF THE FIRE ELEMENT

The test of the Elemental Fire is a two-edged sword. The test concerns control over Fire energy, and also the choice to apply this energy in a controlled and single-minded way. The hermetic axiom involves the test of courage. When you are tested by the Element of fire, it can be very useful to focus your meditations and your rituals on this Element. Work with physical fire in the temple. Study the fire gods. How do they control fire? What attributes do they carry? Write invocations to them, learn what their colors are, read their mythology. In other words: look for what they do exceptionally well and awaken this within yourself. Start to apply this in your life. The art of the Element of Fire is to incorporate within yourself the strength of your opponent.

TRAINING YOUR INTUITION,
THE TEST OF THE WATER ELEMENT

The test of the Elemental Water is about gaining wisdom. It is an intuitive wisdom that grows through connection. It develops by applying all the qualities that involve love. It is gained by sharing love and sorrow, with the impulses coming from the Inner Planes of the divine world. The magical test of love often takes place on what we call the "Path of the Heart Fire." This is the path of development whereupon you walk in your relationship with partners, children, parents, and friends. This path tests you, because your environment reflects your inner state of being.

The path sometimes asks you to stretch your compassion and love past what you think are the outer limits of what you can deal with. Sometimes you need to bend your ego to the limit for the sake of a relationship, or to show compassion for someone else without becoming servile. When, after such a situation, suddenly in a peculiar way the chalice comes toward you, it comes unexpectedly and causes a deep, penetrating realization wherein you *know* that you have passed the test of the Chalice. That is a moment you will never forget. These are the moments when, by means of synchronicity, events take place on the physical plane, or sometimes objects appear. When this happens at a meaningful moment within magic, we call this the earthly check.

MANIFESTING, THE TEST OF THE EARTH ELEMENT

The test of the Pentagram is associated with the earth Element and allows you to give form to ideals in your everyday life. The hermetic axiom "to be silent" can be translated as "don't speak, just do." The results become clearly visible, and nothing needs to be added to them. Or does it?

The Pentagram is the magical weapon connected to the North. It is the most physical and, at the same time, also the most mystical quarter of the circle. The test of the Pentagram is one of stubborn endurance and the no-nonsense attitude of rolling up your sleeves.

You must ask yourself, when you look at the end result, if you have really succeeded at the magical test. Have you applied your spiritual knowledge in your work and made a connection with the divine? Did you truly succeed in making a connection between heaven and earth? Is the end result that you have created a prayer of divine energy in matter? Be still and reflect. Look at your end result and contemplate the thoughtforms you have worked into it. At the moment you connect to your end result, do you feel the spiritual energy flowing or not? That is your answer.

THE TESTS OF THE ELEMENTS IN DREAMS

One peculiar thing that can happen on this road is that you may receive a different type of dream, one that is connected with the psychic and archetypal powers that you are working with or that are influencing you. The tests of the Elements can be recognized in your dreams. A test is often repeated in a dream around a theme. The dream itself can have all kinds of variations. This is not the type of dream that you can look up in books. The meaning becomes clear when you understand your relationship to the dream and the emotion it has evoked.

At the moment when you pass an Elemental test for Air, you can dream of falling down from great heights. The dreams repeat themselves, and that is a sign that you should look to your everyday environment if you are in the middle of situations where you lack clarity and perspective. At the moment where you, in your dreams, have learned to fly, the solution is found and the dreams stop.

The test of Elemental Fire brings dreams in which you are surrounded by fire. This is often in the middle of an area of bushfires, or in burning buildings, or situations of war. You need to fight the flames. The dreams pass when you step through the fire. You need to look again at your everyday life. Are your ideals threatened? Are you not capable of radiating your light? Are you prepared to expose yourself to a dangerous situation and pass through the threat and deal with it?

The test of Elemental Water brings dreams of being under water, aboard a sinking ship, or amid great floods. Often this happens when you are on emotional quicksand, or when you are at risk of becoming psychically unstable, because in this realm, energy is tapped from your system. Here the solution is to learn to breathe under water and learn to swim.

The test of the Elemental Earth is concerned with physically surviving in threatening situations, or the fear of not being able to manifest an ideal. In such a case you may dream that you are buried alive or are locked up in a building with no chance of escape.

Elemental dreams have no relationship with former lives or the end of your current life. These dreams stop when you have resolved a situation in your life. They are bad dreams with the proportions of nightmares. When you have contact with guides who help you with your inner development, they can point out to you that you are going through these tests. When I had a period of experiencing such dreams, I awoke every time with the sentence: "control the Elements, control the Elements, and control the Elements." And that was a reason for me to take a close look at the situation I'd dreamed about.

THE WORD OF GOD

To complete the inner structure of the magical circle, I will give you the names of God that are vibrated to open the four cardinal directions. I will go deeper into these names in the next chapters, where I will explain how to raise energy.

The god-names are Hebrew names for the creator, who is seen as male and female at the same time. In the table you will see the Hebrew letters. Hebrew is read from right to left. In the East you vibrate YHVH, יהוה. This is called the Tetragrammaton. You pronounce it as Yod, Heo, Vav, and Hey. It is the manifestation of the creator on all the levels of the universe. When you go back to the letters I gave you to go with the robe, you will see that these are the same letters. These letters are—with the exception of the Heavenly Man—also representations of the Four Holy Living Creatures in the four cardinal directions. In the South, the divine name Adonai is vibrated. ADNI, in Hebrew letters written אדני, means, "my Lord." In the West, the divine name AHIH, or in Hebrew letters אהיה, means, "the Beginning of the Beginning, I am. I am Becoming." In the North, the divine name AGLA אגלא is vibrated. This is an abbreviation for Atah Gibor, L'Olam Adonai, and these words mean, "you are forever great, my Lord."

These are the classical vibrations that you see in books about applied spiritual magic. These words are not carved in stone. There are a great number of names of power that can be vibrated, and many different methods to open a circle.

SCHEDULE OF THE MAGICAL CIRCLE

ELEMENT	SPIRIT	AIR	FIRE	WATER	EARTH
Time of the Day	Between Time	Sunrise	Noon	Sunset	Night
Direction	Between Space	East	South	West	North
Season	Between Events	Spring	Summer	Autumn	Winter

ELEMENT	SPIRIT	AIR	FIRE	WATER	EARTH
Magical Weapon	Altar/ Temple	Wand	Sword	Chalice	Pentagram
Quality of Consciousness	Spirituality/ Creation	Mental/ Thinking	Energy/ Passion	Feelings/ Emotion/ Intuition	Manifestation/ Crystallization/ Concretization
Elementals		Sylphs	Salaman-ders	Undines	Gnomes
Elemental King		Paralda	Djinn	Nixsa	Ghob
Archangel		Raphael	Michael	Gabriel	Uriel/ Sandalphon
Holy Living Creature		Winged Bull	Winged Lion	Eagle	Winged Human
God-name		YHVH יהוה	ADNI אדני	AHIH אהיה	AGLA אגלא
Symbolic Color	Black or White	Light Blue	Orange	Green	Purple

THE COSMIC TEMPLE—PATHWORKING

The Kingdom of God will come when two and two become one, when the outside equals the inside, when there is no male and female.

CLEMENTINIUS OF ALEXANDRIA
SECOND EPISTLE, CHAPTER XII

Prepare for meditation. Sit down in the meditation posture with a straight back and your feet flat on the ground. Close your eyes and slow down your breathing. Imagine that the ceiling of the room in which you are sitting has been decorated with a painting of a starry heaven. When you look upward with your inner eyes, you see gold glittering stars on a black surface. From far away, some classical music reaches you. You strain your ears to hear the sound. It reminds you of the Mozart's Requiem Mass. The sounds cause a movement within your soul.

———◆———

Slowly you let yourself drift forward on the sounds. It seems as if you drift through the space of your temple on the sounds. The music is tender, like a soft hand touching your inner self. You float on the sounds, and slowly the music peaks. It becomes heavier, and while you look at the ceiling the sounds of deep basses vibrate into the atmosphere.

The space changes, and the painting transforms into reality. From the deep blackness, a column of intense power forms. The music takes you with it, and it is as if soft hands lift up your soul and carry you with them on the music. The ceiling opens and makes space for the night sky. The vibrating power increases, and you realize that you are lifted upward in the hands of an angel.

You ask yourself what angel this could be, and immediately you get the answer. "My name is Sandalphon. I am the archangel who makes a bridge between heaven and earth." On the hands of Sandalphon and on his singing you are slowly lifted into the heights of the cosmos. It is good that he surrounds and protects you, because the ecstasy is so overpowering that you are hardly able to contain it, and these feelings get even stronger when you rise.

As you continue upward, you can hear the voice of Sandalphon more clearly. He is the tallest archangel, the archangel of the temple. He is so enormously tall that he reaches up to the earthly throne of glory in the highest heavens.

You hear Sandalphon and his choirs of angels—called the cherubim—singing, and it is intense and beautiful. Sparks of energy flash from his long black robe. His auric wings fill the entire night sky in all the dimensions. Very slowly you rise on the spiral of power moving upward, in a cascade of sparks. The song of Sandalphon lifts you up further. On the sounds, on his breath, on his directions you rise up through the spheres. You pass the clouds of the earth, you pass the planets one by one.

You ask Sandalphon where he is taking you, and he tells you that you are going with him on this journey to the highest heaven, and he will show you the origin of the throne. He protects you against the exposure of the enormous light. He will translate these divine abstract energies into images for you. By dressing the reality of the highest in images, it becomes possible for you to get a relationship with that which is unknowable and transcending. The veils of the imagination are veils of mercy.

He tells you to look upward. As you rise higher in the column of power, you see that the heaven that is your goal forms itself around you like a tunnel of light. You climb higher with the help of Sandalphon, and as you ascend it becomes lighter in the tunnel. You see that the walls of the tunnel are made of shades of the colors of the rainbow. The light comes down in waves and moves with a fluidity like oil on water.

The colors appear to move in circles without creating depth, distance, or time. You see that the stream moves in two directions: upward and downward. As a paradox, directions appear to be of no meaning here. "This is because we move over the Middle Pillar," Sandalphon tells you. "The Pillar of Equilibrium takes us directly to the highest heavens without delay."

The pillar takes on different qualities. You are not capable of giving words to this. They are very sensitive movements of shades in light and energy that take your soul upward.

"Now you use my steering force to take this journey to the highest realms of the spirit," Sandalphon says. "It is your task to gain this control yourself, by spiritual exercises, by purification and through many incarnations. Until that time, there are many guides and spiritual teachers who have made it their task to support travelers on their journeys in the mind."

In spite of the protection of Sandalphon, you feel that the pressure of these heights increases, and that the singing takes you even higher. You are now no longer conscious of any means of transport. In the safe hands of Sandalphon, and on the sound of the choir of cherubim, your soul is pushed upward into areas of foaming colors and whirling radiations. Then you pass an invisible border of extremely bright light, and everything becomes pitch black.

It is endlessly silent. There is no light visible, and no sound to be heard.

You don't understand this, and this question reaches the archangel. "We have encountered the memories of the creator. S-He grants us the mercy to see how S-He was born. Remember the scriptures about creation, wherein it was written that there was first darkness before the light was born: we are exactly at that moment. It is just before the eyes of God open again and S-He wakes up for a new cosmic day."

Very deep in the darkness, the pressure rises and forms a whirling vortex of power. An area of consciousness is created in the depths where there is no space and no time. The Becoming One collects its powers. The Lords of Form, Flame, and Mind become conscious, and start to weave the Trinity. By gathering the three together, emptiness develops where each single entity used to exist, and this emptiness wants to be filled. And here, through the desire of the One, the Lord of Humanity begins to be created. This causes a whirling movement in the cosmos. The whirling movement reminds you of the propeller of a helicopter. Three of the blades are filled with the power of the Trinity, and the fourth is a vacuum, which is slowly filled by the evolution and the activity of the Trinity.

Because of the rotation of consciousness, an illusion of solidity is created. It is a strange and wonderful world of light and darkness and of consciousness. Because of the movement and more form, the Becoming One comes into existence, and this causes a fourfold outwardly flowing stream. These are the sources from which the rest of consciousness streams. These are the forces that are described as the four Aces of the Tarot: they are the sources of the Four Elements. They are symbolized by the Four Holy Living Creatures.

We have given them a form to be able to understand them. In essence they are formless and consist only of power. The One created the Trinity, and from there the Four Holy Living Creatures were created. In this way, in the next level, the seven are created: seven enormous channels of force that color the forces of the One and descend in all the colors of the light.

Like a mighty chalice, the energy of light overflows in its complete beauty of colors, in an ecstatic radiation, a waterfall in the colors of the rainbow. In the form of ten splendid chalices, all the cups fill each other with light that condenses in the lowest vessel, which receives this concentrated power.

The Becoming One creates an archangel to personify this power. When the forces of the light descend, the shades of colors and the diversity increase. The kingdoms of the mind that they rule become smaller; their tasks become more specific.

Also, the four corners of heaven come under the influence of an archangel, because the power of the Four penetrates all Ten, because every chalice has an existence in the three dimensions of time, place, and space. Where the force of the Four Holy Living Creatures comprises the four archangels of the four pillars of heaven, the force of the One is molded to human consciousness.

Now that Sandalphon names them, they appear very bright and clear before your inner eye. They are enormous beings. Their wings each protect one of the cardinal directions. You can clearly see the difference in their function. Raphael has the rising sun behind him, and his clothes and hair fly on a fresh wind. Michael appears with the sun high above his head, and he appears in the middle of a burning hot landscape. Gabriel appears against a background of a moving ocean and a sunset. And in the North, Uriel appears in a landscape of waving cornfields, which color the landscape in a golden glow. The trees are heavy with the fruit they bear.

"You notice that we have now descended to a more solid layer of consciousness," Sandalphon says. "The powers are as abstract as they were before. But they appear to be more solid because they are dressed in the forms of the inner sight. When you look closely, you see how the Holy Living Creatures tower above every archangel. What you see now is the level of archetypal human consciousness. In this layer of consciousness you also find the world of the gods.

"Now we descend another layer, and we meet the layer of the primordial impulses. Here the instincts to survive dwell. These are important natural forces that are essential for every species. These natural instincts fall under the rulership of the Elemental kings. You can only work with the Elementals when you let them be ruled by their kings, because the kings have a consciousness: the Elementals themselves are but little programs. You can compare them with the electrical currents in computer chips."

On the command of Sandalphon, the four Elemental kings appear. Paralda is as blue as the sky that serves as his background. He is hardly visible and looks like a formation of moving clouds in the wind. From where he comes, the wind speaks of messages of insight and the sounds of birds when morning breaks. On the wings of the breath he carries the Word of God, spoken by all creatures over the earth on the wind. He does this by means of the sylphs who carry these messages on their wings. They ring in wind-bells and whisper in the branches of the trees, and they wave in the moving seas of grass.

In the South, Djinn appears. He has a face that is colored by the sun and is seated on a fiery Arabian horse. His sword radiates in the sunlight. The sala-manders are his creatures; they live in the flames of the inner fires of passion in all these living beings. When they are undisturbed, they warm the houses and the nests of the animals. They are licking warm tongues of motherly and fatherly care. They ensure that the eggs stay warm. The passion and the love for life give them claws, teeth, and stings that they use to protect the highest good: the gift of light and life.

In the West, Nixsa appears. In the moving waves of a moonlit landscape, he appears from the foam of the sea. With him the undines appear: mermen and mermaids, waterwives and mist women. All kinds of water Elementals appear in the sparkling drops and mist clouds that form themselves out of the landscape. The most beautiful of all are the sirens. They sing with the power of temptation, which caused great sea heroes to crash onto the rocks. They give form to the illusions and seductions, and they reflect our inner being. They keep Narcissus imprisoned in his mirror image. In this way, they create self-reflection and also the love for the self.

In the North, Ghob appears, king of the gnomes. He is dressed in earthy col-ors. With him are the gnomes. All beings whose task it is to maintain the physical processes of humans, animals, plants, and minerals fall under the command of Ghob. He is the connecting power of growth. He and his kind live close to the sur-face of the earth and are the steering forces behind the renewal of nature. Every shoot that grows, every lamb being born, every child who grows into an adult, every cell of the body that is renewed falls under the influence of Ghob and his kind, as an image of the great formative forces of the earth herself.

Together with Sandalphon, you watch this beautiful landscape. Around you, you see the representatives of the Elemental kingdoms in their astral shapes. You appear to be standing on the stage of an ancient circular Greek theater, and the tribunes are filled with higher energies. Very high in the sky, the heaven forms a dome, and the four pillars are great transmitters of energies that flow together with the source. Sandalphon calls a sentence back into your mind:

> The Kingdom of God will come when two and
> two become one
> When the outside equals the inside,
> When there is no male and female.

"That," says Sandalphon, "is the work that the magical mandala does. The goal is to unify your soul with your environment and with the creative source. Then you create what in Eastern religions is called enlightenment; what the Jews and the Christians call the kingdom of God; what in Egypt was called the Unification of the Two Lands. That is the goal of the journey and the end goal of the Great Work. For now it is enough. It is time to go back to your own time and place."

And to your amazement you see that the ceiling of your meditation space moves back to its normal place. The dome of heaven disappears from sight. Sandalphon makes gestures in the air, and this causes the tribunes to disappear and all the Elemental forces to vanish from sight. You become conscious of sitting in a chair in a meditation position. Sandalphon stands before you and looks you deep in the eyes.

"When you wish, I will put you under my protection. I am the tallest archangel and my twin brother is the regent of the highest heaven. Through me you can access these high energies while your remain firmly rooted on earth."

You nod your head.

"Then I give you a symbol with which you can call for my help every time you need it. It is the sign of the cross within the circle. It is the sign that the Most High divides into Four Elements. This is the sign that is used as a hieroglyph for earth. This is the *sign that is baked in the bread that is shared on the Altar of Sacrifice to celebrate the unity with the source."*

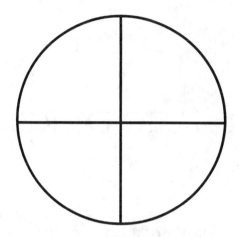

You take the bread of the archangel. He adds: "In your inner temple you will find this sign in the North, wherever you may be."

And as suddenly as the archangel appeared, he disappears. He melts into the symbolism of the ceiling of your temple. It is time to leave this state of meditation. Connect yourself consciously with your body. Stretch your muscles and stand upright. Place your feet firmly on the ground and stamp to feel the connection to the earth again.

7

THE BASIC EXERCISES

O Magician, may it go well with you. Your body of light is your protection. Your soul is within you, your feet walk the right path. You are being renewed with the "Cool Waters" you are getting exalted on this happy day in which you appear in all your glory. Your mother Nut* appears in all her glory. Your mother Nut comes to greet you, together with her sister Nephtys, and she brings you the Eye of Horus. Beautiful is the smell of the sacred oils when they anoint your Eye of Horus with them.

SPELL 840, EGYPTIAN COFFIN TEXTS

The spiritual road of the Mystery tradition is a road on which a good amount of important work is done alone. The daily meditations, the contemplations, the personal ritual, and the study—they all demand the

---

*Nut is the Egyptian goddess of the starry heavens. Nephtys is the goddess connected with the Nile flood.

ability to work in solitude. This does not mean that you need to take the entire journey by yourself. Within the Mystery tradition, it is very important to work together with people who have walked a fair distance on the path, and who know where the pitfalls are—because pitfalls exist. That is the reason why an established Mystery school has experienced supervisors who guide the students.

Working with a group is also essential to the Mystery tradition. Group rituals are complex and must be taught within a working group. I will explain in this chapter a few of the basic principles to individual and group practice, but I will not go deeply into the subject in this book.

INDIVIDUAL WORK

The road within the Mystery tradition can be divided into two parts. The most important part is the buildup of energy that should be done by every magician by means of daily exercises. The exercises consist of study subjects, meditations, contemplations, and rituals. The meditations are, for most people, essential to get the system running, and need to be done on a regular basis to achieve good results. Within a school, you will be offered the content of the teaching systematically. In this way you will not miss important parts. You will give attention to all areas, and you will be helped in areas you find difficult or boring. Because of this, your development will be balanced.

You must invest energy for a long period of time before you get results. Most of the meditation exercises gradually build up to more complex exercises. Self-discipline is necessary. Can you discipline yourself to do your daily exercises? Compare it with learning how to play piano: you see results when you practice on a daily basis and when you also do the boring finger exercises.

FLYING BOOK ROLLS

The quickest way, with the best results, is to work together with people from a Contacted Mystery school in the line of the tradition. Mystery schools often offer good correspondence courses. In this way, it is possible to get a magical education even if you are not able to attend group meetings. Especially these days, with all the possibilities of the Internet, it has become very easy to maintain contact with supervisors, even if they live far away.

Within the world of magic, this way of teaching through correspondence courses has been used for a very long time. This is because our tradition needed to survive beneath the surface for so long. It was not possible to raise temples in very many places.

In the days of the Golden Dawn, the papers of the order were called Flying Rolls, because the papers of the order were sent from one magician to another. A lot of knowledge was transferred without the need to meet on a monthly basis. In these days, qualitative high Mystery schools are difficult to find.

This situation will improve now that the Mystery schools are evolving better relationships with the outside world. Through this, we will be increasingly capable of giving a personal education to people. Our adepts travel often to teach in all possible countries. Mystery temples have gained one important advantage from the years wherein we needed to work within an invisible network: almost no culture of sects has developed.

The individual training is still the red thread of the curriculum, and this will not change. It consists of daily meditations and exercises. In the process of learning magic, the development of independent individuals is central.

STARTING FROM A DIFFERENT PLACE— MODERN PRACTICE

Regular group meetings are luxuries that only became possible during recent years. I had been taught for many years through correspondence lessons and had supervisors whom I had not met. I didn't even know their names. The person lived abroad, and correspondence was passed through "headquarters." Years after I had begun with the lessons, I got to know the supervisors, the initiates, and the adepts personally. When I met these people, I was told that the school was very open to the outside world. In the days that they were educated it was much more restricted! Now, when I travel abroad to learn the praxis, I hear people complain that there is no group in their hometown.

LODGES AND TEMPLES

Today, the group rituals are practiced in so-called lodges and temples. We even teach in workshop form. But the basis of the Mysteries remains the same: individual work. Even if you are a part of a group, the main part of the training has to be done individually. A group can offer moral support. A Mystery lodge is a functional group where people work together. When you meet there, you will get to know people who share your interest and with whom you share wonderful experiences. This can develop into long-lasting friendships.

THE SOCIAL NETWORK OF A SCHOOL

Within a Mystery school, the social network is important and, at the same time, subordinate to the goal, which is the spiritual development of the individual members.

Every magician works from his or her home, individually, within his or her own social network. Friendships between people in a group are based on the work. Mystery schools are not a replacement for a lacking social environment, they are something extra in the life of balanced people who have a healthy network of relationships in their own lives. Attending a Mystery school is an enrichment and an addition to your normal life.

As a magician, you always remain independent. You do not make yourself and your spiritual development dependent on a group. This does not mean that you do not take part in it! You can depend on the friendship; you can enjoy the classes and the shared rituals. But the real work is done by yourself. Even if you work in a group, you must be capable of returning to individual work when the circumstances ask this of you. Individual work is the basis!

THE INSTRUMENT OF THE GODS

To become adept in the Mysteries, you need to be prepared and able to work alone during long periods of time. Patience and diligence are required to train the deeper layers of your consciousness. For the first year you are mainly busy with training yourself in techniques. You can compare the Kabbalistic Tree of Life with a cosmic violin. It is a difficult instrument to learn to play. In the beginning, you explore how to play it, and you need all your attention to produce musical notes instead of noise. Then you start to learn the magical equivalent of chopsticks. At least you are producing music. After a period of simple exercises, suddenly, during the meditation sessions, unexpected realizations come through. Slowly you are being noticed by the gods.

AN ORAL TRADITION: "FROM MOUTH TO EAR"*

Then the tests commence. At the beginning of the path, you are being tested on your endurance. This is when you get the first tests in the astral realm. Supervisors of a Mystery school are people who help you get through difficult periods in your development. They have walked the path themselves. They have gone through the process and know how you feel. They motivate you and give you advice. They have experienced the same kind of things on the Inner Planes, and when they cannot help you themselves, they get in touch with the "older generation," people who have practiced the tradition longer, who are more deeply initiated. In this way, you get access to a range of knowledge that is not described anywhere. The oral practice of passing on the teaching from adept to apprentice: "From Mouth to Ear" is still the core of the tradition.

---

*"From Mouth to Ear" is the translation of the Hebrew name of the Tree of Life Otz Chim.

In our time we, as magicians, have access to sources that were unknown in history. An incredible amount of written sources are available to consult. We can maintain international contacts much easier. The Internet is, for the modern magician, the equivalent of the library of Alexandria. There it was possible to gain access to knowledge after a long search, while we just need a few key words.

The drawback is that knowledge is presented unsorted. Bad material, and even material that is damaging to your psychic health, is also freely available. There are no warning signs, and the quality of this information is dependent on the wisdom of the writer. There is also no division between material for beginners, for intermediates, and for adepts. Also, you must keep in mind that adepts never reveal the full range of their training in public sources.

THE INITIATIONS

In our modern society, people are used to getting everything in the area of recreation presented in easy bites. They expect to be spoon-fed during their spiritual development. They do not want to do the training, but they expect to get mother's milk.

For these people I have got news: the Mystery tradition is not a form of recreation, it is a religious spiritual training, and this takes time and effort. A Mystery school is comparable with a seminary that educates people for priesthood. The initiations are, since ancient times, passed from one adept to another. We do not know of any "instant initiations" that magically give people access to energy.

We give initiations to people who have exercised themselves and worked at themselves. These people receive from this initiation access to a higher wavelength of the energy that makes it possible for them to work with the deeper layers. The training of spirit and body takes as much time now as in ancient times, and needs to become a part of your daily rhythm. The benefits of this training are an enrichment of your soul, an increased intensity in the perception of the beauty of life, and peak experiences of meaning.

An effective training begins with the creation of a firm foundation and builds further from there in increments. You start with a daily investment of five or ten minutes during a build-up period, learning the basic exercises. Gradually you progress to daily exercises that take half an hour to three quarters of an hour maximum. That is the time you need to learn to accumulate the energy and to increase it.

From the beginning, you learn to keep yourself to your own appointments. If you do not keep appointments with yourself, how can you expect the Inner Planes to keep theirs? When you devote a daily amount of time to work with them, they will stretch themselves out to reach you.

THE KABBALISTIC CROSS

THE OPENING MUDRAS

What follows is a series of exercises that consist of energy circulations, vibrations, visualizations, and breathing techniques. The strength of these exercises is in the combination of techniques. Learn to work with these techniques step by step. It works best if you start with the Kabbalistic Cross. When you know this by heart, without thinking too much while doing it, then you start to learn the next step in the series. In this way, you learn the exercises gradually, so that you can perform them without relying on paper.

The Kabbalistic Cross is a series of mudras and mantras you perform at the beginning of your magical work, whether it is in your daily meditations or in a complex group ritual. The Kabbalistic Cross is a way to make a connection between heaven and earth. The exercise has the effect of balancing you. At the same time, it marks the start and the end of magical work and brings the entire practice under the protection and judgment of divinity. The Kabbalistic Cross starts with the Mudra of the Opening of the Veils.

MUDRA: THE OPENING OF THE VEILS

Step forward with your right foot and bring your hands forward from your heart chakra. Make the gesture of opening two curtains at the same time. Visualize pulling an invisible veil sideways, which is the border between two realities: your everyday reality and your magical reality. When that curtain is open, you stand with your left foot next to your right and lower both hands. You have now entered into another dimension.

How to Vibrate Your Voice in the Pathworking Exercises

When vibrating, you use your voice in a certain way. You take a very long breath and you vibrate the words very low, so that you cause a maximum of vibration in your body and in the space surrounding you. When you vibrate in the right way, you can fill a big room with your voice, and other people will feel that vibration too. It is a voice technique that is also used by singers. You use the images and the gestures to lead the vibrations into certain directions. Together with the vibrations, you visualize the images. You try to make those visualizations as clear as possible.

THE CROSS OF LIGHT

Now you start with the Kabbalistic Cross. The movement of the gestures resembles the Christian cross, but the difference is that you do not face the cross—you step into the cross. You raise your right hand and start vibrating the sounds. Vibrate in the way I described in chapter 4.

1. When your right hand is above your head, you vibrate ATEH. Here you visualize that your hand connects to the light of creation. When you stretch out your hand, it becomes an antenna by which you make a connection between yourself and the light of creation. You become filled with this light, and you maintain this connection.

2. After this, you lower your arm and you vibrate MALKUTH. When you lower your arm the light fills you up. It runs down through your spine, while you move your hand downward. You now stand in the middle of a column of light that connects heaven and earth.

3. Bring both hands together at your heart chakra. Between them you collect light from your spine. Then you stretch out your right hand over the horizon. You vibrate VE-GEBURAH. When you do this, the line of light follows your gesture, and stretches out over the horizon at your right side.

4. Then you stretch out your left arm over the horizon and you vibrate VE-GEDULAH. Your left arm also generates a ray of light shining over the left horizon.

5. Bring both hands together at your heart chakra. There you vibrate LE OLAM. Between your hands, a source of intense golden light radiates.

6. Spread both your arms over the horizon and vibrate AMEN. At the moment you do this, a golden sun will start to radiate in your heart.

What you have vibrated means:

Ateh	To You
Malkuth	The Kingdom
Ve-Geburah	The Power
Ve-Gedulah	And the Glory
Le Olam	For Ever.
Amen	So be it.

With this formula you dedicate your magical work (and the energy you generate while doing this) to the great cosmic source. Through this you devote your spiritual work to the divine plan.

When you close a meditation or a ritual, you again use the Kabbalistic Cross, and you close the Mudra of the Veils while you step backward.

THE MIDDLE PILLAR EXERCISE

THE GOAL OF THIS EXERCISE

When you begin a meditation, you start with the Middle Pillar exercise. The name of this exercise comes from the Tree of Life. The Kabbalistic Tree has three columns, which are called pillars. I will explain them later.

The Middle Pillar is the Pillar of Equilibrium between the female and the male side of the Tree of Life. It is the middle road, and this pillar corresponds with your spine. The goal of this exercise is to let go of everyday problems, to cleanse your aura, and to generate magical energy. In later stages of your spiritual development, you use the same principles to empower your magical personality and to work with the assumption of god-forms and angels. This is an exercise that generates more energy over time.

THE PREPARATION

First of all, you sit down in a normal chair with a straight back and arm rests. You can also perform this exercise standing. Contrary to many Eastern systems, in the Western Mystery tradition no lotus or half-lotus positions are assumed. We exercise in the position wherein the Egyptian gods are pictured, with a straight back on a chair, the feet flat on the floor, and the legs next to each other. No crossed ankles or arms. The idea behind this is to become a channel who connects heaven and earth. Crossing the legs disconnects you from the current to the earth.

Also in this exercise, the visualizations and the vibrations go hand in hand. When you vibrate the god names in this exercise, try to direct the vibration as much as possible to the place in your body that belongs to that visualization. You repeat the vibrations three to six times per sphere. First of all, you bring your breathing to rest. You try to stabilize a rhythm whereby you breathe in on four counts, hold your breath for two seconds, and breathe out on four. Then you hold your breath again for two seconds.

THE CROWN CHAKRA

When you have stabilized this rhythm, you start to formulate the first sphere. This sphere is above your head. The name of this sphere is Kether, which means "Crown." I will explain the deeper meanings of these spheres and names in the chapters on the applications of the magical Kabbalah further on in the book.

The sphere of Kether is filled with a radiating white light. The vibration belonging to this sphere is AHIH, the same god-name that is vibrated in the Western quarter. The meaning of this name is "the Beginning of the Beginning." It also means "I am who I am." This name and this sphere connect you with the source of creation, the coming into existence of the cosmos itself.

THE THROAT CHAKRA

When you have stabilized this sphere in your aura, you let the light from this sphere shine through you. The sphere is so powerful that an energy current starts to descend. At your throat, the energy gathers and becomes brighter. The energy changes color. The first sphere, Kether, was a sphere of white light. Here at your throat the sphere is called Da'ath, which means "Knowledge." The color of the second sphere is lavender. Kether is connected to the source of creation, Da'ath is connected to the star Sirius. This star was known in ancient times as the "Sun behind the Sun." You visualize a sphere of lavender-colored light, and you vibrate YHVH-Elohim. YHVH is Yehovah: the unspeakable name of God. Elohim is a strange word. It is a word that means "Sons of God," but the ending of the word is female. Elohim is the connection between the male and the female aspect of God.

THE HEART CHAKRA

When the sphere of Da'ath has become stable, you let the energy lower through your spine and you formulate a golden yellow sphere at your heart chakra. This sphere is called Tiphareth. The name of this sphere means "Beauty." This sphere is connected to the sun. The god-name you vibrate here is YHVH Eloah Va-Daath. This name means the "all-knowing God." Again you let the sphere stabilize itself. The sphere overflows, and the energy falls further downward in a stream of light. This gathers together in the next chakra.

THE GENITAL CHAKRA

Here a sphere of violet forms. This sphere is called Yesod. The name means "the Foundation." The god-name that you vibrate here is Shaddai el Chai. This name means "Almighty God of Life." This sphere is connected to the moon. Let this sphere stabilize, and, as with the former spheres, you let the energy stream downward. The stream of energy forms a ball under your feet.

THE EARTH CHAKRA

Under your feet a sphere made of earth colors forms itself: black, russet, olive green, and yellow. The name of this sphere is Malkuth, and it means "Kingdom." The god-name that is vibrated here is Adonai Ha Aretz, and this name means "Lord of the Earth."

You have made a column of light through your spine, from the source of the cosmos to the earth. You have created five spheres in different colors, which are located at different places on your body. You have energized these parts of your body through vibration. Your body sparkles because of the extra oxygen and the vibration. You now start cleansing your aura.

THE FIRST CIRCULATION OF POWER

In your mind you go to the sphere above your head. You imagine that you are surrounded by an egg-shaped energy field. This is the most important layer of your auric field. You start to clean this area with the cosmic energy that enters into your head in the sphere of Kether. From the cosmos, Kether will be refilled automatically. You imagine a constant stream of white sparkling energy filling your crown chakra.

On your in-breath you pull the energy inward through Kether. On the out-breath you let the energy stream downward along the front and sides of your aura. Imagine that this energy refreshes your aura. The energy streams into the earth, is filtered here and mixed with earth energy. Then the energy streams upward on your in-breath, along your back and sides, back to Kether. There a new energy reservoir is ready for the next circulation. You repeat these circulations six times at a minimum. It is important to work in a very concentrated way to get the visualizations as clear as possible.

THE SECOND CIRCULATION OF POWER

The second circulation resembles the first one, except that the energy is now focused to the sides of your aura. You start with Kether. Now you let the energy go down along the left side of your aura and purify it and filter it. The energy returns to Kether along your right side. Again, you repeat this circulation a minimum of six times. Visualize this energy also as a white sparking energy.

THE FOUNTAIN

Now concentrate on your crown center again. The energy stream refills this chakra automatically. You take the cloud of energy that is waiting ready for use in your crown chakra, and at your out-breath you let it flow through your spine and through the soles of your feet into the earth. Here the earth energy connects with the core of the earth. Both energies mix and then shoot through your spine back to your head. In your crown, they explode like fireworks and, from this explosion, the sparks fall down into your aura through your out-breath. Your aura sparks and twinkles because of the energy. As the sparks fall downward, you gather new energy from under the soles of your feet. As you breath in, the energy stream shoots from below to above in your crown chakra and explodes again. Again, you repeat this circulation six times.

THE EXERCISE OF INTERWOVEN LIGHT

Concentrate on the sphere under your feet. In Malkuth, your energy reservoir is filled with a mixture of earth energy and cosmic energy. Now you visualize yourself being wrapped in this energy like a mummy. You can do this very literally by imagining the energy rolled up like a bandage. You start by drawing the energy under your right foot. The bandage of energy passes across your back, and comes around to the front. The movement of this energy is from below to above, and the spiral moves across your front from right to left. You need several breathings to wrap yourself in this energy until your entire body, including your head, is covered. See yourself wrapped in light, vital, and sparkling with energy.

With the exercise of the Interwoven Light, you have the energy stream activated around you, and it is ready to work with. The most difficult part of this exercise is to refresh it. When you have worked with it for several months, you will know it by heart, and then boredom becomes your biggest challenge. There is the possibility that you will start to do it sloppily, and then, of course, it becomes less effective.

THE INVOKING RITUAL OF THE PENTAGRAM

This ritual is often called the Lower Banishing Ritual of the Pentagram. This name is confusing. It is shortened into "LBRP." A banishing ritual is done to send energy away, for example to cleanse spaces from unwanted energy. When you want to raise a magical circle, then you want to call up energy to use on behalf of your ritual. This is why you use the Invoking Pentagram: you banish the mundane and invoke spirit.

The Invoking Ritual of the Pentagram is, in fact, the opening ritual for a magical circle. During the closing of a ritual, this procedure is mirrored, and in this way the energy is neutralized again. There are a number of methods to open and close a magical circle, and many include the use of the pentagram to do this. But this is the basic method.

The Invoking Ritual of the Pentagram is a basic ritual you will be using during your entire career as a magician. In chapter 5, I showed you the basic plan of the magical circle. You have seen that the circle opens to the four cardinal points. In the figure below you see a five-pointed star in every cardinal direction. Each of these stars is drawn at the point where a pentagram is projected when raising the circle. In the picture here, you see that every point of the pentagram represents each of the Elements and connects them. You can draw a pentagram in one fluid movement.

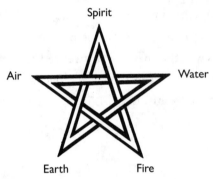

The pentagrams are projected in every one of the four cardinal directions, according to this method:

1. Start in the Eastern quarter, and begin your ritual with the Mudra of the Opening of the Veils.
2. The next step is to vibrate and visualize the Kabbalistic Cross.
3. You step forward with your right foot. You stretch out your right arm, forefinger and middle finger pointed, and you use the full length of the arm to draw the pentagram. In this way your pentagram is more than one meter high. You start with the highest point of the pentagram—symbolic for the Element of Spirit—and draw down the first line to earth. You bring down spiritual energy to the earth plane.

    You project a line of light of blue flames. It is the same color blue that comes from a lighter or a gas flame. When you project the pentagram in this way, the energy must be sealed and the Eastern quarter must be opened. You do this by vibrating a god-name into the quarter. In the East you use the name יהוה: YHVH, Yod-Heh-Vav-Heh. While you vibrate this name you touch the core of the pentagram with your outstretched hand. This causes the pentagram to grow so big that it covers the entire eastern wall of the temple. In the core of the pentagram two big wooden doors form, and they open to the Inner Planes of the Eastern quarter.

4. Now you walk with an outstretched arm to the Southern quarter. Here you project another invoking pentagram, in the same way as in the Eastern quarter. Only the god-name differs. You vibrate here אדני, Adonai. At the moment that this quarter opens, you see the Inner Planes of the Southern quarter.

5. Walk toward the West. You draw the invoking pentagram in blue fire in the same way. Vibrate the god name, which here is אהיה AHIH, and visualize the Inner Planes of the West.

6. Now you go to the North and repeat the procedure. Here you vibrate אגלא, AGLA, and you visualize the Inner Planes of the North.

7. Now you stand amid four gigantic flaming pentagrams that form the gateways to the other dimensions.

8. Standing before these gates, you call the four archangels and invite them to appear in your temple. Face the East and say: "Before me: (vibrate) Raphael." Now you visualize that Raphael appears through the opened gate of the Eastern quarter and enters your temple.

Say: "Behind me: (vibrate) Gabriel." Now you visualize Gabriel appearing through the opened gate of the Western quarter entering your temple.

Say: "At my right side (vibrate) Michael." Now you visualize Michael entering through the opened gate of the Southern quarter entering your temple.

Say: "At my left side (vibrate) Uriel." Now you visualize Uriel entering through the opened gate of the Northern quarter entering your temple.

Say: "Around me flame the pentagrams." While you say this you activate the visualization of the pentagrams again.

It is important that you make your visualization three-dimensional. In fact you are in the middle of a sphere of light, where the pentagrams touch each other and form the gates to the other dimensions.

9. Stretch your arms and legs and vibrate yourself in the middle of a gold-colored hexagram. Next say: "In the middle stands the six-rayed star."

10. You close the Invoking Ritual of the Pentagram by repeating and vibrating the Kabbalistic Cross.

When you have finished your ritual, you close it by making the movements in the reverse order. You start in the North and you wipe away the blue fire energy. You start at the point of earth and go to spirit. From the North you close the West, the South, and the East. Then you seal the closing with the Kabbalistic Cross. You close the Mudra of the Veils. Then you leave your ritual space and ground yourself by eating and drinking something.

THE DIVISION OF POWERS
IN A GROUP RITUAL

SOLO RITUALS VERSUS GROUP RITUALS

Individual ritual and group ritual have similarities in technique. The main altar is in the middle of the ritual space, between the four cardinal directions. The principle of opening and closing is identical. During a group ritual, however, different tasks are created. Because of this, the possibilities of the ritual increase enormously. By working together in a team of people who are used to each other, the power of the ritual increases.

When you practice alone, you can invoke one type of divine energy. Invocation is calling up a projection of a divine thoughtform inside yourself and inside a magical circle—you call the god or the angel inside yourself. You then assume a god-form. Assumption of a god-form is an ancient Egyptian magical technique whereby you project the human image of a god-form on your aura during a ritual and act as if you are that god yourself.

The rest of the energies you need to evoke. Evocation is calling up a projection of a divine thoughtform outside yourself and outside a magical circle. When you look at the Invoking Ritual of the Pentagram described previously, you can see that the four archangels of the four cardinal directions are evocated.

In a ritual with more people, you can invoke as many different divine energies as there are participants. A group ritual is a high-pressure area of spiritual energy. The energy can cause strange phenomena such as astral fog or an objective increase in temperature. For this reason rituals within the Mystery schools are designed in advance and are written down on paper. We work in a very structured way. Within our tradition a ritual is not left open to spontaneous ideas or the mood of the individual participants.

The goal of the ritual is also carefully planned. Rituals are not meant to create material effect; rather, the goal is to generate magical and mystical experiences in the consciousness of the participants, both during the rituals and in their afterglow.

These experiences cumulate into the realization that the entire world, your environment and your life, is inspired and penetrated by the divine. This goal is described in mythological terms in different ways. "Healing the King of the Wounded Land" is, for example, an expression coming from the Arthurian mythology. In Egyptian mythology, there is reference to "Unification of the Two Lands," where the two lands are Upper Egypt and Lower Egypt. This is, as well as being a historical event, also a mission statement: to create a connection between heaven and earth. Within Christian gnosticism, this is called "Entering the Kingdom of God on Earth."

So structure is important within the Mystery tradition. The placement of the participants within a setting and the division between the different tasks is precise. The participants are placed in concentric circles.

The simplest form for a collective ritual is a group of four people, in which each participant personifies one of the cardinal directions. The leader of the team is the Magus, the person who works with the energy of the East. Ideally a group consists of an equal number of males and females. In the table at the end of this chapter I have written down the basic energies of the Officers. This does not mean to say that these quarters need to be fulfilled by a male or a female. Every initiate works with both types of energy. The indication of gender expresses the movement of the energy: expressive (male) versus creative (female). Within a group these functions will always appear in one form or another.

THE OFFICER OF THE EAST, THE MAGUS

The Magus is the leader during a ritual. It is the function of the most experienced initiate within a group. This person is responsible for the content of the rituals and for the training of the group. The success of a ritual is dependent on the Magus, as is also the work of the lodge. Within a magical school, the Magus works very closely together with the head of the school, so that the group is coached in an optimal way.

As a Magus, you take part of the responsibility for the spiritual development of others. A Magus is an initiate in the tradition with a long practical and theoretical training, and he or she works under experienced people before starting a group. The Magus is the Officer of the Eastern quarter. He does not only hold the Wand, he IS the Wand. He stands between the two pillars of the temple. The Black Pillar at his right side is the Pillar of Form, called Boaz. The left pillar is the Pillar of Force and is called Jachin. These are the two side pillars of the Kabbalistic Tree. Between them the Magus stands, personifying the Pillar of Equilibrium.

THE PSYCHIC FORCES OF AIR

The East is the quarter of the Element Air. The Element of Air represents the space around you that is filled with breath. By the movement of air, vibrations that cause sound are transported; this includes the vibrations of the Word. Patterns such as the vibration of thoughts also move through air.

Air as a cardinal direction represents the psychic skills that have control over the mental level. A part of this is control of thoughts. Thoughtforms are mental images, patterns, or ideas that want to realize themselves. When a thoughtform is more specific and detailed, it is closer to the earthly realm. The buildup and visualization of thoughtforms is the task of the Magus.

Air as the transporter of vibrations also carries the sound of the Word of Creation. From the vibration of the Word of Creation the entire universe was formed: this is the direction of the Word of Power. From here, all the other words of creation come forth, and the Magus in this way becomes the Officer who pronounces the Words of Power.

THE MAGUS AS A CONDUCTOR

The task of the Magus is to lead a ritual group and to ensure that the different energies of the participants mix harmoniously. The Magus is the one who, like the conductor of an orchestra, directs the energies of a ritual and steers them. By his gestures he determines the tempo. By his directions, which he gives in words and body posture, he determines how the energy of a ritual is built up, how the thoughtforms are created, when the energy peaks and lowers and comes back again. The Magus balances all the energies of the ritual: he connects them, directs them, lets them circle around, and corrects them when necessary. He is responsible for the opening and closing of a ritual. The Magus is the one who writes most of the rituals for a group. A ritual that is well written is a prayer in movement and entails careful choreography of the energies and the thoughtforms.

THE OFFICER OF THE SOUTH, THE TEMPLE GUARDIAN

In the South, the Officer is the temple guardian. As the Magus is the Wand, so the Officer of the South is the Sword. It is the archetypical warrior, and represents in a group the defense of the temple and the Defense of the Light. A classical image is that of the archangel Michael, who overcomes the opponent during the War in Heaven. With a drawn sword, he has the dragon under his feet and controls it. This is an excellent image for the Officer of the South to identify with.

The Officer of the South is the one who is responsible for the defense of the temple as a delegated responsibility from the Magus. Ideally this is someone who has a good background in martial arts. It is someone who is trained, and who can scan energies that do not belong in the temple and can neutralize them. The Officer of the South has developed a good sense of ethics and justice.

THE PSYCHIC FORCES OF FIRE

The Southern quarter is the place of Elemental Fire. You can feel this in a temple. In the South it can get enormously hot, in the same way that you can sometimes feel wind in the East. The South is the Element where courage is tested. Handling the Sword requires one to have control over the weapon, as well as the ability to work actively with it. The forces of the South consist of passion and desire. Sexuality is also one of the forces that belong to the Southern quarter. They are strong forces having to do with the capacity to survive, and must be brought under the control of consciousness.

THE OFFICER OF THE WEST, THE ORACLE

The Officer of the West is the channel for Elemental Water. Water is the Element of intuition and self-reflection. Creative ideas and realizations reside in the West. At the same time, this is the direction that is deeply connected to the Inner Planes. From this quarter, contacts with the divine energies are made. Energetically this is a reflective, receptive, and passive quarter of the temple. On the inner levels, this officer is the most active of all.

THE PSYCHIC FORCES OF THE WEST

This is the quarter of psychic gifts, of contact with the unseen realms. The Officer of the West works in polarity with the Magus. The Officer of the West brings in the energies from the Inner Planes, and they are transformed by the Magus into active energy. This officer is the living grail, the portal that gives birth to unseen energies. The Officer of the West is the Messenger of the gods. She is a pool of silent water wherein the images are mirrored and carefully registered. The West is the quarter of medium skills. The Officer of the West opens herself to receive the images that are called up by the rituals from the Inner Planes.

During a ritual, you create thoughtforms as a group, which you send to the Inner Planes. The Officer of the West receives the answers of these inner worlds. In the Chalice of Reflection the visions appear of what will be born out of the ritual. From the West one can see if a ritual "takes." The West is a very popular place in temples, as there are many people who think they are psychic or who want to become so. It is an incredibly difficult place, because the result is directly interconnected with the capacity of the officer to see herself. It is the place where the greatest humility is needed. It is the place of the greatest illusions, because many people tend to mistake their fantasies for divine visions.

Humility in magical temples is the virtue that needs the most attention and practice. The images with which we work are big and exalting, and they have a great influence on practitioners. It is understandable that people tend to identify with them. This is a mistake. It means that your ego is attached to your practice. You become a good channel for spiritual forces when you succeed in keeping your ego out of the work.

THE OFFICER OF THE NORTH, MANIFESTATION ON EARTH

The quarter of the North is connected to Elemental Earth. The earth is the place where everything needs to manifest. Spirituality must gain a solid hold on your life, in your actions, in the way you balance your life, in your choices. Matter is crystallized divine energy, and is just as sacred as the most beautiful visions. The Officer of the North is the one who earths the forces of the ritual. The magical weapon belonging to this quarter is the pentacle—a flat disc, a plate whereon the fruits of the earth are represented in the temple. Instead of a pentacle, a horn of abundance can be used as an instrument representing the earth.

The Officer of the North is ideally a person with the skills of a crafts-person. She creates concrete things. It is someone who has a love of nature and takes care of plants and animals. The North is an important place in a ritual. Without manifestation, spirituality is an illusion in this world. Within certain traditions, and in some temples, the North is regarded as so important that this is the place of the Magus. In the North sowing and harvesting take place. It is the most spiritual quarter. The sun passes through the Four Elements. It rises in the East, peaks in the South, descends in the West, and there it creates a twilight space. In the North, the sun travels in its most mystical form. The *Sun at Midnight* is a term that was in use in antiquity to indicate the Great Initiation. This is the initiation in the Element of Earth that was generated by means of ritual drama.

THE POWERS GATHER TOGETHER

Earlier in this chapter, I told you that people within a group ritual are divided in concentric circles. In a ritual with a central altar, the partici-pants will be divided equally over the four cardinal directions.

Above the altar, a great spiral of magical energy gathers together. This energy will be building up during the ritual and is then concentrated and pointed toward the goal of the ritual.

A PRAYER IN MOVEMENT

As I stated earlier, a ritual in the Mystery tradition is a prayer in movement. Spiritual exercises train an initiate to increase the buildup of power in a ritual. Techniques are used that have their sources in ancient shamanism. Exercises that work upon the energy system of the individual candidates are intertwined amongst the different participants during the rituals.

After the opening ceremony, a group builds up a magical landscape. This practice places the entire group in one of the cultures of the Mystery tradition. Within this magical landscape all the participants are manifestations of divine forces and are grouped within a myth or a spiritual reality.

As an example, we can use the Christian Mass to explain what happens. At the highpoint of the Mass, bread and wine are consecrated. The priest speaks the words of blessing over what was until then ordinary bread. Through the consecration by this anointed priest, spiritual energy that was generated throughout the Mass is concentrated, and it penetrates the bread and the wine. Through this, the bread and wine become the body and the blood of Christ. This is not symbolic: according to the church it has become a fact through transubstantiation.

Transubstantiation

During the celebration of the Mass, bread and wine are changed into the body and blood of Christ. This is called transubstantiation. The priest blesses the bread and wine and says: "*Hoc est enim corpus meum.*" These words, spoken by an initiated priest, create inside the Mass the miracle of transubstantiation. These words are in folk magic degenerated to "hocus-pocus."

I remember the story my parents told of a priest, after Mass, taking bread and wine to visit some sick people. When the priest walked through the villages or over the fields, altar servers preceded him. The villagers and the farmers knelt on the land when the priest passed. They did not kneel for the priest, but for Christ, who was passing. The priest was carrying the consecrated host.

Similarly, within a magical temple every object that is used is charged with magical power. It flows into the robes, the temple, and the people who work in the temple. Within a ritual, the temple as a whole is changed into a holy mythical place.

SYMBOLIC GESTURES

After the opening ceremony, the intention of the ritual is gradually built up by means of words, symbolic gestures, and language. The word *symbolic* has become associated with empty gestures or objects that "represent something." Cutting a ribbon is a symbolic gesture for "opening a doorway." When, in ordinary language, it is said that you get a "symbolic gift," you know you will not get rich.

In contrast, a deeper meaning of the word *symbolic* points toward an unseen reality that is represented by the image. Magical symbols are objects and images that carry a reality within themselves. The symbolic objects used during ritual are charged with magical energy and become a living reality through transubstantiation.

Symbols deepen layer by layer. The world of one single symbol is complex and forms gateways to increasingly deeper spiritual and mystical meanings. Symbols are like keys to a reality that we can experience in trance. Symbols form a language with which we can communicate with the unconscious mind. Under the layer of our consciousness, which we use to suppress facts and fears, there are deeper layers of consciousness that can exalt the soul to mystical, ecstatic experiences.

FROM SYMBOLS TO VISIONS

The subconscious is regarded in the Mysteries as an incredible source of power. You contact these layers by means of the language of symbols. The language of symbols must first be learned, like an ordinary language. However this language is not learned by rote, like vocabulary lessons. This language develops through meditation. When you start meditating, you start with placing one symbol in your consciousness and associating upon it. In the deeper levels of meditation, symbols become living realities with which you develop a relationship. In even deeper layers of consciousness, the symbols draw together in patterns and generate complex visions. This is the language of mystics and magicians.

These symbols are related to nature and natural events. They have an intrinsic meaning. It does not matter in which culture and in what time you live, the symbol of a lightning flash will always be associated with a thunderstorm. A deeper layer indicates a sudden total enlightenment as a result of an action from the divine world. The symbols are a language that connects us with cultures thousands of years old. The language of symbols is the language of which the Bible speaks. It is also the form of communication that was understood by all tribes and all races, but was gradually forgotten. This caused the Babylonian confusion of languages.

QUALITIES IN THE MAGICAL CIRCLE

FUNCTION	ELEMENT	BASIC ENERGY	MAGICAL WEAPON	PSYCHIC QUALITY
Officer of the East/Magus/ Messenger	Air	Male	Wand	Mental Plane/ Thinking
Officer of the South/Temple Guardian	Fire	Male	Sword	Vital Power/ Passion

QUALITIES IN THE MAGICAL CIRCLE (continued)

FUNCTION	ELEMENT	BASIC ENERGY	MAGICAL WEAPON	PSYCHIC QUALITY
Officer of the West/Oracle	Water	Female	Chalice	Intuitive Force/ Creativity
Officer of the North/ Manifestation/ Magus	Earth	Female	Pentagram	Concrete Plane/ Realization/ Fertility

A TOWER TOWARD THE GODS— PATHWORKING

I have made the oldest monument of Babylon complete in its greatness with silver, gold, other metals, stones, glazed tiles, spruce wood and pine wood: the House of the Bridge between Heaven and Earth. I have restored it. I have put the roof upon it from brick and copper. This building is the House of the Seven Lights of the Earth, the oldest monument of Borsippa. It was built by a former king, but he did not finish the roof. It has been abandoned for ages by the people without any clue as to the reason for this. After this earthquakes and thunder have crumbled the sun-dried clay. The bricks have fallen apart and the earth of the interior is spread in heaps. Marduk, the Great God, inspired my mind with the idea to repair this building.

KING NEBUCHADNEZZAR, 605 BCE

This time, you start your meditation with the Kabbalistic Cross. Assume your meditation position. After this, you generate energy by doing the Middle Pillar exercise. Breathe deeply a few times and let all tension fall from

Reconstruction of the Isthargate

you. When you hear sounds, recognize them for what they are and then let them go. The outer world becomes less important when you turn toward your inner world.

When you bring your concentration inside, you build up a gate before your inner eye. The gate is arched and is closed by two wooden doors. The doors are made of cedarwood, a type of wood that was already known in the ancient world for its fine smell. Cedarwood was expensive and was used for the decoration of sacred spaces. To what sacred space will this door bring you?

———◆———

You knock on the door to get access, and at the moment you do this the doors swing open. You are approached by a man with a long beard and long hair. His clothing is made from a piece of fabric draped over one shoulder and laced with tassels. He has folded his hands over his chest. He bends toward you and speaks. He tells you that he is your inner guide during this journey. The journey will give you insight into the primordial language in which all the knowledge of the Mysteries is written down.

He has brought an animal—a camel. The guide gestures you to sit on the camel, which has knelt before you. The camel is dressed with a saddle and cloths decorated with geometrical patterns. The guide helps you to climb onto the camel and, as you hold yourself steady by its humps, the camel rises and causes you to swing from side to side. Now you have a high seat and look over the road before you. The guide closes the gate and takes the reins of the camel.

Before you is a landscape of sand dunes. Far away on the horizon you think you see a piece of green land. The guide tells you that he will lead you in that direction. You can hardly see the road here. The guide tells you that this is because the gate through which you entered is not a part of the normal caravan route. It was the gate that connects the worlds of time.

You climb the sand dunes of the desert and descend slowly to a broad river. The green land consists of palm trees. As you approach the river, you see a city form from the contours in the distance. It is built from sand-colored stones. You see very clearly a city wall appearing before you. The broad city wall connects to the towers that form the corners of the city. The guide now leads you toward the bridge that spans the two banks of the river.

At the same time, students from all directions of the Mystery tradition gather together, each one accompanied by a guide. You hear all kinds of languages; it is a pity that you cannot understand your fellow students. In an amazing way they appear from all directions. Together they form a caravan that enters into the city at a slow pace. The caravan is welcomed by the inhabitants of the city. At both sides of the bridge people gather together, looking in expectation at the long row of people coming from all countries, cultures, and time zones.

To your amazement, the crowd does not enter the gate of the city that is directly connected to the bridge. The crowd veers to the left on the other riverbank, toward the North. The guide tells you that you walk along the banks of the Euphrates. The city you find at your right hand is Babylon. The guide tells you that Babilani is a name from the ancient Akkadian language. The word means "Gateway to the Gods." The goal of this journey is to enter through this gate and learn from the gods themselves in the holy language that connects the worlds of the gods and humanity.

The crowd walks on the road along the city wall to the North, following it as it curves to the right. The walled city is surrounded by a channel that is directly connected to the Euphrates. The sun sinks slowly and lights the clouds. This causes a rainbow to form before you.

"A good omen," the guide says. "It is the sign that the gods wait for you and welcome you. This is one of the favorable omens that often precede important meetings between gods and people. It is the sign of the connection between the gods and humanity that appeared after the Great Flood, the bridge between heaven and earth. It is a covenant written in light in all its colors to indicate that the One divided itself in a multitude of forms, which caused heaven and earth to come into being. All colors are equally important, and although their shades are different, they are all made of the same light. Now you need to pay attention, because you will soon discover how this city got its name."

The procession walks around a curve, and now you enter onto a breathtakingly beautiful processional road. The guide tells you that the road toward heaven starts here. You have arrived at the place where, before you, great prophets and saints began their journey to the heavens. The road alongside the city wall now takes you into the city, crossing the water. You walk over the bridge. You enter a street that is surrounded by walls on both sides. On both walls you see pictured a row of lionesses, which approach you. The walls are covered with glazed bricks. The lions walk toward you over a bed of white roses. The guide tells you that the row of lionesses indicates that the goddess Isthar approaches you. You will enter through her gates. When you enter through her portal, you will walk into her realm, the most holy place of Babylon.

Then you see the Isthargate before you, and an exclamation of awe sounds through the processional crowd at the spectacle of the beautiful gate. Built in lapis-lazuli blue bricks, you see the gate against the evening sky. At the gate are pictured the Holy Bull of the god Marduk and the dragon of the god Nabu. The guide explains: "When you pass this gate you come onto the purest ground. Here all the sacred buildings of Babylon have been built. The ground is as pure as the holy Heavenly Waters: the Abzu itself, wherefrom everything came into being."

The metal knobs on the poles of the banners that are at both sides of the road shine in the evening sky, just as clear as the sunlight on the antlers of the holy deer in the Abzu. The view is as breathtakingly beautiful as the appearance of the new moon in the heavens. Against the background of the evening sky, the gateway through the blue wall is really a gateway to the celestial realms.

The caravan passes though the round gate. Now the camels that carried the students through the gate have finished their task. It is time to descend. At the caravanserai, priests are ready to purify the travelers before they are allowed to enter sacred space. On foot, the crowd walks further along the processional road. The road turns, and then you see the purest soil on earth. This is the axis mundi of the heavens. On this sacred ground two buildings have been built. The guide points them out and says: "The building at your left side is the Esagila; it is the center of the world. It was built by the god Marduk himself. But this is not the goal of this journey. The goal is the building on the right." The guide points toward a great ziggurat, which is seen against the evening sky. In this light it looks like a gigantic staircase leading to the heavens.

"This is the E.temen.an.ki," the guide tells us. "The name means 'House of the Bridge between Heaven and Earth.' This building is a throne, a worthy residence for the mighty gods from the starry heavens."

Every step of the building, which is built in the form of a staircase, is dedicated to one of the heavenly lights. Every circuit takes you along the four cardinal directions of heaven. In this way every circuit will initiate you into the secrets of the heavens, which follow each other. The first floor is dedicated to the Moon god, the second to Mercury, the third to Venus, and the fourth to the Sun. The fifth floor is dedicated to Mars, the sixth to Jupiter, and the seventh to Saturn. Of course these are the planetary gods as you know them in your time. In ancient Babylon their names were different. The eighth floor consists of seven temples that are all dedicated to one of the heavenly gods. And at this place you can connect yourself to the most holy part of the starry heavens: the fixed stars, and the inexhaustible stars, which turn around the most sacred point on the heavens. There live the seven sages of Babylon. And in the center of this, you see the polestar.

The procession is now led to the E.temen.an.ki, and you find yourself at the bottom of the road that turns upward in the form of a spiral. The road follows the direction of the Sun. You start the long climb. When the first pilgrims set foot on the stairway to the heavens, a monotone song is sung. You cannot understand the language. According to the guide, the song is sung in the ancient Sumerian language because that is the sacred language that is a legacy from the time before the Great Flood. The guide tells you that the secret name of the tower is the "Tower of the Tongues," Borsippa. On the top of the ziggurat the Babylonian priests study the movements of the gods in the starry heavens, and communicate intensively with the heavenly lights to unravel their plans and to learn to understand their omens.

On the way up you see how the evening sky slowly deepens in color: the pastel-shaded air changes into deep purple, to blue, and finally to black. With the increasing darkness the heavenly lights appear in the firmament. The guide points toward the gods as they let their lights shine one by one. The god who just appeared below the horizon is Shamash, the Sun god. The god who now becomes visible when Shamash is descended is Nabu, who in our time is called Mercury. Nabu is the bringer of messages. The bright star next to him is the goddess Isthar, whom we know as Venus. She is the goddess of the Holy Marriage. The big clear disk is the light of the Moon god; Sin is his name. The red light that appears in the heavens is Nergal; we know him as Mars. Now Marduk appears in the heavens; we know him as Jupiter. The god who indicates the borders of time is Ninurta, and we know him as Saturn.

You have now almost arrived at the top. Before you, you see how the roof with the seven chapels comes nearer. The guide explains: "The first chapel is dedicated to the god Marduk and his wife, Sarpanitum. The second chapel is for the god Nabu and his wife, Tashmetu. The third chapel is for Ea, the water god. The fourth chapel is for Nusuku, the light god. The fifth chapel is for the heaven god, An. The sixth chapel is dedicated to Enlil. The seventh chapel is the most important: this is the House of the Bed and the Throne. In this chapel a priestess lives who has dedicated her life to the god Marduk. In this chapel is a couch that is richly dressed. Next to it is a golden table. There are no images in this sanctuary.

"The god Marduk visits this temple every night and uses the bed to honor the Marriage between Heaven and Earth. Every night the bond between the gods and humanity is honored. It is time for your meeting with Nabu, because this god is the reason why you came here to the heavenly chapels of the Tower of the Tongues." The guide leads you to his chapel. When you arrive, you see a colossal image of the god, made of wood and covered in gold, with eyes inlaid with mother of pearl and lapis lazuli. The god wears a crown made of horn. The presence in this chapel is so penetrating that you can feel it physically. The entire chapel is loaded with a heavy energy. When you enter into this chapel you feel a pressure increasing on your third eye.

You sacrifice some incense on the burning charcoals that are before the god. You suddenly see the head of a lioness, flanked by two torches. You take your place on one of the seats in the chapel. It is clear that the god wants to speak to you. As soon as you have entered into meditation, you hear the sounds of the words of Nabu resonating in your head.

"Be welcome, seeker of knowledge and wisdom. My name is Nabu. I am the god of the arcana of the concealed and the invisible. I am the god who engraves the goal of every human being into the Tablets of Destiny. I see that you have come to learn the essence of the secret knowledge. I feel a question has formed in your mind, the desire to learn to speak the language of the gods, the language the gods use to communicate with humanity. How comes it that the gods speak to the earth, you may ask yourself.

"Can we gods speak to the earth? The earth speaks! Can we speak to the water? But the water speaks as well. As does the fire. The Elements speak and we gods recognize this language. Why am I the god of writing? In the air you find my signs, in the fire you see my visions, in the water and on the earth letters form. Learn these signs and your eyes will speak to me with these signs. The black people, the yellow people, the brown people speak. We gods hear. We listen but we do not understand their language. But, written in the signs of the earth, we can understand their language. Your eyes must make the signs and learn to recognize it.

*"Why am I the god of science? I communicate through the laws of the animals, the laws of the arts, the laws of growth and decay, the laws of the time to sow and the time to reap. The laws of disease and health. The laws of Water, Earth, Fire, and Air. When we recognize them, we know how we need to proceed, on the easiest path with the best result."**

The guide adds: "When you learn to understand the language of nature, you have access to the symbols with which you can speak to the gods. Nabu is the god of communication: the laws, the signs, and symbols. They all come from him—the eyes, the ears, the mouth, the nose, the fingers—all information of the senses and of common sense, and of numbers.

"The language of the oldest writing is written in the language of the earth herself. It is in the language of the wind and of the seasons. The language of the birds and of the animals. The language of rocks and rivers. From here came the language of talismans and of the holy signs, written by the gods themselves. With your inner eyes you can speak to the gods and the gods will answer in this language. When you know the language of nature, you can speak with the gods. This is the language you need in the Mystery tradition. This is the One Language that is taught in this sacred place. This is the reason why this place is called the Tower of the Tongues. The ziggurat is the House of the Bridge between Heaven and Earth—the E.temen.an.ki—because in her structure the key to the language of the gods is hidden."

Nabu says: "The E.temen.an.ki has physically disappeared from the earth. In Babylon nothing is left but heaps of mud of this once-so-famous ziggurat. The tower to the gods, however, has survived on the Inner Planes. The stairs to the sanctuary can be climbed, and with every step you take while going upward, you tread on all the stones that have been laid down by the people who went before you. Every stone from which the tower is built is a clay tablet whereon, in the language of the earth herself, the messages of the gods are written down. By reading this ancient language—the One Language that connects all humans of all cultures—you ascend the great stairway to the heavens.

---

*Quote from the god Nabu from the Phoenician letters.

"Here, at this high place, every night when it is dark the gods will come to the earth to unify with humanity. When you enter into meditation and close your eyes, you will be able to hear their voices, and will gradually be initiated into their wisdom. They will light their lights, and shine and raise their voices, for now and ever. In the dark loneliness of deep meditation, you find the Chapel of the Bed. To this place the gods descend, to unite with the people who have taken upon themselves the obligations of the priesthood, to commit to the Holy Marriage. I also participate in this Holy Marriage." At the moment Nabu speaks these words, the eyes in the head of the lioness spark, and the torches flame.

"You who are a student of the ancient wisdom tradition, listen to my words. The One Language never disappeared. The language is hidden in nature. It is locked into the Tree of Life and is woven into the clothing of the Heavenly Man. Return to your normal consciousness. It is now time for you to learn this language. I, the god Nabu, will help you with this and explain the language of the symbols to you, and teach you how to preserve this by making of yourself a Heavenly Human and a memory castle."

Then—suddenly—the energy freezes and, with it, the vision of the god Nabu interconnects with his statue and sinks into it. Slowly you rise to leave the chapel. At the exit you turn around for a last view of the statue, and you bow in respect. At the moment you do this, the eyes of the lioness spark off fire, and with your inner ear you hear her roaring.

You descend the stairs. As you do this, your fellow students gather together as well. The sun slowly rises as the procession moves downward. The people are very excited. The sacral mood that was present while climbing the ziggurat has now become exalted. Obviously all the seekers have made a contact. Slowly people start to have conversations on their road downward. Suddenly you realize that this is in fact impossible. On the way up nobody could understand one another. A raw noise sounds from the tower of the ziggurat. You look up and see how a winged dragon flies away from the top of the tower, disappearing to an unknown destiny. Your guide says, "That is the god Nabu in his animal appearance."

Downstairs, the camels are waiting. The journey back goes quickly. When arriv-

ing at the river, the procession divides itself into all directions. The guide leads your camel over the bridge, into the desert. Before you the gate of cedarwood appears, the gate between the worlds. Walk through this door. Behind this door your physical body is resting. Connect yourself to your body and breathe deeply. Stretch your muscles and yawn, stamp your feet on the floor to connect yourself with the earth again. After this exercise you eat and drink something.

8

THE DIVINE TRINITY

THE KABBALISTIC TREE OF LIFE

THE KABBALISTIC TREE OF LIFE
IN THE WESTERN MYSTERY TRADITION

In general, the Kabbalah is divided into three categories, the theoretical, the meditative and the Magical. The theoretical Kabbalah, which in its present form is based largely on the Zohar, is concerned mostly with the dynamics of the spiritual domain, especially the worlds of the Sefirot, souls and angels. Meditative Kabbalah deals with the use of divine names, letter permutations, and similar methods to reach higher states of consciousness, and as such, comprises a kind of yoga. The third category of Kabbalah—the Magical—is closely related to the meditative. It consists of various signs, incantations and divine names through which one can influence or alter natural events. Many of the techniques closely resemble meditative methods, and their success may depend on

*their ability to induce mental states where telekinetic or
spiritual power can effectively be channeled.*
QUOTE FROM: *SEFER YETZIRAH:*
THE BOOK OF CREATION IN THEORY AND PRACTICE
BY RABBI ARYEH KAPLAN

The Kabbalistic Tree of Life has a central role in spiritual magic. The
Kabbalistic Tree is a part of the Jewish tradition. The basis of the Tree is
described in two books. The first book is called the Zohar: this is the Book
of Splendors. The second book is called the Sepher Yetzirah, the Book of
Creation. The first comments from this book date from the tenth century

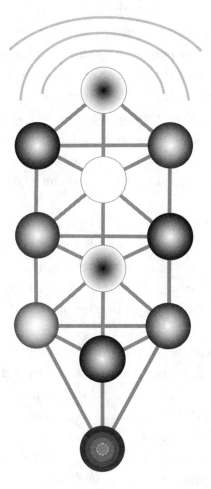

*The Kabbalistic
Tree of Life*

CE. But there are already references to the Sepher Yetzirah from the first century CE, and there is enough indirect evidence to assume that the Kabbalistic Tree was known in Alexandria around the year zero.

The idea of bringing mystical and magical knowledge together in one symbol is a well-known phenomenon, even in antiquity. The Huluppu tree, from the Mesopotamian Uruk, is thought to be an early form of the Kabbalistic Tree of Life. The German Yggdrasil tree was a tree representing the world and magical reality.

THE TEMPLE NOT BUILT WITH HANDS

Contrary to the trees I have mentioned, the Kabbalistic Tree has been used throughout history and has remained a part of the living tradition. Jewish society has suffered immensely throughout the centuries because of intolerance and suppression. Jewish adepts have learned, as a result, to keep their spiritual knowledge safe, refraining from putting their practices and beliefs into writing. When the Jews were dispersed after the second destruction of the Temple of Solomon in 70 CE, they had already learned to wear the temple around them as a thoughtform by means of spiritual exercises and visualization. This is what is meant by the "Temple not Built with Hands."

In times when the tradition needed to go underground, the Kabbalistic Tree could always be passed on easily because the basic plan is easy to memorize. For people who are not introduced to the secrets of the Kabbalah, they were only strange drawings. The explanation of how these pictures could be used was passed on through oral tradition, "From Mouth to Ear."

From ancient times through the Middle Ages, the Kabbalistic Tree was in use. The Jews were not the only ones to use it. The history of the Tree is an example of how an esoteric teaching can develop itself and can become available for other schools of thought, yet still remain intact. Christians, scientists, and magicians used the Tree of Life. As more schools made use of the Tree of Life, other association chains were developed based on the plan of the Tree. One of these variations is the Magical Kabbalah.

THE KABBALISTIC TREE IN THE GRIMOIRES

It was necessary for Jews to carry the hidden knowledge descreetly. The Kabbalistic Tree was an ideal solution for them. Where the knowledge surfaces, the so-called grimoires appear. These are magical diaries. Examples of these are the *Key of Solomon, The Grimoire of Armadel,* the prophecies of Nostradamus, the *Three Books of Occult Philosophy* of Agrippa von Nettesheim, and *The Book of the Sacred Magic of Abramelin the Mage.* They are just a few examples from the extensive curriculum of magical texts that have been preserved. They are written in Kabbalistic symbolism.

The Kabbalistic Tree of Life has two main traditions that all the old Mystery traditions share. The first tradition is to find the key—when you have the key to open the door, you can slowly unravel the deepest secrets. With this key, the Kabbalistic Tree initiates you deeper, assuming that you maintain your search. The second characteristic is that the Kabbalistic Tree has a language of images that is related to nature. The language of nature does not change; it is independent of culture and time, and so it is universal.

The beauty of the Kabbalistic Tree is that the glyph is so flexible. The Tree takes on association chains very easily. It accepts the symbols and the inner worlds of all kinds of traditions and, at the same time, remains itself. In this way the glyph becomes a road map of the Inner Planes. You can take this map with you through the traditions, and through meditation you discover how these traditions fit on the map. In this way you can—through the language of nature—compare mystical and magical techniques and understand how they relate. You can, for example, compare the archetypes from the Arthurian tradition with Greek mythology, and compare the Jewish tradition with the Egyptian.

The Kabbalistic Tree of Life is used in the Mystery tradition to let the energies—which are necessary for the practice of spiritual magic—flow through the Body of Light. The Tree forms the basis for the buildup of the so-called magical personality. It is an incredibly handy key when you want to access other magical systems. The Kabbalistic Tree at the same time remains a mystical and magical system on its own.

ADAM KADMON

BUILDING THE BODY OF LIGHT

As a magician, you build up your Body of Light gradually in the form of the Kabbalistic Tree of Life. The picture here shows you that the Middle Pillar—the Pillar of Equilibrium—is the central pillar to do this. On this pillar, which runs through the spine, are located five spheres. Adam Kadmon is the Heavenly Man, or a human who has realized his fullest potential. This is, of course, a symbol of an ideal. Such an ideal provides a matrix through which you can develop yourself in this direction. Of course you need to look constantly into the mirror of self-reflection to have an image of yourself that is as objective as possible. A clear perspective on your strengths

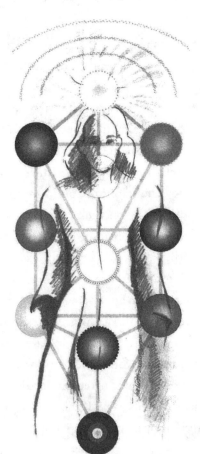

Adam Kadmon

and weaknesses is a presumption for healthy spiritual development.

Within a Mystery school, we assume that daily functioning and social relationships are normally developed before you enter this road. This is the basis. From here the Heavenly Man is built up. When the basic needs are met, a foundation is available for self-realization and transcendence of the mind. The purpose of magic is not to use sorcery to deal with feelings of powerlessness or incapability.

THE MATRIX OF PERFECTION

The work of the initiate starts with repeatedly aligning oneself on the Matrix of Perfection by means of meditation exercises and ritual work. This is done by working with Adam Kadmon. Through this work on the Self, you are confronted with the deviations that always will appear in your life. The work on the Tree of Life will shake up your life, and situations that are not in balance will show themselves. In the beginning this causes personal upheaval—your life is turned upside down. You have two choices: work on yourself and your life, or stop the Great Work.

The *Great Work* is a term used in high magic and spiritual alchemy. In the Mysteries we assume that we, in our material reality, live in a state of imperfection. This is caused by the Descent of the Spirit into matter. We ourselves are often unaware of our divine nature. The Great Work is the work that is done to resolve this imperfection. It consists of two parts. First, there is the knowledge and the techniques that make it possible for humans to become aware of their true nature. The second part of the Great Work is to devote one's self to the healing of the world.

In your preparations and your meditation exercises, you tune in to the Matrix of Perfection. By doing this, you steer yourself and your spiritual exercises in the right direction. This is the reason why you place yourself in the cross while performing the Kabbalistic Cross, instead of looking toward it. The ritual garments serve the same goal: to reflect the inner world of perfection. In this way, the initiated Magus remains constantly conscious of the matrix upon which he or she works.

The temple in which the Magus works is a representation of the creation myths. In this way, the temple becomes a miniature example of the kingdom of God, and the Magus relates this example to the daily world around him—to nature and to his everyday experiences. Following the mechanism of "As Above, so Below," you tune into the Matrix of Perfection with every exercise.

THE HEAVENLY MAN

Specific qualities are inherent in the archetype of Adam Kadmon, the Heavenly Man, and these aspects are the focus of the systematic training provided in the Mystery schools. The initiate dresses himself in this Body of Light of perfection and builds up all the spheres of divine energy within him. By doing this, he gets access to the different dimensions and manifestations of the divine, to the varying heights in the heavens. This ability to travel through all these different dimensions and to reach all these different heavens is called "Rising on the Planes."

SEPHIROTH AND NATIVOTH

When you look at the picture of the Kabbalistic Tree, you see spheres and lines. The spheres are called Sephiroth. Singular is Sephirah. They represent the different emanations of divine light. The connecting lines are the paths, called the Nativoth.

Adam Kadmon, the Heavenly Man, carries all these possibilities within himself. He represents the Kabbalistic Tree of Life and the total sum of the ensouled universe, the spirit of divinity. He is the model for the human world, the original human. He is the one who is mentioned in Genesis: "Let us make a human after our own image." He is as big as the cosmos, his body is the earth itself, and his soul is the sum of all souls.

Adam Kadmon has his feet on the earth. He is gigantically big. His genitals start at the moon. His heart is the sun itself. His throat reaches the star Sirius and his head comes forth from the big bang itself, which caused the universe to manifest. Adam Kadmon is the model used by the initiate to awaken the forces of the Tree of Life within himself, and to metabolize it into his psyche and body.

TEN SEPHIROTH BLIMAH

PEELING THE ONION

The word *Blimah* means "unnameable." Blimah in relation to the ten divine emanations means that you can get into contact with them by entering into a state of divine receptiveness: you need to enter into silence and into meditation. Then the Mysteries of the ten unnameable Sephiroth can be experienced and will come alive. At the same time, it is important to keep seeing the Sephiroth as interconnected.

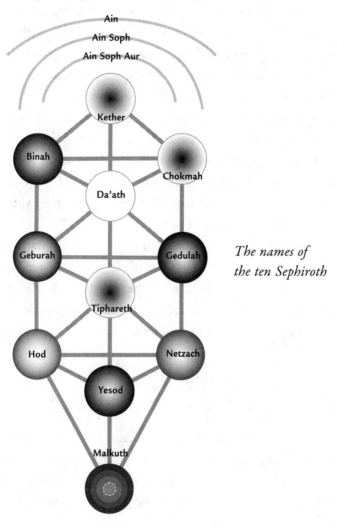

The names of the ten Sephiroth

You can understand the Kabbalistic Tree of Life more easily when you tune into one layer of meaning and then go through the entire Tree. You make it more difficult for yourself if you zoom in on one Sephiroth and try to understand it on an intellectual level. There are people who make it a sport to learn all the correspondences and associations and, like a walking encyclopedia, learn everything by heart. For a magician, this is not of much use. For us it is important to learn the inner reality, and from there assign meaning to the symbols. You should learn the deeper meanings gradually and reveal the Sephiroth slowly, like peeling an onion.

The Sephiroth and the paths must be discovered through meditation and contemplation from one's own inner worlds. In books with the correspondences of three, you find incredibly long lists with associations. These long lists have been developed because people, through the centuries, have added their inner experiences to the Tree. They have added their experiences as correspondences to the existing lists. The correspondences are useful as indicators when you want to encounter the inner worlds. But if you do it the right way, you will, over time, develop an opinion of your own, and add your self-discovered correspondences. Then you can, from your inner experiences and with argumentation, explain why you disagree with Aleister Crowley's book *777*.

The Kabbalisitic Tree is a model that explains how things come into creation. It is the history of creation itself. It is, at the same time, the underlying structure of the human psyche. For the magician it means that, when you apply these principles to yourself and to your own life, you follow the natural pattern of manifestation.

FOUR LAYERS OF CONSCIOUSNESS, PER SEPHIRAH AND PER PATH

The Kabbalistic Tree is built up in four layers. They are layers of divine consciousness. Every Sephirah has those four different layers. Compare them with the different layers of an onion. The innermost layer is the most abstract and the most spiritual, whereas the outer layer has the

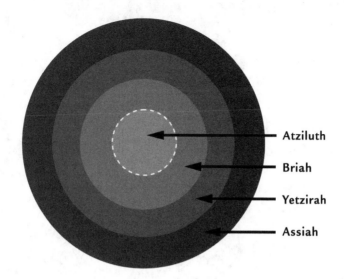

The Four Worlds

appearance of the object, or the symbol. The outermost layer is how you usually look at things in your everyday life.

In some illustrations you see the Tree pictured like four trees on top of each other. Then Malkuth—the lowest Sephirah—is pictured in the same place as Kether of the Tree below. This is called Jacob's Ladder. The name comes from the Vision of Jacob, who saw a ladder on which all kinds of angels walked from Below to Above, to the highest heaven. In every Sephirah, and on every path, you can divide the different layers, which I will explain in the next paragraphs.

Atziluth

The most divine layer of the Tree is Atziluth. It is the causal world of pure spirit. From here the Root of the Element of Fire comes forth. It is the most abstract layer of the Tree. Images or words are not capable of expressing these energies; they are pure energies and resplendent light.

Briah

The second layer of the Tree is Briah. It is the archetypal world of the pure intellect. This layer forms the Root of Elemental Air. In Briah you

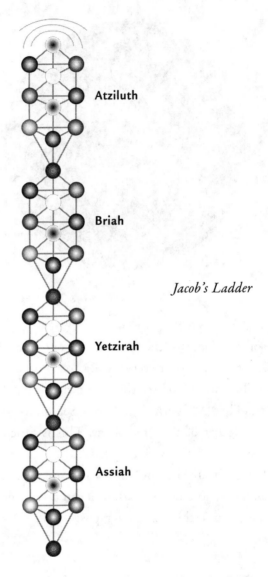

Jacob's Ladder

find all the archetypal images. You will meet the archangels and the gods here.

One of the goals for which the Kabbalistic Tree is used within spiritual magic is to create relationships with the gods from the different pantheons. The gods are then personified, and Briah is the starting point of the magical work.

Here you find the so-called telesmatic images. These are the images of the divine forces clothed in human form. The magician is capable of taking these forms into his Body of Light and of working with them. In this way the god-forms are assumed. This makes it possible to perform magic with the help of gods and angels. This is the reason why, in spiritual magic, the Briatic layer of the Kabbalistic Tree is used the most often in practice.

Yetzirah

The third layer of the Tree of Life is Yetzirah. It is the formative world wherein the matrixes are found of every form and idea that comes into existence. Here matter condenses according to fixed patterns. Here we find the Root of Elemental Water. In this layer of the Tree of Life we find the angelic choirs. In the Kabbalisitic tradition there is an entire hierarchy of angels.

The archangel is the regent within one Sephirah, and the angelic choirs are all helpers that rule a specific cosmic current in the smallest detail. We are used to seeing angels and gods in a human form, but in fact they are abstract patterns of consciousness.

Compare archangels and gods with natural phenomena such as gravity or electricity. They are abstract natural forces. They are not physical forces, but waves of consciousness, natural laws within the universe of consciousness.

Assiah

The lowest layer of the Tree of Life is Assiah. This is the most earthly form of consciousness, the Root of Elemental Earth. It is the physical world, the world of bodily sensations and the unseen natural laws. It is also the world of the involuntary bodily processes such as digestion and the hormonal feedback mechanism. Within the Sephiroth this is the layer of planetary forces.

THE UNMANIFESTED

The Kabbalistic Tree starts with absolute Nothingness. In the beginning there was nothing at all—even the concept of nothingness did not exist. An absolute emptiness, a complete vacuum, an incomprehensible void. This is expressed in the Kabbalistic Tree with three circles above the Tree. These are called the Three Veils of Negative Existence. These three rings were called, by the magician Samuel MacGregor Mathers, the Ocean of Negative Light. They are the Ain, the Ain Soph, and the Ain Soph Aur. The highest of the three—the Ain—is the most unmanifested of the veils, and this is God.

The Ain

At a certain moment, the Ain started to concentrate upon itself and pressed together inwardly. The Nothingness imploded. This is incomprehensible on its own. I always get images of a Nothingness that turns around in spirals and pushes itself together in the center of the spiral. But there is still nothing. Only the pressure on the core increases. God is a pressure building up, but there is still nothing.

The Ain Soph

The Nothingness concentrates, but because this happens in the unknowable, we cannot understand how and why this happens. By the increasing pressure, the Ain Soph came into being. The Ain Soph is endless, unlimited. It is something that is still built up from nothing. It is the idea of endlessness, not endlessness itself. In the Ain Soph, the Heavenly Waters come into being. Even stronger: the Ain Soph are the Heavenly Waters. This area raises feelings of awe. It is an awe-filled power that gathers together in the endless Nothingness.

ש The Ain Soph Aur

The Heavenly Waters of the Ain Soph Aur start to move. By this movement, light comes into existence. This is an endless light. It is a threefold light, represented by the Hebrew letter Shin, which also indicates the spirit of God. When the Ain Soph Aur comes into existence, then light is created. At the moment that light is created, the first emanation comes into being, the first Sephirah. It is a sphere of endless light, and this process causes an intense joy. From this point on creation starts.

KETHER, THE CROWN

*The First Path is called the Admirable or Hidden
Intelligence because it is the Light giving power of
comprehension of the First Principle, which hath no
beginning. And it is the Primal Glory, because no created
being can attain to its essence.*

SEPHER YETZIRAH

When reaching this point in the process of the creation—indicated by the Sephirah Kether—we have arrived at the first path. The Sephiroth of the Tree of Life, together with the paths of the Tree, form together the Thirty-two Paths of Wisdom of the Tree. The Sephiroth themselves are the first ten paths, then the connecting paths are numbered from top to bottom.

The unending light dances in circles and flows together at one single point. This point is called Kether. Imagine that incredible spiral of Nothingness, turning around itself, the pressure increasing. The first movement of Nothingness exists. In this way, an ocean comes into existence with waves of Nothingness and Cosmic Tides. This causes resistance and, through that resistance, light comes into being. By this means, the entire creation process is in motion.

Kether is a sphere of a constant creation process. From the Nothingness, the universe comes into being. Kether is in fact the opposite of a black hole. The light of Kether contains all the possibilities of All that creates Itself. Kether is a unity that streams out in big waves from the Nothingness. In Kether there is no diversification and no specialization. The light cannot yet be divided here. There are different symbols connected to Kether.

GOD IS PRESSURE

In Kether there is no form yet. There is only consciousness. This consciousness is indicated with: I Am, or I Am that I Am, or in other words: I Am Becoming. This consciousness is created because the Nothingness comes under so much pressure. Kether is a very strange point. It is in fact a vulnerable balance. The balance between unmanifested being and manifested being hangs on a silk thread. It is incredibly thin. From the other side, the force is so big that this causes an entire universe to be born. This power cannot be measured with the best instruments. The All consists of Mind, the hermetic laws tell us. The All, the universe is built from consciousness.

MALE AND FEMALE IN ONE

Because Kether is a unity containing the male and the female, you could use the yinyang symbol for a sign of Kether. Both are not divided and carry the seed of the counterpoint within themselves. The light and the unmanifested are rolled into each other, and one creates the other. The manifested returns to the nothingness. Negative light and positive light are together at the point of manifestation. The point in the circle is another symbol for Kether. It is a point without dimensions, without length, depth, or height.

Classically, the symbol for Kether is the Crown. The Crown is symbolic of the chakra—the Sephirah—that is located above the head. The Crown flows out in all directions above the head of Adam Kadmon. In the yoga system we find the chakra of the thousand-petaled lotus here. These are two symbols to explain the same principle.

In Kether, God is called AHIH. In the Middle Pillar exercise, you start formulating the Sephiroth from the highest Sephirah: Kether in Atziluth. You start with the vibration of this divine name. AHIH represents the unmanifested cosmic principle of God before the creation happened: I Am Becoming.

KETHER IN THE FOUR WORLDS

Kether in Atziluth is the most unmanifested energy that exists. This highest sphere is expressed in images of an incredible brilliance. A sparkling light that is greater and more brilliant than the sun. You cannot look directly at it, and you cannot develop a relationship with it in this way.

The gods from other pantheons who are associated with Kether are, for example, Uranos from the Greek tradition, Atum-Ra and/or Khephri from the Egyptian tradition, and Anu from the Mesopotamian tradition. From the Kabbalistic tradition we find here the association with the archangel Metatron.

The angelic choir that belongs to Kether is the Chaioth ha Qadesh, the Four Holy Living Creatures. You remember that they have their places within the magical circle as well. They are associated there with the highest order within the hierarchies of the Elements.

There are no active planetary forces in Kether. Kether is too unmanifested for this. To Kether is given the name Rashit ha-Gilgalim. This name means "First Whirlings." They are the first movements of cosmic consciousness coming into manifestation from the nothingness. From this is created one of the magical images of Kether.

MAGICAL IMAGES OF KETHER

Imagine the swastika, the cross with sidebars that point in the direction of the movement of the sun. Compare the swastika in this case with a cosmic fan. When a fan stands still, you see that it consists mostly of the space between the blades. When a fan starts whirling, you had better not put your arms between the blades, because then the empty space between them becomes a part of a force field. In Kether, the swastika functions like a cosmic fan. The Four Holy Living Creatures, as representatives of the root forces of the Four Elements, stand at the ends of the blades. This enormous mill starts to turn around. This creates the illusion of matter, but in fact it consists of very quickly whirling consciousness: Nothingness in the form of the consciousness of the Lords of Form, Flame, Mind, and Humanity.

I am now speaking in the form of magical images. The magical images are important in the Mysteries. In an earlier chapter I talked about the language of nature, the One Language that forms the key to a deep understanding of mythology and the Mysteries. The magical images are the symbolic language you use to get started. The magical image of Kether is an old bearded king, seen in profile.

TITLES OF KETHER

Every Sephirah has titles that belong to it. Some of the titles of Kether are: Existence of the Existence, the Concealed of the Concealed, the Old One of the Oldest, the Most Holy Old One, the Ancient of Days, the Primordial Point, the Point in the Circle, the Most High, the Vast Countenance, the White Head, the Head that is Not, the Macroprosophos, the Occult Light, the Inner Light, the Unending High. It is a good idea to meditate about these titles and images, because doing so will produce images in your own subconscious that will increase your understanding of the Sephirah.

Every Sephirah belongs to a part of the human body, and the body part that belongs to Kether is the head.

SCHEDULE OF KETHER

WORLD	DIVINE ASPECT	TAROT ASSOCIATIONS
Atziluth	God-name AHIH	Ace of Fire/Root of the Element Fire
Briah	Archangel Metatron	Ace of Air/Root of the Element Air
Yetzirah	Angelic Choir/Chaioth ha Qadesh/The Holy Living Creatures	Ace of Water/Root of the Element Water
Assiah	Rashit ha-Gilgalim/ The First Swirlings	Ace of Earth/Root of the Element Earth

THE BLUE LOTUS—PATHWORKING

Prepare for meditation. You do this by reading this exercise very carefully and memorizing the images. Then you perform the Mudra of the Opening of the Veils and the Middle Pillar exercise. When you have created all the energy circuits around yourself, you connect yourself in your imagination with the sphere of Kether above your head. You vibrate the mantra that connects you with Kether. Ehieh Asher Ehieh: I am that I am.

Visualize a sphere of a sparkling white light above your head. As you put this sphere above your head, you vibrate repeatedly the god-name of Kether: AHIH. When you vibrate the name, you realize what this name means. The name is the mantra of the source of the universe, at the moment that this beams outward from unmanifested nothingness to light. The light streams into manifestation above your head. It flows from above in your aura. To the rhythm of a beating heart, this sparkling light embraces you. Within yourself you formulate the wish to make a connection with the Sephirah Kether, the highest sphere of the Kabbalistic Tree of Life.

At the moment you do this, the archangel Metatron appears before you. He offers himself as a guide of the inner worlds of Kether. He appears as a whirling movement of light. The light moves so fast that it seems to cause rainbows on the movement of the lightning energy of the archangel. It is an incredible Fire energy that moves before your eyes. He stretches out over the entire horizon of the visible universe before you. He has thirty-six wings, which all spark off this rainbow-colored light. He has an endless amount of eyes, which look in all directions. He has access to the Crown of the Universe itself. He offers you his help to make a connection with Kether. He turns around, and you see that behind him is a gigantic Ladder of Light. The ladder goes directly into the highest heavens.

The ladder spirals around an enormous pillar. The pillar is engraved with four letters. At the top of the pillar stands the Yod, then below it comes the Heh, followed by the Vav, and at the bottom of the pillar the second Heh is engraved. The

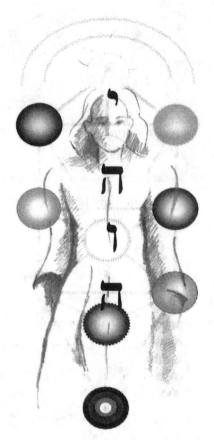

*Adam Kadmon in
the Tree of Life*

pillar is the spine of Adam Kadmon himself. As an enormous wand of power he
stands before you. He reaches to the highest heaven. Metatron tells you to watch
exactly where the Crown of Adam Kadmon is located. You see that the figure of
Adam Kadmon reaches up to the north polestars. Archangel Metatron walks in
front of you, and you climb the spiral staircase upward. On your way you pass
angels and archangels, who move to the Above and the Below. In this way they
connect the force fields of all the heavens.

When you reach higher heavens you feel that the pressure and the energy intensify and become more difficult to bear. It appears to become darker, but Metatron
assures you that this is not the case. You have difficulties perceiving the light at these
heights as the frequency becomes higher. You approach the L.V.X. Occulta:* the

---

*L.V.X. is Latin for "light."

dark light. This light is, in fact, so bright that it is unbearable if you are not of the right purity and resonation. That is why this occult light is equal to the inner light.

When it gets too bright to receive, the souls who reach this height are protected. The light is veiled, and this is why it is called the dark light. Metatron takes you with him, and you climb even higher on Jacob's Ladder—higher than the rainbow bridge. The archangel takes you with him over the Great Abyss to the point where this bridge ends in nothingness.

You look around you. On all sides you are surrounded by a midnight blue. In a sea of deep lapis-lazuli blue, you stand at the end of the ladder on the rainbow bridge. You are in the company of the archangel amid the Primordial Waters: the waters of creation itself.

"Look to the secret of Kether," the archangel says. "Because of my presence the secret of Kether will become visible by the visions I give you. The reality, however, is much more abstract. I, as an archangel, have the key to the sphere of Briah of Kether, so that I am able to give you the images. Be aware of the fact that these are but symbols for the reality behind this, which is unknowable."

You stand in the middle of this enormous sea of deep blue Cosmic Waters. Around you it is dark. Suddenly, you become aware of an intensely beautiful scent. Slowly it becomes stronger, and the deep black darkness starts to move. Something whirls. You look intently at this motion. You are reminded of the bud of a flower, which slowly forms from the circling of the primordial ocean. The water whirls together with the flower bud. The flower is deep purple; it has the color of the Primordial Waters. The scent becomes stronger. Before your eyes the flower opens, pulsating with the rhythm of your heart. It opens very slowly while it moves on the momentum of the whirling Primordial Waters.

The flower opens further and the scent gets more intense. The atmosphere starts to spark because of the unknown energy of the occult light whirling around.

"These are the First Whirlings," Metatron says. "They form the Beginning of the Beginning, the Concealed of the Concealed."

Suddenly the blue lotus opens, and in the middle four great golden pistils become visible. On the pistils you see the Root of Air, the Winged Bull; the Root of Fire, the Winged Lion; the Root of Water, the Eagle; and the Root of Earth, the Winged Human. These are the essences of all of the Four Elements, the Chaioth ha Qadesh. These Four Holy Living Creatures are the consciousness of the great form-giving powers of the cosmos. They appear here in the middle of the Cosmic Ocean.

The lotus starts to turn more quickly. With an increasing speed, the energy spins around. The atmosphere sparks because of the charging power. You stand beside Metatron to see how this energy whirls and turns. By the movement of the concealed light—because of the enormous pressure—consciousness slowly awakens.

Then you hear the sound that the Becoming One causes: AHIH. The energy builds up in power. Then, very suddenly and unexpectedly, all this tension results in a gigantic cosmic lightning flash. You follow this intense light with your eyes. When you look down along the spine of Adam Kadmon, you see that the lightning flash has caused ten gigantic spheres.

"Ten Sephiroth Blimah," says Metatron. In deep silence, surrounded by the cosmic primordial ocean, you see the ten spheres before you. They are connected through a path of intense light.

"The ten Sapphires* are connected through the Path of the Lightning Flash," Metatron tells you. "This is the road we need to follow to connect you to your physical body. Follow me over the Path of the Fool." You ask the archangel what type of path this is.

"It is the path of the divine sparks. Every Yod, ', every soul follows this path when he incarnates in a physical body. This is the road of the incarnation into matter."

You follow the archangel downward over the Path of the Lightning Flash. He calls the names of the Sephiroth as you look downward: "Kether, Chokmah, Binah, Chesed, Geburah, Tiphareth, Netzach, Hod, Yesod, Malkuth."

You have arrived in your physical body again. When you turn around, you see once more the Pillar of Equilibrium with Jacob's Ladder turning around it. At the

---

*Sephiroth means sapphires.

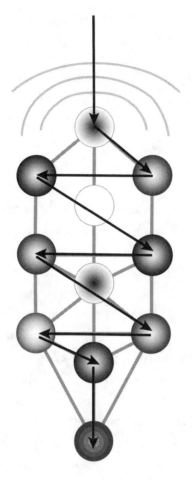

*The Path of the
Lightning Flash*

top, in the endless heights, you see a Head Which Is Not. It has the profile of an
ancient bearded king. You see it in a flash and then it disappears. The archangel
stands before you. You thank Metatron for this experience. He bows to you, and
then his image slowly blends into the background. Like a fata morgana, it disappears as if it never existed. You know, deep inside, that at any moment you can call
upon this archangel.

Now breathe deeply in and out. Connect yourself with your body. Stretch your
muscles and turn your head to the left and the right. End your exercise by writing
down your experiences, and close by eating and drinking something.

CHOKMAH, WISDOM

The Second Path is called the Illuminating Intelligence.
It is the Crown of Creation, the Splendor of Unity,
equaling it. It is exalted above every head and is named
by Qabalists, the Second Glory.

SEPHER YETZIRAH

The second Sephirah of the Tree of Life on the Path of the Lightning Flash is called Chokmah: Wisdom. We now leave the sphere of Kether. We leave the sphere of the growing pressure and creation. The pressure has built up until an enormous explosion followed: the big bang. You can see Chokmah as explosions of cosmic gasses. Chokmah is pure stellar energy that is unformed and undivided. Kether is the birthplace of consciousness itself, Chokmah is pure cosmic energy. Kether is the place where the consciousness of the All is born. This is symbolized by a point without dimensions. Chokmah is expanding force. This is symbolized by the line, as a metaphor for this unendingly powerful explosion of pure force.

To get an impression of the whole, you could imagine Kether as a miniscule hole between two spheres. On one side of the unmanifested, an enormous pressure builds up. On the other side of this hole, pure force comes out when it has forced itself though the hole. That is Chokmah. Like an exploding volcano or like a penis ejaculating.

These are images that are used for Chokmah—an explosion of pure raw male force. The lingam is used as a symbol. Also the Yod ' from the Tetragrammaton is a metaphor for the male sperm. The Yod is the symbol for the sparks of Fire that form the core of the souls of living people.

THE VISION OF GOD FACE TO FACE

Chokmah is a straight line, endless, without dimensions and without direction. It is an outburst of pure spiritual force. This force does not meet any resistance, and will go on endlessly with the same intention.

This force is not yet capable of causing any effect. To cause effects, a force needs to work upon something else, and that is not yet present at this stage of the creation: there is no form yet.

But there is consciousness when Chokmah is created. Both the force of Chokmah and the consciousness of Kether have come into existence now. Because of this, reflection is possible. This reflection creates the Vision of God Face-to-Face. God—the consciousness of the All, the almighty spirit—looks into the Waters of his consciousness and sees himself reflected in it.

The consciousness sees itself and calls itself by the name Yehovah: YHVH, the Word of the creation itself. The Word contains all the Elements on the highest level. It is male and female at the same moment. The letters Yod and Vav of the Tetragrammaton symbolize the male force. The two Hehs represent the female part of the divine force. In Chokmah, the Word of Creation is born. From this word all others come forth. In Chokmah, pure sexual force is sublimated to the highest spiritual experiences. This is why the ejaculating penis is an excellent metaphor: it spreads the seed of life itself, the Yod. This letter even has the form of the male seed.

THE BOOK OF RATZIEL

Archangel Ratziel is the archangel who brings the knowledge of the zodiac to the people. The book of the archangel Ratziel contains all human, heavenly, and earthly wisdom. The book was made of sapphire, and Ratziel gave this book to Adam, but other angels got jealous because of this and threw the book into the sea. Later, this same book came into the possession of Enoch and Noah. Noah locked it up in a golden chest and used the knowledge to build the ark that saved him and the animals during the Great Flood. He took it with him to divide the day from the night, as long as the Flood lasted, and neither the sun nor the moon shed any light on the earth. Later, this book would be in the possession of King Solomon.

THE AUPHANIM, THE WHEELS

The angelic choir that is associated with Chokmah is the Auphanim: the "Wheels." These can be visualized as the stars that turn around the invisible point of the north pole heaven, the stars that never set. They turn circles, and are described by Ezekiel (Ezekiel 1:15–18) in his vision of his ascent to heaven:

> Now as I beheld the living creatures, behold one wheel upon the earth by the living creatures, at the four faces thereof. The appearance of the Wheels and their works was like unto color of a beryl: and they four had one likeness: and their appearance and their work was as it were a wheel within a wheel. When they went, they went toward their four sides: they turned not when they went. As for their rings, they were high and they were dreadful: and they four had their rings full of eyes round about.

In Kether, the Middle Pillar starts, the Pillar of Equilibrium of the Kabbalistic Tree of Life. With Chokmah, the so-called Silver Pillar starts. This pillar is called the Pillar of Mercy: Jachin. This is the Pillar of Force that is created when the Path of the Lightning Flash comes into being and strikes Chokmah. The lightning zigzags to the other side of the Tree of Life and here Binah comes into being and, at the same time, the Black Pillar of Severity: Boaz.

Another symbol for Chokmah is the zodiac. The Kabbalists call it Mazloth. The zodiac is a ring of cosmic forces projected around the earth. More symbols and magical images of Chokmah are: the supernatural father, Abba, the Great Procreator, the Standing Stone, the Tower, the Upraised Wand of Power, the Inner Robe of Glory, Male potency, the Logos. The body part belonging to Chokmah is the left side of the face; in fact, you might say the left side of the brain. Examples of gods belonging to Chokmah are the Mesopotamian god Anu, the Egyptian Horus the Elder, the Greek Zeus, but also goddesses such as Neith, Nut, and Athena belong here.

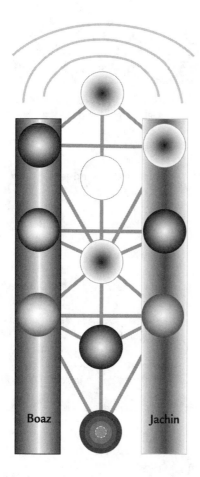

*The side pillars of
the Tree: Jachin and
Boaz*

Chokmah will become clearer when I explain Binah—the next sphere
on the Tree of Life. Chokmah and Binah polarize each other on the Tree.
They are opposites of complementary forces that balance each other.

SCHEDULE OF CHOKMAH

WORLD	DIVINE ASPECT	TAROT ASSOCIATIONS
Atziluth	God-name Jah/Yehovah/YHVH	King of Fire/Lord of Flames and Lightning/King of the Fire Spirits/King of the Salamanders/Two of Wands: Lord of Dominion
Briah	Archangel Ratziel	Lord of the Winds and the Breeze/King of Air/King of the Spirit of Air/King of the Sylphs and Sylphides/Two of Swords: Lord of Peace Restored
Yetzirah	Angelic Choir: Auphanim—the Wheels	The King of Water/ Lord of the Waves and the Waters/King of the Hosts of the Sea/King of the Undines and Nymphs/Two of Cups: Lord of Love
Assiah	Mazloth/Sphere of the Zodiac	King of Earth/Lord of the Wilderness and the Fertile Land/King of the Spirits of Earth/King of the Gnomes/Two of Pentagrams: Lord of Harmonious Change

THE BOOK OF SECRETS—
CONTEMPLATION EXERCISE

In this contemplation exercise you take the different stages of the exercise into yourself in pieces. You can use the different parts as meditation exercises. I have divided the pieces by putting stars between them. You can take the text with you to your meditation space where you have projected your magical circle. Then you can relate to the space of the circle that you have created around you.

Read every part of the exercise thoroughly and commit the images to memory. Then perform the Mudra of the Opening of the Veils and the

Middle Pillar exercise. When you have created the energy circulations around you, you connect yourself in your imagination with the sphere of Chokmah at the left side of your head.

Vibrate the Word of God while you visualize the sphere. Yod-Heh-Vav-Heh. While you do this, you see that the four cardinal directions become solid before your inner eye. When you vibrate the letters, the Heavenly Man forms in the North, the Winged Lion appears in the South, the Eagle comes flying toward you and takes his seat in the West. The Winged Bull with his mighty appearance comes forth in the East. The First Whirlings have taken their seats in your meditation space.

———————◆———————

For the second time you vibrate Yod-Heh-Vav-Heh, and on the sounds of this vibration an angel forms before your eyes. He is dressed in a robe of deep midnight blue, a robe made of the starry heaven itself. He has a splendid appearance. The fire of the stars is so intense that he is dressed in a shower of sparks. Your heart starts to beat quicker when the shining appearance of the archangel materializes before you. The archangel bows, and you bow back. He asks you why you have called him. You answer that you are searching for the Wisdom of Chokmah.

Ratziel answers that, if you want to receive this Wisdom, you need to become one with the Word of God.

"You yourself must become the Wand," he says. "When you can become one with the Heavenly Man, then you represent one of the Holy Living Creatures in the universe. The Point of Creation Cosmic Source itself is in a constant state of creation. When humanity strives toward unity with the divine, then he drinks from this source of eternal becoming. So vibrate the divine name once again, and become one with Adam Kadmon."

When you vibrate the name now, the letter Yod descends into your head, the letter Heh forms your arms, the letter Vav connects your head and your arms with your spine, and the last letter, Heh, forms your hip joints and your legs.

"Excellent," Ratziel says, "now then has come the time to form the dimensions of the universe. The first three dimensions form the First Wheel. They are the three Mother Letters. The first letter that forms itself is the Aleph **א***.*

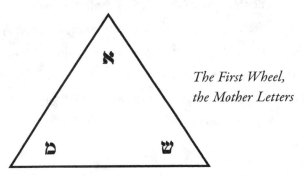

The First Wheel,
the Mother Letters

"Aleph is the breath of the ox, it is the divine Wind that whirls around and on whose wings the Four Holy Living Creatures stand, who set the entire vortex of power into motion. The second letter is the Mem **מ***. These are the Waters of Space, also called the Waters of the Deep, the Tehom, the Primordial Waters. The Primordial Waters are divided by the breath of the ox, and this causes the Above and the Below. The third Mother Letter is the Shin* **ש***. This is the power of Rising Fire, which connects the Waters of Below with the Waters of Above. And you, Adam Kadmon, you are the Wand. You are the Wand of Power that connects the Below and the Above to each other. The snake lies at your feet, and the Crown is above your head."*

Now it is time to connect the Word of God to the four cardinal directions of the magical circle. The Yod represents the in-falling light. The Yods are the flood of divine sparks, the souls that descend to the earth. The letter Yod is symbolic here of the Heavenly Man. The letter Heh forms the first gate through which the light interweaves itself in a physical enclosure. The Vav is the nail that nails the soul to the Cross of the Four Elements. The last Heh is the second portal of light. This is the goal to which the soul develops itself by taking the path through the earth. In this way it finds its Way Back to the unmanifested God itself.

Within this universe of the holy magical circle, you are Adam Kadmon the Fool and, at the same time, Adam Kadmon the Magician, because you manifest your own reality by what you create with the Four Elements.

There is more, Adam Kadmon. You will get seven helpers. These seven helpers will advise you time and again. They are the seven archetypical forces. They are also called the Seven Pillars of Wisdom. They are the seven primordial forces that are available to every magician and every mystic.

These seven letters together form the rainbow of the Word of God. They constitute each one of the seven rays of colored light that form aspects of the self wherein Adam Kadmon can wrap himself. Each letter is one of the creative forces that are personified by the world of the gods and the archangels to rule in the lower universe. You can find them in every tradition under the force fields of the classical planets.

These seven Double Letters form the Second Wheel of the Word of God. You, Adam Kadmon, are the Wand of Power, surrounded by the four cardinal directions and the Four Elements. See how the planetary spirits turn around you in the form of the Double Letters of the Word.

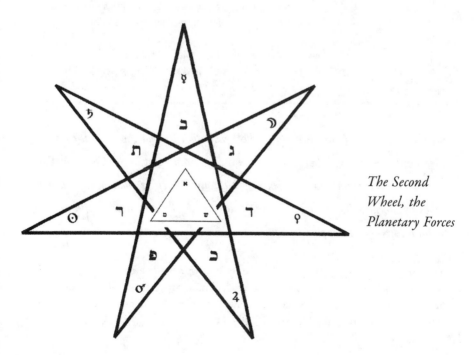

The Second Wheel, the Planetary Forces

Beth House	ב	The letter Beth is the mantra that forms the House. In this house Mercury lives, the Messenger of the gods.
Gimel Camel	ג	The letter Gimel is the mantra that opens the path to the moon and, like a camel, this mantra will carry you faithfully through the desert of life itself, and carries you over the rainbow bridge to the world of the gods.
Daleth Door	ד	The letter Daleth is the mantra that opens the portals to fertility in your life. With her sweet sounds she opens the portal to Venus, the love for the self.
Kaph Palm of the Hand	כ	The letter Kaph opens with its sounds the palm of the Hand of God. In his hand your destiny is written. In the form of the planet Jupiter he shows you who leads you.
Peh Mouth	פ	The letter Peh opens your mouth. The sounds of your mouth open the path to Mars, the energy of The Warrior.
Resh Face	ר	The letter Resh lets the sun shine in your heart, when you vibrate this mantra. With this letter you connect yourself with the Light of the World.
Tau Cross	ת	The letter Tau forms with its sounds the crossroads between the visible and the invisible worlds. The rings of Saturn are the bridge to the universe.

But there is more, Adam Kadmon. The heaven is rich and the stars turn as big wheels of power around the point of the unseen—the Point in the Circle. Look to my heavenly robes and read my Book of Wisdom. The circle encloses my heavenly Robes of Eternity like the cord around your waist. The cord around the waist of Adam Kadmon is the zodiac.*

---

*This paragraph—like all other Pathworkings and rituals—is written in mystery language. It is a part of the training for the student to meditate on the riddles and to resolve them. The Book of Wisdom is the stars. The circle is a metaphor for the Zodiac belt, and the heavenly robe is the Mantle of God—the stars.

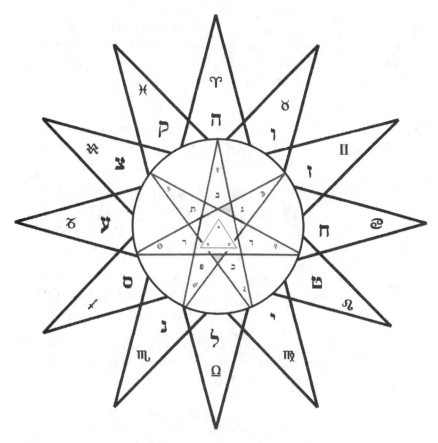

The Third Wheel, the Zodiac

Here, the Forces of Activity are described. Through these starry gates the One filters its consciousness in the form of the temples of the zodiac. Each temple forms a sacred center of divine power. All these forces together form the great cosmic lyre whereon the all-embracing One plays the heavenly music of the spheres.

These sounds bring the All into vibration. Listen to the sounds of the mantras of the zodiac and hear what they tell you. They are the vibrations of the angels who sing together the Word of Creation.

Heh Window	ה	My name is Heh, and I am the first one of the animals, the announcer of the Light. In the form of the heavenly ram I am the first one who opens the portals to the Light.
Vav Nail	ו	My name is Vav, and I am the Heavenly Bull. I connect heaven and earth with each other. I am a fixed sign in the zodiac and a lower form of the Winged One of the First Whirlings.
Zain Sword	ז	My name is Zain, and I am the sword. In the sign of Gemini I show the essential of the connecting forces of polarity. I cut the unity so that the force of attraction is created.
Cheth Fence	ח	My name is Cheth, and I am the fence. Like the Crab I enclose and harness, because the holiest part of the inside cannot be exposed.
Teth Snake	ט	My name is Teth. My form is the snake; my essence is the fiery force of the Lion. Also, I have been deduced from the Winged One of the First Word.
Yod Hand	י	My name is Yod. I am a spark that springs forth from the Hand of God. The Virgin carries me as one of the seeds of her ear of corn.
Lamed Ox Goat	ל	My name is Lamed. I am the ox goad used to lead the ox. In the sign of Libra I show that there is one straight way leading us to equilibrium.
Nun Fish	נ	My name is Nun. I am the fish, the heavenly food of Wisdom. In the sign of Scorpio I show that true Wisdom is captured in the unseen. I transform this knowledge by means of the Eagle of the First Whirling.
Samech Prop	ס	My name is Samech. I am the tent pole that supports the House. In the sign of Sagittarius I show that I shoot my arrow, using the rainbow as my bow.

Ayin Eye	ע	My name is Ayin. I am the Eye of the All. In the sign of Capricorn I show you that I take the Light of the World on my back when I jump out of the heavenly ocean and land in the House of Bread.*
Tzaddi Fishhook	צ	My name is Tzaddi. I am the fishhook. I capture fishes in the sign of the Watercarrier when he pours the heavenly flood out of his jar, and the water streams over the land.
Qoph Back of the Head	ק	My name is Qoph. I am the back of the head, the subconsciousness. In the sign of Fishes I show that I have the ability to get access to the most exalted spiritual knowledge.

*"House of Bread" is the physical body in the Mystery language. The Hebrew word for it is better known: Beth Lehem.

These—my dear Adam Kadmon—are the sounds coming forth from the Word of God. They form a heavenly song that is sung in all languages and in all traditions. Hear the song of the Auphanim, the heavenly Wheels.

> Holy art Thou, Creator of the Universe.
> Holy art Thou, who nature has not formed.
> Holy art Thou, oh vast and mighty one.
> Creator of light and darkness.

And while this singing sounds, the archangel Ratziel rolls up the papyrus whereon the Book of Wisdom is written. Now separate yourself slowly from the figure of Adam Kadmon. Let the letters of the Tetragrammaton slowly shrink until they are as small as the top of a nail. Let the images shrink into a silver ball. Connect this with the left side of your brain. This makes it easy for you to store the thoughtform and let it grow in power every time you use it.

BINAH, UNDERSTANDING

The Third Path is called the Sanctifying Intelligence,
the Foundation of Primordial Wisdom: it is also called
the Creator of Faith, and its Roots are in Amen. It is the
parent of faith, whence faith emanates.

SEPHER YETZIRAH

Binah is the third Sephirah that comes forth from the unmanifested. Kether was male and female at the same time. Chokmah is male. Binah represents the female quality of divinity. Binah is the Sephirah that stands at the top of the female pillar, the Pillar of Severity. This pillar is called Boaz. If the Silver Pillar is the Pillar of Force on the Kabbalistic Tree of Life, then the Black Pillar is the Pillar of Form. The ability to create form is the essential characteristic of Binah.

In Kether, consciousness comes into existence, and this generates the process of creation. In Chokmah, there arises a gigantic outburst of energy. The energy spreads in all directions without any connection or any resistance. In Binah, the energy is limited. If there is no limit, then energy is nothing more than power flying around without any result.

The meaning of Binah—Understanding—needs to be read in two ways. When you understand something, you stand under something, supporting it, giving it a foundation to stand on and a structure so that it does not collapse. The skeleton of a building is an image to express this aspect of under-standing. There is also emotional understanding. Can you understand why a person acts in the way he does? Can you place yourself in another person's shoes? By doing this, you step into the world of another and pour your empathy into another form, temporarily experiencing someone else's emotions.

Binah's Understanding is a combination of both aspects of the word. It is about the form-giving aspect and the emotional, empathic aspect of consciousness. These are two results of the same principle.

In this connection, the mathematical symbol for Binah—the

triangle—is very beautiful. Kether had the point in the circle—a sphere of pure being, without dimensions. Chokmah had the line—an explosion of force, a movement between two points that form God Face to Face. In Binah a third point is added, and this causes dimensions to come into existence: the first form is created that can contain something. Through this, a vessel is created that can contain power.

A VESSEL FOR POWER

Consider steam as an anecdote to explain the above idea. Steam itself is nothing more than rising gasses, like formations of clouds. We are surrounded by steam our entire life, without giving it much attention. But as steam starts to condense, as it becomes denser, it takes on a form. It flows in rivers and small streams. Because of the combination of the energy (the movement of the water) and the enclosure (the riverbanks), complete energy production can be put in motion. In this way, entire cities and countries are supplied with electricity. That is what the combination of energy and form brings about.

Pressure is produced by a limitation or a curtailment of energy, which causes resistance. Resistance results in the friction caused by limitation. Free power cannot flow unrestricted, but will bump against the borders of the container, searching for a way out.

Limitation created by form is the characteristic of Binah. This is connected with the female. Females have the ability to give life and bear children. This form-giving force is seen as the ability to encapsulate cosmic consciousness in a form. The divine spark is given a body, a house for the eruption of the male energy of Chokmah.

IN-FALLING LIGHT

The first Heh ה of the Tetragrammaton is associated with Binah. The letter has as hieroglyphic root the symbol of the window—in other words, in-falling light. The letter is built from two parts: the Daleth ד, which signifies a door, and the Yod י, the divine spark of consciousness itself. By the combination of these two energy forms, an enclosure is made that the light can fill.

Another metaphor is the womb in which the seed of consciousness is sown. Through this, life unfolds. This last principle is characteristic of Binah. The creation is still in the very primal stage of germinal force. With Binah, we are still in the highest triangle of the Tree of Life: Kether, Chokmah, and Binah together form the so-called divine or spiritual triangle of the Tree of Life, the Trinity. Also, on this highest level, the Trinity creates the triangle of form. Creation is simply not possible without the Trinity, because this is the spiritual womb of the All.

S-HE

The god-name of Binah is Yehovah Elohim. Yehovah is the same name as YHVH (Hebrew is written almost without vowels). The word *Elohim* is special. It explains different concepts of divinity. The stem of the word comes from the word *El,* which means divine. The word is then extended further to *Eloah,* which makes it plural. But because of the last extension, the word *Elohim* is formed, and that is a female plural addition.

The word *Elohim* is used throughout the Bible, appearing in the very first sentence of Genesis. If you wanted to translate Elohim, which indicates divinity, in English, an accurate approach would be "S-He," which is male and female as well as singular and plural all at the same time.

TZAPHKIEL

Tzaphkiel is the name of the archangel who belongs to Binah. The name means "one who perceives the divine." This is the observing consciousness. In everything you do, you keep one part of your consciousness separate to observe. With this observing part you ask yourself questions, and you look to see if you are still on the right track. Tzaphkiel is seen as the watcher, the observer.

The term *Watcher* is very interesting in this connection, because this is also the name that the Mesopotamian angels had; the Annunaki were the Watchers. In the Mesopotamian Mysteries they were "they who were sent from the heaven to the earth by Anu." They were also called the

Nephilim, "they who descended." The stem of the word *Nephilim* has the same source as the word *Neteru,* the Egyptian term for the gods.

The ancient Semites were very suspicious about those Watchers. They thought that they were a kind of spy who informed God about the mistakes of humans. That is why they got bad press, both in the history books and in the Bible.

Tzaphkiel within ourselves is the piece of our consciousness that constantly watches to ensure that what we are doing conforms to our higher mission as well as to the general interest of the cosmos. Tzaphkiel fits in very well with the divine energy of Binah, as this angel watches us like a mother. In this way, Tzaphkiel also forms a bridge between heaven and earth. This angel keeps us conscious of the unseen and unmanifested worlds. Tzaphkiel receives the light of divinity that enables divinity to see itself and becomes all knowing and all conscious.

THE ARALIM, THE THRONES

The angelic choir of Binah is the Aralim, "the Thrones." The name means the strong ones, the powerful ones. They are the supporters. They are the angels who give power and support so that wisdom can grow. A throne was, in ancient days, a chair for a god or a goddess. A throne lifts you up from the crowd, and underlines someone's function.

In the Book of the Angel Ratziel, it states that there are seven Thrones. Seven is, of course, a very frequently used number within magic, and in this case, it is also very important. Binah is a Sephirah who is a part of the divine triangle. This means that we are, in Binah, still within the sphere of pure, unmanifested spiritual energy. In Binah, the birth process of the material cosmos begins. In Binah, the Thrones provide form for this birth.

The seven Thrones are: the Mesopotamian Annunaki, the seven archangels of the Tree under the Great Abyss, the seven Khuti from Egypt, the seven sages of Sumer, and the seven archfathers of the Bible. These seven Thrones all get an area in the heavenly temple. In the divine triangle, the Holy Marriage takes place between Chokmah and Binah and, as a result, the other seven Sephiroth are born. These are the Sephiroth who form our microcosmos.

Kether and Chokmah are Sephiroth who are completely pure and untouched. Their only characteristics are virtues. Because of the fact that in Binah the divine forces are poured into a vessel, it is here that the first resistance grows, the first friction—the vices.

To stretch the metaphor of water a little further, you can compare the vices of Binah with the inevitable erosion of the banks when water streams through a riverbed. This is why, apart from the virtues, now the vices also appear in the perfect plan of creation. This is why the Thrones are associated in connection with justice. The vices need to be corrected to keep us all on the right track of the divine plan.

SCHEDULE OF BINAH

WORLD	DIVINE ASPECT	TAROT ASSOCIATIONS
Atziluth	God-name Yehovah Elohim	Queen of Fire/Queen of the Salamanders/Three of Wands: Lord of Stabilizing Force
Briah	Archangel Tzaphkiel	Queen of the Thrones of Air/Queen of the Sylphs and Sylphides/Three of Swords: Lord of Sorrow
Yetzirah	Angelic Choir: Aralim— The Thrones	Queen of the Thrones of Water/ Queen of the Nymphs and Undines/ Three of Cups: Lord of Abundance
Assiah	Shabbatai—Saturn	Queen of the Thrones of Earth/ Queen of the Gnomes/Three of Pentagrams: Lord of Material Work

THE DESCENT AND THE GREAT FLOOD— PATHWORKING

"I am dried out and I die because of thirst."
"Drink from me," says the always flowing source
which whirls up from under the beautiful cypress.

"Who are you? Where do you come from?"
"I am a child from the Earth and the Heaven,
but my race comes from the stars."

POEM FROM THE ORPHIC TRADITION THESSALY

Read every part of the exercise thoroughly and memorize all the images. Then perform the Mudra of the Opening of the Veils and the Middle Pillar exercise. When you have created the energy circulations around yourself, in your imagination connect with the sphere of Binah at the right side of your head.

———————◆———————

Vibrate the name of God in the sphere of Binah: YHVH Elohim. While you do this, you see that the four cardinal directions open up before your inner eye. At the moment that you vibrate this, the air before you starts to shiver. The nightly heaven moves, and from the waves of the All a black goddess forms.

A deep feeling of love streams toward you from this goddess. Although the image is difficult to understand, you feel the love of this goddess entering into your heart center. In waves, you feel an understanding and a security coming toward you that is unknown in the world. The deep joy is so intense that you react with tears. They are not tears of sorrow. Your heart is touched with a soft compassion to which you react with so much joy that you are almost unable to bear the intense spiritual love.

You hear her soft voice. "Tears of joy," she says. "That is pure melting water. They are very healing for the soul. These are the tears I give you. With these tears I wash away pain and sorrow from your soul. See, my tears cause the Great Flood.

"In my presence your heart is lifted, so that you can experience the unity of the All for short moments. Let me tell you who I am and what my titles are. My name is Star of the Sea. I am the great Primordial Ocean, the great cosmic womb wherefrom all life came forth, and whereto everything returns.

"My Waters are not of this world. My Waters are the waters of consciousness, the waters of the mind. My Waters were called Nun in Egypt. Tehom—'the Deep'—in Hebrew. They were called Abzu in Mesopotamia. All the old cultures had names for my Waters. My Waters still consist of Nothingness.

"The Nothingness became conscious of itself, and this caused friction in the All. Because of this friction, foam arises from the Cosmic Ocean. From this foam I spin robes. My foam is the first moisture—Prima Materia—because one of my appearances is the Egyptian goddess Tefnut. I am the great goddess of heaven. My skin is as black as the night itself. In the daytime I dress myself in heavenly blue, and I weave my robes from the clouds. Every night I descend to make love with the earth, and because of this unification I get pregnant. I get pregnant with life itself.

"Every night I hope that my beloved waits for me again. He appears to me in the form of mountains and sacred buildings. In the form of a ziggurat or an obelisk, the tower of a cathedral. Every night I descend again and take the sacred tower into myself. I bear fruit and give birth, and I create seven temples of wisdom. Seven spheres will hang like apples in the Tree of Life.

"I am Isthar, queen of the seven temples. I am the cosmic mother, the giver of life. But with the gift of life comes unavoidable death. So I also give you the gift of death.

"When you are born on earth, you die in the heavens. When you die on earth, you will be born in the heavens. That is the reason why I have two names. Under the name Aima Mater I am the heaven at daylight. Then I am the fertile mother. Under the name of Ama Mater I am the heaven at night. As the dark sterile mother I take all the souls within myself and give birth to them in heaven. I am the limiter. As Saturn I slice time. I hack eternity into pieces, and in this way I cause the Great Abyss between heaven and earth.

"I am also the Khorsia, the Throne that supports the entire creation. All gods use me as their seat, and I support them. All divine forces, all the angels and archangels, all plants, animals, and humans are born from my womb and return to me.

"From my womb, the sun is born every day. The red of the dawn colors the heaven, and is the birth blood, a sign of the Great Flood of life that I pour out over the earth time and again. The Great Flood of Heavenly Water, from which the First Land is born, is my gift. In the Great Flood the Annunaki descend to take their seats in my seven temples. The seven holy forces bring civilization and law. They will teach humanity to read and write, and they are an inexhaustible source for their development, wisdom, and spiritual growth. This is why I say these words to you."

Khabs Am Pekht,

Konx om Pax,

Light in Extension!

And at that moment, a bridge forms at the other side of the cosmic Primordial Waters, a gigantic rainbow bridge. The One Light is divided into seven rays of cosmic consciousness. Over the rainbow bridge the gods descend. The Descent has begun.

The seven divine rulers each take a throne in the Sephirah under the rainbow bridge. The Great Work has begun. The work whereby the divine one will experience itself in diversity.

In the lower heavens it starts raining—Manna from heaven, divine nectar. Large waves fill the oceans on the earth. The entire earth is covered with water. A great flood covers all the lands.

You witness the sorrow of the Great Mother. Her tears accompany you when you descend as well. Your soul tumbles down, and you feel how your soul gets heavier as you fall deeper. There is no land to be seen. It appears to be flooded everywhere. But when you look carefully, you see that at the end of the rays of the rainbow bridge, the First Land arises: in the form of holy mountains, holy temples, and pyramids. The First Land rises from the flood.

See how all these images crystallize. Each of the rays of the rainbow ends in a sphere of colored light. "The seven temples are active," the Great Mother says. "The descent has been completed successfully. Now we need to prepare the right steps to create the Way Back."

It is now time to go back to your physical reality. Take the images and let them shrink into a black ball. Store this ball in the right side of your brain. Repeat the divine Trinity in your mind one more time. Kether is stored in the whirling Crown above your head. Chokmah forms a silver ball at the left side of your head. Binah is the black ball at the right side of your head. Take your time to ground yourself and thoroughly connect with your physical body. Eat and drink something.

9

THE ETHICAL TRIANGLE

DA'ATH AND
THE GREAT ABYSS

I have explained to you the core of the three divine Sephirah. Now you come again to a place that is difficult to understand. The next place on the Tree is Da'ath,* which means "Knowledge." It is Knowledge at the highest, most abstract level. Da'ath represents a state of consciousness wherein you receive knowledge that you did not know—and could not know—logically. The Knowledge is received by inspiration. Every human can receive this Knowledge from Da'ath. You cannot understand Da'ath and the Great Abyss by logic. Da'ath is a paradox, and behaves as unperceivably as a Zen koan. It is an area that you can understand when you put off your logical thinking. It is apprehended through symbolic language. By pausing your logical mind, you force it to contact the Mysteries from another area. I will explain some of the symbols through metaphoric images.

_____

*Da'ath has no Yetziric text to describe it.

222

THE PRISM

Within the Trinity, creation is a continuous process that happens on the most abstract level. The energies need to find their way into matter. Otherwise experience is not possible. The reason for creation is that the source wants to experience itself. This cannot happen when you are one. You can experience something when you are in interaction with something else—something outside yourself. That is why the source split itself in the first instance into the seven rays of light. The consequence of this is that God is both permanent and transcendent. This means that divinity is present in everything and every being, and at the same time divinity transcends everything.

When the light has divided itself, these seven rays are divided even further. Every ray becomes a cascade of divine sparks. As a metaphor, the Kabbalah states that the pure white light is broken into a prism. Through this, the seven colors become visible. The prism is one of the symbols for Da'ath. The three Sephiroth form a whirlpool together. Because of the whirling forces, resistance is caused, and this resistance creates light. That light is broken in Da'ath by a prism, and this causes the rainbow bridge. The rainbow bridge is the road over the Great Abyss. There is only one way to get from one side to the other, and that is by an absolute and blind faith in divinity.

THE HIDDEN ROOM

Another image of Da'ath is the Hidden Room, the Empty Space, or the Upper Room. This image was already known in the old kingdom of Egypt. In the temples and mastabas, they created inside the building an empty space as a symbol for Osiris. The god Osiris was sometimes drawn in the shape of a circle. It is the earliest picture of the snake Ouroboros. Da'ath is the space within the Ouroboros circle. What does this image mean?

When unity separates in a cascade of sparks, light, and color, there must be space in which all this can happen. The Cosmic Waters need

Marduk has beaten Tiamat and split the vault of heaven.
He plants a pole, which separates the seas.

to be divided. You do not only find this image in Genesis, it is a basic image in all kinds of creation myths. In Egypt, the earth god Geb and the heaven goddess Nut lie together in an eternal embrace. Then Shu comes, the god of Air, and he lifts Nut up, which causes the heavenly vault to become separated from the earth.

In the Mesopotamian myth *Enuma Elish,* the god Marduk divides the chaotic forces of the heavenly dragon Tiamat. He places a pole between heaven and earth to divide them. This pole is very important. It is the axis between the earth and the north polestars. It is the stem of the Tree of Life. It is the spine of Adam Kadmon. The north polestars are essential to understand the old magical symbols.

At the north pole heaven, several constellations turn around an invisible axis. These stars never disappear below the horizon. They are the eternal stars, the inexhaustible ones. It is the invisible center around which all the stars turn: the creative source. In other words, behind this invisible point is God. The stem of the Tree of Life is placed as the axis between the earth and the north pole, the axis mundi. This creates a space. This is the division of the Cosmic Waters. This space is, at this stage of creation, still empty and is not populated yet.

A HEAD WITH TWO FACES, EACH LOOKING IN A DIFFERENT DIRECTION

This image is complicated if you do not know in what direction you need to look for the solution. You must realize that Da'ath is a point at crossroads. Da'ath is a combination of the divine unmanifested world of *solitary* consciousness and the ensouled universe where a force field is created between all kinds of divine energies. You can regard the two faces of Da'ath as a coin that has an image on each side. The paradox of Da'ath is that God is both permanent and transcendent. Those are in fact the two faces of the heads. At the same time, they remain one at-one-ness. Seen from Da'ath, God manifests and remains nothingness at the same time.

The Egyptian god Horus-Seth

THE STAR SIRIUS

As you have seen, every Sephirah has a so-called mundane chakra—a planetary energy that is connected to the energy of the Sephirah. The mundane chakra gives us a physical focus to work with the energies. At the same time, it is a physical point in the starry heavens. From here you can also work astrologically. At the time when the Kabbalah was developed, the Mystery planets had not yet been discovered. Uranus, Neptune, and Pluto are recent discoveries. There are only seven classical planets. Now some people want to connect the Mystery planets to the higher Sephiroth. This is a mistake that disturbs the structure and the connections of the Tree. It causes confusion if you want to understand the energies of the Tree. The connection between very old mythologies must remain undisturbed.

The higher Sephiroth have their own mundane chakras, and this cannot be changed without cutting down the Tree, or letting it grow higher with fertilizer. The mundane chakra of Kether is the invisible point around which the north polestars circulate. The mundane chakra of Chokmah is the zodiac. The mundane Chakra of Binah is Saturn, and to Da'ath belongs Sirius. Why is this? And what do you need to do with the Mystery planets?

A STAIRWAY TO THE COSMOS

As you look at the Tree, you follow the Middle Pillar from Below to Above. Then you see a staircase of energies. You start with Earth itself, in Malkuth. From here you go deeper into the universe. First you reach the Moon in Yesod. Then you go to the Sun in Tiphareth. The next step is that you leave our solar system, and you reach with your consciousness to the next star system: Sirius. The following step is to become one with the beginning of the big bang: Kether. The Three Veils are an abstract concept. They represent the unknown source of causes at the root of creation.

In this way, the Middle Pillar is a staircase you can walk to raise your consciousness to become one with the source. The Mystery planets are still part of our solar system. Uranus is an exaltation of Mercury, which is

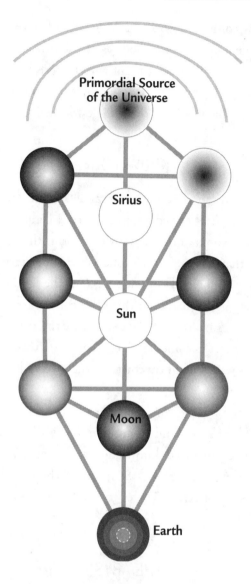

created by the higher level of the in-falling inspiration from Da'ath. The stars outside our solar system also raise Neptune to the higher levels of the Mysteries of Venus. Finally, Pluto raises Mars' energy to a higher spiritual level. Da'ath is the X-factor: an unforeseen Element that turns the system upside down and raises everything we know to a higher level.

The star Sirius was called the "Sun behind the Sun." It is a channel for the star energy of the goddess Isis. It is a very important star in mythology. It is connected with the Mysteries of redemption, with the Mysteries that give insight into the laws of the divine. It is the star traditionally considered the contact point with the great Masters. Isis is the goddess, the energy that leads us over the abyss. She is the "Priestess of the Silver Star": this is the magical title of the tarot card the High Priestess.

KNOWLEDGE

Da'ath is not a Sephirah. The Sepher Yetzirah says that there are ten holy Sephiroth, *not* nine, *not* eleven, and yet there is Da'ath. In this way, the Yetziric text gives words to the paradox that forms the core of Da'ath. Of Da'ath it is said that it is the consciousness of the meditating Logos. *Logos* is the name for enlightened consciousness on the level of the sun. The great world religions are based on this solar consciousness. It is the consciousness where our heart is deeply touched by the redeemer. The soul is raised here. The heart becomes the conscience, and through here the love energy streams. I will explain this further when we look at Tiphareth, the Sephirah of the sun.

Highly trained mystics and magicians connect themselves with the highest level of Tiphareth, and from there they walk the path to Da'ath. Here one receives inspired knowledge and mystical visions. These are described by mystics such as St. John of the Cross, Hildegard of Bingen, and Teresa of Avila. To get to this level you first need to pass the Abyss.

THE ABYSS

Da'ath is often connected with the top of a holy mountain where a cloud suddenly appears that protects the mystic from being seen by others. What is meant here is that the energies with which Da'ath worked become too high for most of us to even notice. Our spiritual senses must first be sufficiently developed to perceive these heights. If you are not capable of seeing these heights, then suddenly there appears to be nothing, and you feel torn apart.

THE DARK NIGHT

This is an experience that exceptionally talented magicians and mystics who have been doing intensive spiritual work will go through. It is a different experience than the Dark Night of the Soul. The mystic St. John of the Cross describes in his work *The Dark Night of the Soul* two different types of nights. The experience of Da'ath is the second night: the Dark Night of the Spirit.

When, as a practitioner, you arrive unexpectedly—it is always unexpected—on this part of the path, you need to exalt the events in your life in a totally different way than what you have learned before. You will likely not succeed in getting into this new spiritual flow, let alone maintaining it—the light simply has too high a frequency here. You could compare it with working in purple light and then from there you step into invisible ultraviolet light: the result is that you suddenly appear to be surrounded by darkness. You are still surrounded by the gods, but the frequency is too high for you to perceive them. You get glimpses of a state of consciousness that makes your heart burst, and you shed tears because of the absolute beauty of the energies. It is such an incredible stream of love and beauty that it is simply unbearable. So you are thrown directly out of the experience, and you walk around in a darkness in which there appears to be no spirituality at all.

Because of the increased sensibility of your heart, you pick up all the astral and mental movements and are completely open to all the thoughts and emotions that surround you. You could close yourself down, but this is not fruitful if you want to develop further. The intention of the practice is for you to transform within yourself what you perceive and that you become stronger. Not by defending yourself better and closing down, but by training yourself in compassion and detaching yourself from your ego.

By getting glimpses of these high-level spiritual experiences, the peak experiences of earlier periods appear to be less intense and even childish. This phenomenon repeats itself, and the darkness gets denser. You are tested until your bones are totally stripped, both magically and spiritually.

There is but one thing left, and that is discipline and the knowledge that the glimpses of the higher frequencies were real! You know that you are now in the Dark Night of the Spirit . . . and that it takes a few years to get through. That is not a very encouraging thought. The only way to get over this abyss is to have blind faith in the divine guidance that you have had on your spiritual path time and again.

SCHEDULE OF DA'ATH

WORLD	DIVINE ASPECT	TAROT ASSOCIATIONS
Atziluth	God-name Yehovah Elohim	There are no Tarot Associations with Da'ath
Briah	Archangel: The Four Archangels of the Cardinal Directions: Raphael, Michael, Gabriel, and Uriel	
Yetzirah	Angelic Choir: Winged Serpents	
Assiah	Sirius	

THE RAINBOW BRIDGE
OVER THE ABYSS—RITUAL

PREPARATION FOR THE RITUAL OF DA'ATH

The exercise, which works with Da'ath, is in fact a mini ritual. In this ritual I bring you from the top of the Tree of Life down over the Abyss. A ritual is actually an active form of meditation. In a ritual, you create a place of action where an important spiritual event takes place.

By means of this role-playing, you place yourself in the middle of a mythical story and, with your imagination, place yourself in a sacred space. A ritual always consists of a very precise combination of actions, meditations, contemplations, spiritual techniques, and prayer.

In a ritual, you apply in a precise setting the techniques you have learned so far. In this way, these techniques will support one another, and the energies will become stronger. This helps you develop a solid and active internal temple. Within a ritual, you turn your magical circle into a three-dimensional mandala wherein you practice your art. It is a miniature cosmos that you create for a short while.

In this way, the magical circle becomes a powerful seed that you sow in your subconscious mind. It forms the core of a hologram of psychic patterns. They will translate from the circle into your daily life and will influence your feelings, actions, and reactions to what comes toward you. There is a lot more to rituals, but for the moment this is enough.

Necessities:

Fire
One white candle
Charcoal for incense in a burner
Incense
Seven candles in the colors of the rainbow: red, orange,
    yellow, green, light blue, indigo blue, and purple
Twelve tea lights
  Music: the sound of the sea

Look for a place where you can be undisturbed for forty-five minutes. You begin with a meditation, which you start in the Ain, the sphere where there is nothing. Take care that you sit relaxed and with a straight spine. Your feet are flat on the floor, no crossed legs or arms.

Put the white candle on a table in front of you, together with a match or lighter. Place the incense and charcoal on some dry sand. Place the tea lights in a circle around you. With the seven rainbow-colored candles you create an inner circle around you. With this exercise, the sound of the sea in the background would be a good choice.

When you do a ritual, always consult the instructions. First you read it through so that you know what it is about and so you know you have all the necessities at hand. During the ritual, you read little pieces of the instructions, and then you concentrate on the action. You meditate about it briefly and use your imagination to build up the images that belong to the psychic scenery. Take your time to form the images and connect with them, so that you feel an empathic relation to them. Within the Western Mystery Tradition, the rituals are put on paper. Nothing is left to chance. In the ancient Mystery temples, the texts that were used were inscribed in holy signs on the walls.

Rituals connect students and initiates with matrixes of harmony. This is where you want to make a connection. The rituals and pathworkings are techniques to tune in to these patterns. The fruits of this method will become slowly obvious after having worked with it for a while. The experiences become deeper and start to have an influence on your dreams and on your feelings.

Before you start with a ritual, you relax and begin with the Middle Pillar exercise.

IN THE CENTER OF
AN OCEAN OF NEGATIVE LIGHT

Close your eyes and concentrate. You focus on the dark that you now see around you. You are immersed in an ink-black endlessness. There is a total absence of everything. Endlessness stretches out everywhere you look: beneath you, above you, in all directions. When you move your eyes, you float and move into that direction. You are floating without any weight. You float without direction, because there is no direction.

———◆———

The darkness is very comfortable, enclosing you like a protective mantle. There is no heat or cold here. There is no smell, no tactile sensations. A body does not exist here, and so there are no physical feelings. There is no history, no future, and there is no time.

Floating is the sensation that best describes what you experience here. There is no height, no breadth, no depth; all is spread and diffused. You cannot imagine how big this place is, or what your size is, because you yourself are endless in all directions. It feels very secure here. You are one with everything around you. There is no difference between you and your environment. You are so diffuse and expansive that you are All. You are the ocean itself, endlessly stretched out to the furthest distance, floating and drifting. Timeless and eternal. You are All and All That Is.

Contemplate your drift in the Sea of Consciousness. Your consciousness creates circles around you. You expand and touch the shores, then you concentrate on the

center and gather in the middle. There your consciousness peaks like a big wave in the sea and floats outside in circles toward the edges. Here you feel that you gain speed.

You clearly sense the borders of eternity and endlessness that surround you. You use these to feel yourself, to bump against for your movement back to the center. Here you gather all your consciousness in a feeling of intense happiness. You are conscious of yourself.

Again you spread out your consciousness and let it expand to the furthest edges. Now you know the sensations that you are experiencing. From the peak in the center you float in all directions. Then you come into very turbulent waters wherein the two tides—the outgoing and inflowing—bump into each other.

This is the energy of the Ain Soph, the chaotic energy of the Ring Chaos. You push yourself off against the edges of the Ring-Pass-Not. You are in the middle of the Ocean of Negative Light: this is the Ain. Then you float and gather in the center. You go upward on the wave. This is very powerful now. . . . You feel the sensation of ascending. You lift up very high and then you feel "I am." I am becoming! I am in an Ocean of Negative Light. I am *an Ocean of Negative Light.*

Kether

In the universe of the Primordial Waters, the Ocean of Negative Light, the consciousness of God comes into being. You vibrate with an intensive joy, "Ehieh Asher Ehieh"—I am who I am. I want to experience. You are the Cosmic Ocean yourself. Timeless, endless, negative light. And you long to see who you are.

Chokmah

Can you see yourself? As you are, here in this floating environment? You raise your consciousness, peaking on the waves of the depths. You look at yourself: God sees himself from face to face. You vibrate Yah. And at the moment you do that, light comes into being.

[Here you light one candle as a taper and contemplate the flame.] Now there is a light in the middle. There is one light in the midst of the darkness of the deep. The light is the day and the darkness is the night.

You are still within the darkness, but now there is a light in the darkness. One radiating light. One sparkling light that burns so beautifully, and brightly, that it becomes bigger and fills the center of your consciousness. Fill yourself with the light. Feel how the light penetrates you entirely.

Take your candle and say:

"Let there be a firmament in the middle of the Waters."

One by one you light the twelve tea lights. You walk counterclockwise and call the zodiac by name: Aries, Taurus, Gemini, Cancer, Leo, Virgo, Libra, Scorpio, Sagittarius, Capricorn, Aquarius, and Pisces.

Binah

Visualize how all this light flashes within the negative light, like a spark of fire in charcoal. Light the charcoal and look at it. See red sparks radiate in the darkness of the black charcoal. You hear the noise and feel the heat.

The Working of the Divine Triangle

Now you put incense on the burning charcoal. See how the smoke rises and forms clouds. The clouds of smoke form a mist that penetrates light and darkness.

The Waters of the Deep are now lit by the starry heaven. Through an activity of the Great Mother of Creation, Binah, a mist is formed from the primal sparks. This mist is Prima Materia, the dew of the alchemists. This is what the ancient Egyptians called Tefnut, heavenly moisture. There is now darkness that reflects itself in the form of you and the flame. There is light and darkness. There is a firmament, and the creative forces of the Great Mother have started with weaving the Web of Creation.

The first thing that needs to happen is to divide the Waters of the Below from the Waters of the Above. You need to create a space, because otherwise the Prima Materia has no place to go. Then it is just damp in the endless oceans. So you divide the Primordial Waters.

The Empty Room

You are Adam Kadmon. Your spine forms the pole that divides the Waters. Your body reaches from Below to Above, it reaches the north polestars wherefrom everything comes forth. So Adam Kadmon, lift the stars and the darkness with your mind to the Above. They form the Waters of the universe. Under you, at your feet, the Waters of Below gather. They form together all the oceans of the earth.

Now you have an empty space between the Waters of Above and the Waters of Below. The space is filled with moisture. In the moist landscape the light burns. The light spreads. One light lights the other. The flame multiplies itself without becoming dimmed. The light glows at the horizon and becomes more intense.

Visualize a landscape now. The starry heaven above your head is a deep blue darkness filled with stars. The dark blue is crowned with a ring of lights that together form the zodiac. The oceans below are light blue and are spread endlessly. The space between them is filled with mist: Prima Materia, the gift of the Great Mother. It is the dew on the morning of creation. The light increases in intensity . . . and breaks because of the moisture. Suddenly there is color:

The Rainbow Bridge

Now one by one you light the seven candles that form the rainbow bridge. As you light each candle, say the invocations listed for each below aloud.

The rainbow forms a bridge between the divine world and the world of humans. The light falls through the prism of water damp with the first dew. The light is lit. The seven rays of the rainbow together form the Seven Pillars of Wisdom.

1. The blue candle:

"Here I raise the blue Pillar of Mercy. This pillar represents the Vision of Love. Let the Waters collect themselves and let dry land appear."

2. The red candle:

"Here I raise the red Pillar of Severity. This pillar represents the Vision of Power. Let the earth bring forth grasses and the herbs that produce seeds."

3. The yellow candle:

"Here I raise the yellow Pillar of Beauty. This pillar represents the vision of the Mysteries of the Crucifixion. Light the lights in the firmament to divide the day from the night."

4. *The green candle:*

"Here I raise the green Pillar of Victory. This pillar represents the Vision of Beauty Triumphant. Let the waters bring forth the moving living creatures and all the life that flies in the open firmament of the heaven."

5. *The orange candle:*

"Here I raise the orange Pillar of Glory. This pillar represents the Vision of Splendor. Let the earth bring forth beings of its own kind."

6. *The purple candle:*

"Here I raise the purple Pillar of the Fundament. This pillar represents the Vision of the Machinery of the Universe. Let us make people in our own image, in our likeness."

7. *The light blue candle:*

"Here I raise the light blue Pillar of the Kingdom. This pillar represents the Vision of the Holy Guardian Angel. God blessed them and said: be fruitful and multiply. God saw everything he had made and saw that it was good."

After you have lit these seven candles, you contemplate the images this brings you. You are now sitting in the middle of the rays of the rainbow. Wasn't this traditionally the place to find gold? I will tell you the secret of the rainbow. Your heart is the gold. When you are capable of exalting your heart toward the Light, then you can cross the abyss by means of the rainbow bridge.

Let the images disappear slowly and come back to yourself. Maybe you want to let the candles burn for a while. You can also snuff them out, in the knowledge that when you do this, you take the flames, the light, and the images deep into yourself: you store them in the Treasure House of Images.

CHESED, MERCY

The Fourth Path is called the Cohesive or Receptive
Intelligence, because it contains all the Holy Powers, and
from it emanate all the spiritual virtues with the most
exalted essences. They emanate one from another by virtue
of the Primordial Emanation, the Highest Crown, Kether.

SEPHER YETZIRAH

You have now passed the Great Abyss. You arrive now in the so-called formative world. You start at the second part of the Tree of Life, the Ethical
Triangle. This triangle contains all the energies of Chesed, Geburah, and
Tiphareth. Another name for Chesed, which you will also read in some
texts, is Gedulah.

It is very important that you realize that the Tree of Life repre-

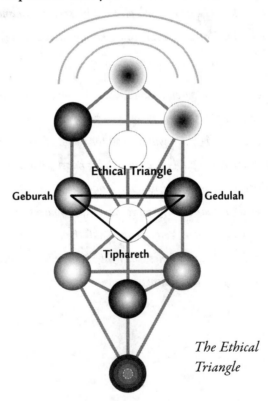

The Ethical
Triangle

sents consciousness. The Tree illustrates how the primordial energies of consciousness—and by implication also the human mind—are interconnected. Creation takes place from Above to Below. From the nothingness toward matter. The Three Veils of Negative Light symbolize the absolute nothingness. From there, consciousness changes in character. Finally, crystallization of consciousness takes place in Malkuth—not earlier. When I talk about the formative world, this does not mean that matter has formed in this part of the Tree.

FOUNTAINS

You must try to see how the Kabbalistic Tree is interconnected. Every Sephirah is the source for the next one. You can visualize this in the form of a fountain. Starting with Kether, the most pure form of consciousness streams into the universe. It is totally undifferentiated and all containing. You can imagine every Sephirah as a cup of a fountain. At the moment that the cup is filled with water, the water streams over the edge and is gathered in a lower cup. At the moment that the I-Am consciousness fills up the cup of Kether, it streams over in Chokmah. Then there are two cups that reflect one another, as Chokmah's color, gray, acts as a mirror.

When Chokmah is filled, the cup streams over to Binah, where Prima Materia is created. In Kether, the energy is pure white. In Chokmah, as I already described it is gray—mirroring. In Binah it is black, but more precisely it is black light. Then you get a "chemical reaction."

From the moment that these three supernatural Sephiroth have been filled, all three start to cooperate like a sort of machine, and a consciousness of another quality is created. The previous text from the Sepher Yetzirah points toward this mechanism. The "exalted essences" are the divine Sephiroth, and the text says that Chesed is created from a mixture of all three supernatural Sephiroth, which come forth from the One. And the highest Crown is pointed toward Kether.

From Chesed the consciousness gets more specific, and gradually it will be fine tuned in the lower Sephiroth. It will find its final form at the end of the creation process, in Malkuth.

THE NATURE OF THE CREATION PROCESS

To create spiritual magic, it is very important that you realize how this creation process works. From the moment you begin to create changes in your consciousness, your environment will change as a consequence. That means that most people can be surprised on their spiritual path!

When you start to practice the system of the Kabbalistic Tree of Life, you will first connect yourself with all the Sephiroth and the paths of the Tree. This is an intensive process that will take some years. Some people get a great fright when they find out that, when working on a specific Sephirah, this Sephirah becomes active in their life as well. Meditating on a Sephirah or on one of the paths generates events!

THE ETHICAL TRIANGLE

The Ethical Triangle plays a major role in this process. The Ethical Triangle balances the so-called virtues and vices. You could say that the Ethical Triangle is the part of the Tree that discriminates between good and evil.

From the divine triangle Four Rivers of Purification start to flow. They are the Euphrates, the Tigris, the Gihon, and the Pheison. They carry the Waters of the virtues from the divine worlds to the worlds below. It is the biblical place where you eat from the Tree of Good and Evil. The Ethical Triangle is the force field wherein you brood and balance. It is the place where you can get a divine revelation of truth.

It is very important to keep nurturing the relationship between the human body and the Tree of Life. For instance, in the vestments of the magician and the priest, all the energies of the Ethical Triangle are summarized in the robes and the symbols that are worn on the chest, like the breastplate of the High Priest or the crook and flail of the Egyptian pharaoh.

In the Creative Triangle, the spark of the soul is sent into a new incarnation. In the Ethical Triangle, a soul gets its destination in life. The consciousness that thinks and decides according to its conscience and the goal of its life gets its form in this triangle. Its essence is personified in the image of the holy guardian angel.

CHESED

Chesed is the highest state of enlightenment that we can reach while being in a physical body: the union with the holy guardian angel. As we go higher up the Tree, we will pass the border of death. The planetary energy belonging to Chesed is Jupiter. Jupiter is traditionally connected with the highest manifested god-form within a pantheon. In mythical pantheons you will first find the creation myths, wherein the primordial gods play the major roles. In Greek mythology, for example, these are the Titans. Then come the gods that rule the world of the humans. Zeus is, in the Greek pantheon, the god connected to Chesed.

Chesed is a sphere where you come into contact with divine power. You can imagine Chesed as a landscape in which all the possibilities for the future are open. There are no concrete structures or plans yet. There is no building yet. The land is your life, and you are the architect of your future. What do you want to build here? In this landscape one thing is set, and that is a source that brings in the Waters from the highest spiritual regions. This Water carries the blessings of the highest Sephiroth. The source is a source of love, which gives rise to mercy and expansion. It is an ongoing source of goodness. The sphere within the landscape is an atmosphere of peace and stability.

THE MASTERS

Because Da'ath is a nonexisting Sephirah, the contact point with the Masters is located in Chesed. This is a concept that causes a lot of confusion in esoteric circles. You can see the masters as beings whom you can compare with gods and angels. They exist on the inner levels. They are not objective beings. The fact that they exist on the Inner Planes does not mean that they are just meaningless fantasies.

The Inner Planes are the imaginations of the force fields of our own consciousness. Here the human spirit has raised some intensely powerful monuments during the millennia. The potential of these images is burned into the essence of humanity. When you get in touch with such an image, the knowledge it holds can unfold at an amazing tempo.

The masters are the concentrated powers of consciousness of the best of certain human characteristics. They are the matrixes for the talents of the human species, which have been transmitted since primordial times through mythology. At certain times, a human is born who is almost similar to the matrix of this ideal image. Such a person can become the personification of such an Inner Plane monument.

There are different types of masters. Some have clearly specialized themselves in one area. Others have a range of talents and excel in all areas.

CONTACT WITH THE MASTERS

When a human makes contact with a master, you will know the contact has occurred because of recognizable signs. The most important sign is the rise of an incredibly strong current of inspiration. The person who makes the contact gets access to unwritten sources of inspiration, which raises an undeniable feeling of truth and authenticity.

Masters are not only active in the Mysteries. Masters exist for every talent or profession. For example, Mozart is a master of music, and Einstein is a master of physics. Aesculapius is a master of healing, and Imhotep is a master of architecture. When you are training yourself in a professional area, it can be very helpful to connect yourself with one of the masters. In this way you will get more feeling for the specific "wavelength" of consciousness whereon this talent resonates. Talent is the extent to which you are capable of connecting yourself to such a wavelength of consciousness. The better you can connect yourself with such a psychic highway, the more authentic and inspired your work will be.

A master is not necessarily always connected to esoteric knowledge. The Masters are connected to Chesed, and there are Masters that are especially connected to the Mysteries. But there are also other masters of other areas, such as music and so forth. Of course there are masters who are specifically connected with the esoteric highways. Examples of these are the great prophets and saints. They are often chosen as a patron for a specific religious group. You can see from the choice of the patron what energy current a religious group is developing.

SCHEDULE OF CHESED

WORLD	DIVINE ASPECT	TAROT ASSOCIATIONS
Atziluth	God-name El	Four of Wands: Lord of Perfected Work
Briah	Archangel: Tzadkiel	Four of Swords: Lord of Rest from Strife
Yetzirah	Angelic Choir/Chasmalim/ the Shining Ones	Four of Cups: Lord of Blended Pleasure
Assiah	Tzedek/Jupiter/Justice	Four of Pentagrams: Lord of Earthly Power

THE INTERIOR CASTLE—
RITUAL

PREPARATION FOR THE RITUAL OF CHESED

The exalted consciousness of the adept rises in his occult
meditations to the sphere of Chesed: it is there that he
receives the inspirations that he works out in the world of
form. The spirit rises to the highest modus of the contact
with the masters, and he connects from mind to mind in a
sphere of exalted consciousness.

DION FORTUNE, *THE MYSTICAL QABALA*

Necessities:

A small table with a piece of fabric in indigo blue
A bowl with water
Picture of an orb
Picture of a crown
A wand or a pointed crystal that is used especially for this
  goal
Picture of a royal mantle
Picture of Jupiter
Picture of an ancient king
Four blue candles
A golden candle
  Incense: cedar

It is very helpful to make a focus point for your exercises and rituals of the spheres. You can make a simple altar or decorate a meditation
room. Put the necessities together on a small table in the middle of your
meditation room. The act of decorating your room already focuses your
consciousness strongly on the goal of your meditation or ritual. For this
mini ritual you can make an environment in blue: indigo blue. The color

is strongly associated with kingship. The magical image of Chesed is a mighty crowned king.

Put the pictures associated with Chesed on the altar: an orb, a crown, a wand, a blue altar cloth, a royal mantle with a fur collar, and a picture of the planet Jupiter. I would not advise you to choose the picture of a living king, because you have associations with living persons. Pictures of ancient kings or kings coming from mythological stories keep you more focused on the archetype of what a king should be.

Of course instead of kings you can also use famous queens from the past. Chesed is a Sephirah from the male pillar. This means that the energy is active and dynamic, not creative and receptive, but this does not mean that females are not able to work with this energy.

Put four blue candles on the corners of the altar and one golden candle in the middle. If you love incense, then cedar incense is a good choice. If you like to use meditation music in the background, then choose a piece of music with a full orchestra that you can put on repeat. The sphere of Chesed is royal and rich. Here you do not use the sound of a floating stream or a panpipe. The music must give you the feeling that you enter into the hall of a royal palace. But you start with silence.

These suggestions are, of course, not essential to making a connection with the sphere of Chesed, they are just aids. You can visualize the scenes as well. The great benefit of a ritual is that you can enter totally into the experience. In this way, your spiritual experiences are not only lived in your imagination, but through your body consciousness also anchored in your subconscious.

Now go into meditation, first focusing on relaxation and breathing. Take care that you have your feet flat on the floor, and that your back is straight. You start with the Kabbalistic Cross and the Middle Pillar exercise as usual. Read the instructions, visualize the scene, and then follow the instructions. Then you visualize the effect of your actions.

THE INTERIOR CASTLE

When you have finished the initial exercises, imagine yourself standing before a great castle. In your hands you hold a staff. You are dressed in simple clothes that are held together at your waist by a rope. On your feet you wear sandals made of leather. When you look around you, you see that the landscape is barren and totally empty. You are surprised about this. Your feeling tells you that it is very early in the morning, before sunrise.

Sunrise

You see a desolate, endless plane as far as you can look. A cold wind blows over the landscape. The castle appears to be abandoned. It is the only building in the environment that will give you some protection, so you try to get inside. First you must cross the canal. The castle has no bridge. You walk toward the castle, but you let the idea of swimming over the canal go when you look over the edges. The canal is empty and endlessly deep. How can you get inside? At the same time, you watch the sky getting grayer. It looks as if a thunderstorm is approaching. The wind increases in strength and you feel it pull at all your clothes.

You feel lonely and desperate in these rude circumstances. Then you suddenly hear a voice on the sound of the wind. The sound tells you that you need to use the knowledge you now have to solve your problem. You must get access to the castle. You think deeply; what knowledge do you have that you can use at this moment?

The voice continues: "Remember the creation story. Remember the information you have received about the Great Abyss and how you cross it. You have come forth from the Divine Triangle. You are now in a desolate plane that gives you access to the castle of the world. Remember what the Great Mother taught you. Creation is built from moisture. From the Divine Triangle a fountain flows, which produces moisture.

The Castle of the World

"Look to the clouds over your head. See how moisture and the possibility of life hover about this landscape in potential. Look at the Wand of Power you hold in

your hand. With this Wand you can call up the Elements that you need to give your-
self access to the castle of the world. What do you need first?" the voice asks.

You think and conclude that, if there was water in the canal, you could get into the
castle. "Then call upon the Waters," a voice says. "Call them down." What waters,
you ask yourself. "Call upon the Four Rivers of Purification," the voice says. "They
stream downward from the Divine Triangle. They will form a protection around your
holy heart. They will purify your heart continuously from the events of the world. Use
the waters of these rivers to fill the canal. Use your Wand. Use the holy name."

Cleaning the Circle

Now you take your wand in your hand and walk to the eastern side of the altar. You
raise the wand and call:

"In the name of El I call upon the powers of the River Pheison: stream
down from the highest heavens and surround the Castle of the World with
the virtues that will give me the power to correct my behavior. In this way I
can always renew the connection with the place from where I come."

Sprinkle water in the East, so that this quarter is purified. To your amazement
you see that the canal at the Eastern side slowly fills itself with water bubbling up
from below. It looks as if the canal is filled from an unseen source.

Now you walk to the South and again your raise your Wand of Power. Say:

"In the name of El I call upon the powers of the River Gihon. Through
here I have access to the virtue to clean my heart and reconnect time and
again with my highest goal."

Sprinkle water in the South, so that this quarter is purified. In the Southern
canal the water starts to flow. Slowly the canal fills itself with water.

Walk to the West. Raise your wand and say:

"In the name of El I call up the powers of the River Tigris. I call up the
river that contains the virtues to cleanse myself from desires so that I can
judge clearly in the Castle of the World."

Sprinkle water in the West, so that this quarter is purified. And here also the
canal starts to fill itself with the pure and sparkling waters of the virtues.

You walk to the last quarter, to the North. You raise your wand and say:

"In the name of El I call upon the powers of the River Euphrates. This river protects the Castle of the World and encircles it with the virtues of justice."

Sprinkle water in the North, so that this quarter is purified. And as in the other cardinal directions, the canal fills itself with water. At this point you light the incense so that your altar slowly fills with smoke.

You see that, as the canal gradually fills itself with water, the land develops a smell—the aroma of cedarwood. In a mysterious way the landscape is filled with this splendid scent. Again you hear the voice in the wind, which tells you: "The rivers of purification flow downward from the highest heavens and they fill the entire landscape with the Fluid of Life. They also protect it against evil." Moisture fills the air. A mist forms and hangs over the landscape. Again you hear the voice. "Now you call upon the Light!" You look around you to see from where it comes. It appears to come from the nothingness. You decide to follow the advice of the voice.

You raise your wand and turn yourself to the Above.

Invocation of the Divine

In the name of YHVH I call upon the Light of the World. I call upon the forces of the covenant. Give me access to the Castle of the World.

Here you light your golden candle, which stands in the middle of the altar. You see how the air slowly starts to color. The deep black makes way for the purple and red pastel colors. The colors of the air deepen in shades of blue. The clouds color orange and red, and very slowly the sun rises in the East. You are witness to a beautiful sunrise. You are not expecting the miracle that you see before your eyes. The rising light is broken in the moist atmosphere of clouds and over the canal forms a rainbow of light.

"You see, here is your access to the Castle of the World," the voice says. You walk to the canal, and you notice that the rainbow is strong enough to hold your weight. At the moment you put your feet on the bridge, the portals of the castle open slowly.

You enter into a hall that is totally empty. Again you hear the voice. "Walk further into the castle. You are expected in the chapel of the king." Before you a blue color forms; it moves in the direction of a staircase. You decide to follow the cloud. You climb the staircase. It is a bare stone staircase without any decorations. The steps are worn. Your footsteps sound hollow in the space. Then you stand before a *round portal. The doors swing open and you enter into a great hall. It appears to be some kind of a tower room. (You should turn on the music at this point.)*

The Council Room of the King

The hall is lit by enormous windows that look out over the four cardinal directions of the land. The entire hall is decorated with blue velvet. In the middle stands a great round altar. The altar cloth is made of blue silk, and on the altar you see a miniature castle. This castle also is surrounded by a canal. Around it you see an entirely barren landscape. The altar is a perfect copy of the landscape outside from where you came. Above the altar drifts the planet Jupiter, clearly recognizable because of the red spot. Around the altar are four big chairs in a circle, all furnished with blue velvet. On the altar are four blue candles.

"Sit down on one of these chairs," a voice says. You take a seat. "Now light the blue candle that is directly in front of you," the voice says.

You light all four blue candles.

When the candles are lit, three figures appear at the table. You cannot see who they are. They are energy fields, like the blue cloud. Then the voice speaks again: "You are here in a world where you can create your internal landscape. At your table are sitting three sages whom you can ask for advice. They are people who have lived in the past, and who have represented an image of perfection within their profession. They are here to advise you in building your sacred landscape. You will always find me here as well.

The Holy Guardian Angel

"I am your holy guardian angel. I am the best part of yourself, which will always be in contact with the source of where you come from. Your internal castle will be filled with gods and angels. They will help you to give form to your experiences. They will constantly be available to give you advice and help. You will encounter me in every sphere, because I am the best part of yourself.

"I will take care that you will always remain in touch with the source of your existence. I will communicate with you by means of my voice. We will discuss if what you want is in accordance with the task that you took upon yourself in this life. I will

connect myself energetically with you. You feel my influence entering you from the back. Now it is time to talk with the kings of the cardinal directions."

The Kings of the Winds

The kings tell you that they are the builders of your internal and external worlds. They are the architects who create all potential possibilities by means of thought power. They can show you all kinds of experiences as thoughtforms. The thought-forms of the kings hang around the castle as three-dimensional images. They hang in potential above the interior landscape that surrounds the castle.

The thoughtforms of the kings are powerful projections of ideals and can materi-alize in your life. The three of them build the most beautiful forms and project the possibilities onto the landscape as if it were a movie screen. You look at their game and you see that they create all kinds of new possibilities for you. This could be you; this could be your life! All kinds of desires and ideas form in dream dust and circu-late around the altar. You now feel the power of the holy guardian angel very clearly standing behind you as an entity. You hear the voice of the angel speaking to you.

"Study the thoughtforms made by the kings. If they create a form that is ben-eficial for you, one that can be a blessing in your life, then we can decide to fix this form in your interior landscape. That is the reason why you sit in the North—because you are the king who will manifest. The landscape you build in the Inner Planes will crystallize in your daily life. That is why it is important that what you store and save here in the Inner Planes is in line with your goal of life, and with the divine task that you have taken upon yourself."

The Divine Regalia

It is important that you dress yourself in robes that are worthy of a king. First you take the under robe. It is made of blue silk. On top of this you wear a blue velvet cape with a mink collar. The blue color of kingship is meant to keep you conscious of the powers with which you create; they descend directly from heaven. The orb is a symbol for the earth—the land that is under your care. The Wand is a shepherd's staff. You care for the land and for everyone who lives there. The crown points toward the starry heaven. Compare the crown with antennae that transmit to you what you are expected to do in the context of the divine plan. The first thing that needs to happen is that the landscape becomes fertile.

You see that the holy guardian angel concentrates now on the dark clouds of the thunderstorm that floats over the miniature castle. He tells you to use your hands and stretch them out over the water you find on the altar. You do this, and the clouds now seem to drift under your hands. The archangel tells you to connect yourself with the source from which you come, the sphere of Kether above your head. You feel the sphere light up like a great ball of energy. Then you hear the voice of the angel, loud and clear:

"Let the divine light descend!"

You see and feel how the crown on your head is touched by a lightning flash. From the top of your head, the lightning flash zigzags down, and energy rushes through the palms of your hands. You see that the water under your hands lights up and radiates energy.

"Now let it rain over the landscape," the angel tells you.

You take the bowl of water and sprinkle this over the altar. You say:

"I hallow and bless my internal landscape, that it may bear fruit and will be a continuous inspiration and that it may mirror my spiritual growth."

As you bless the altar, it starts to rain outside. It is a fruitful spring rain. Once you've blessed the altar, you see that the landscape slowly transforms to a green color because of the little germinating plants starting to grow.

Meditate for a while and collect all the images you receive. Write them down in a diary. By writing the images down, they become more concrete and stay in your memory better. When you are finished, you gather all the images and store them inside a blue sphere. This sphere contains all the experiences you had, and those that are yet to come. This sphere changes into a round pin that you fasten on the left shoulder of your magical robe. With this you can make a connection that enables you to call up these images and this scene. When you have done this, you close this ritual. You do this by making the Kabbalistic Cross. You leave the candles burning for a while. As long as they burn, the experience will be fixed in your inner being.

GEBURAH, SEVERITY

The Fifth Path is called the Radical Intelligence because it resembles Unity, uniting itself to Binah. Understanding, which emanates from the primordial depths of Chokmah.

SEPHER YETZIRAH

Geburah lies straight opposite Chesed on the Tree of Life. Now you cross over to the other side of the Tree and to the other side of the spectrum: from the White Pillar to the Black Pillar; from the Pillar of Force to the Pillar of Form. Geburah is the second Sephirah on the Black Pillar of Form. Chesed and Geburah are each other's opposites. Chesed is Mercy, Geburah is Severity.

In Chesed you create an internal landscape that starts to grow. In Geburah the wild growth is cut down. The planetary influence on Geburah is Mars, and by means of this image Geburah becomes easy to understand. What is such a warriorlike Sephirah doing on the Tree of Life, you might ask yourself? Isn't the Tree a collection of the forces of light? And what is that warriorlike energy of Mars doing in the divine scheme?

AWE

Chesed is like a fountain of blessings that streams outward endlessly. In Geburah, the most important emotion is awe. In Chesed the emphasis is on enjoying the beauty and a beneficial outstreaming of divine blessings. In Geburah, divinity lets you feel its powers and forces clearly. The feeling of awe is connected to Geburah; a divine reverence that is a mixture of fear, beauty, and power. In Hebrew this is called *pachad*. The godname for Geburah—Elohim Gibor—points in this direction. The name means the "creative forces of power."

The experience of awe with which you regard Geburah is as follows. You walk into the mountains and you stand on a mountaintop. Then suddenly a thunderstorm breaks loose. The sound of thunder and the forces of nature make you feel tiny in the perspective of the eternal. You are smaller than a fly on the wall in the perspective of the cosmos. You are caught in the middle of an experience of beauty and, at the same time, you feel the power and the force that make you shiver.

A MIGHTY WARRIOR IN HIS CHARIOT

The magical image of Geburah is a mighty warrior in his chariot. It is the image of a king who defends his land. The creator structures the creation and weeds out the wild growth and everything that does not belong to the divine plan.

From Binah on, the divine energies are not pure virtues any longer. The vices have become active as a result of erosion and because of the resistance that is caused because of materialization. These vices cause impurities. Geburah is the Sephirah that weeds out these impurities. This can happen in a careful, tender way on a miniature level, but if it is necessary, also with great violence on a cosmic scale. The power that causes the pendulum to change its direction from Gedulah (Chesed) to Geburah is closely related to the dynamic when a situation has grown out of balance, and how big the impact of the changes are to find a new equilibrium. The equilibrium of the newly developed situation we find in the Sephirah Tiphareth.

MERCY VERSUS JUSTICE

The energy exchange between Gedulah and Geburah can be observed very well by studying the big political climate changes. You must observe the movement between what will expand itself and what will need to be limited. Look without judgment. When you start to think about whether or not you agree with the politics, then you lose your objectivity and your ability to see the underlying mechanism. Look at mechanisms like liberty versus structure. See how certain ideas suddenly expand, and how they create an opposition to change. The continual conflicts over borders between nations is a good example of how Gedulah and Geburah are in a continuous interaction.

Gedulah and Geburah can also be studied in connection with natural balances. Within ecological systems, the food chain creates balance in the populations of different species. For example, if there are too many wild rabbits, then there is enough food for the natural enemies of rabbits. Foxes, dogs, and wolves find more to eat and can also raise more young. However, when the surplus of rabbits is eaten, the predators face a food shortage, because their numbers have now increased due to the previous abundance of rabbits, but the rabbit population has now decreased.

When you apply this mechanism to the human population, you can ask yourself how long it is possible for humankind's unlimited expansion at nature's expense, and how long we will be able to survive this way. What would be necessary to restore this natural balance on earth? In cultures where people see themselves as dependent and interconnected with the earth, they do not plunder their natural environment.

DEFENSE OF THE LIGHT

The cosmic source protects what it has created. The cosmic source creates the "God-Experiencing-Itself." Divinity achieves this by mirroring itself in everything it creates as well as what comes forth from the source. The inevitable erosion must be contained. This process falls under the Defense of the Light, and this defense and protection of the light is a central task of Geburah and is why Geburah also has weapons. If the symbol for Chesed is the crook, the symbol for Geburah is the flail. You will also find the spear and the chain. To get a musical impression of Geburah, you could listen to the music of the Kyrie from the Requiem of Verdi.

SCHEDULE OF GEBURAH

WORLD	DIVINE ASPECT	TAROT ASSOCIATIONS
Atziluth	God-name, Elohim Gibor	Wands Five: Lord of Conflict
Briah	Archangel Khamael	Swords Five: Lord of Defeat
Yetzirah	Angelic Choir, Seraphim/ Fiery Serpents	Cups Five: Lord of Blended Pleasure
Assiah	Planet, Madim/Mars	Pentagrams Five: Lord of Earthly Problems

THE HALL OF JUDGMENT—
RITUAL

PREPARATION FOR THE RITUAL AT GEBURAH

*O my heart, my mother! O my heart that I got from my
mother! O my heart that feeds me in all my different ages!
Do not stand up as a witness against me in the Hall of
Judgment, be not hostile against me in the presence of the
Watcher of the Scales.*

THE BOOK OF COMING FORTH BY LIGHT
(THE EGYPTIAN BOOK OF THE DEAD)*

SACRIFICING

The ritual attitude belonging to Geburah is that of the sacrificial priest.
The sacrifice that is asked of you is to bring yourself into harmony with
the cosmic balance. You sacrifice your vices and your character flaws to
the creative source on the altar of Geburah. You put your queries on the
altar, and you open yourself to the correcting influence of the holy guardian angel. The emotions and feelings responsible for your development's
stagnation are weighed and judged on the balance of the cosmos. To see
yourself in this light requires great courage. To place yourself in the burning bright light of the Hall of Judgment is something you do throughout
your spiritual development. Transforming your ego in the light of balance
is a permanent part of the Great Work.

The angels of Geburah are described as Seraphim: the Burning Ones.
Cleaning and purification are, since antiquity, connected with fire, and
are inherently difficult processes. A sacrifice is made to serve a higher

---

*The "Per Em Heru" is the Egyptian name of the so-called Book of the Dead. The name
is now translated to "Coming Forth by Day," but in my opinion this translation does not
reflect the magical and philosophical content of the text. A better title would be: "Stepping Forward into the Light."

goal. A sacrifice is a transformation of something ordinary—something common—to something exalted. Through this, a higher energy becomes available. To clarify, consider this example from ordinary life: If you spend less time in the pub and instead devote that time to your spiritual practice, then you sacrifice your time and your money to that higher goal. In contrast, you could also sacrifice your spiritual work for your nightlife.

THE JUDGMENT IN
THE LIGHT OF YOUR DESTINY

Your sacrifice for your higher goal is not to be judged by the world. That is the task of your holy guardian angel. This is your guide on your path of life. He always shows you where you can find the light, independent of the situation you are in. Look again at the example of the person who chose to devote his or her time to nightlife over university study: maybe this choice was made by a local bar talent whose sacrifice then led to he or she becoming a genius concert musician.

The holy guardian angel is that part of your inner self wherein you decided what your contract would be for this life, the goal of your life. It is the higher goal in your life that you want to accomplish. This is what is meant by the so often wrongly understood "true will." The true will is not a stamping impetuous child who shouts, "I want it, I want it!" To live your true will requires considerable courage and self-awareness, as well as sacrifice. It is a will that is free of ego and is a servant of the higher goal. Individual's higher goals are always compatible with a bigger divine plan. Within this framework, everybody has free will. Whether you choose to focus on that goal is up to you. That is the issue by which you will finally be judged in the Hall of the Judgment.

Everybody needs to make choices in life, and limitation is one of the characteristics of Geburah. By delimiting something, it becomes stronger. By means of this ritual, you purify your heart of things that are not compatible with the light or the divine plan. From the moment you are capable of transforming vices, or blockages, you will get more energy. You can use this energy for things that are important for you in the long term.

Transcending is something different from suppressing. You first need to look very carefully at what your vices bring you—you developed them because they served you in some way.

MAGICAL WORLDS

When you do a ritual, you connect yourself with a mythic reality. Mythic realities are magical worlds. They exist internally in every one of us. They are inner landscapes. They have existed throughout our history in the jungle. They awaken very quickly, even when you do not have much training. This is also the trigger point. A magical world can open so quickly that you may feel overwhelmed. This can bring you out of balance. A stable magical training develops you slowly and under the guidance of people who know the path throughout.

PREPARATIONS

Necessities:

> A picture of scales
> A red altar cloth
> Five red candles
> Incense: dragon's blood
> A personal question, written down on paper
> A picture of a flail
> A red shawl or sash
>> A cup with water

For Geburah, you make an altar in blood red. Red is the color of Geburah and the color of sacrifice. Red is also the color of the Hall of Judgment. In mythology, this hall is seen as surrounded by the waters of life, and when you cross these waters you arrive at an Island of Fire. Place four red candles at the corners of your altar table. In the middle place the fifth one, next to the incense burner.

We will go a little step further with our minirituals. We will start to work with some correspondences of Geburah. I explained some of the correspondences in the text. Below is a list of the correspondences that you work with in this ritual. Following the list I describe how to use the symbols to create a magical reality:

The color red
The Element of Fire
The Hall of Judgment
The Seraphim
The sacrifice
The virtue of justice
The number five
Creating a protection of the light
  The pentagram

The pentagram is one of the symbols that are used to indicate the "man made perfect." Within the Mystery schools, we work toward the perfection of ourselves. By putting the pentagrams around you, you create an enclosed atmosphere in your meditation room wherein energy can be built up. This energy you use for your ritual, and the goal is purification of the self.

THE FIRES OF PURIFICATION

When you have prepared your altar, you start by calling up the Pentagrams in the way I described in chapter 7.

*You start with invoking the Pentagrams. Every time you have opened one cardinal direction, you turn back to the altar. Then you light a red candle belonging to the cardinal direction, and you vibrate **"Elohim Gibor."***

Once the four candles are burning, approach the altar and light the fifth candle in the middle of the altar. You raise this candle and say:

In the name of the Light of the World,
In the name of the most high light,
I open my heart for the Hall of Judgment.
I call upon the divine in the name of Elohim Gibor.

Put the candle back in the middle. You have now lit four candles for the cardinal directions and a fifth candle for the Element of Spirit. Sit down and take time to visualize the burning pentagrams around you.

Now take the cup of water and bless the space in which you work. You do that with the waters of life. Here again, take a little moment of active meditation. Walk a spiral around your altar and sprinkle water.

I call upon the ferrymen of the Inner Planes:
Let me sail safely over the waters of life.
Bring me to the Island of Fire,
So that I can purify myself in the Hall of Judgment.
I will accomplish my task in life
In accordance with the light.

Sit down at the altar. Visualize yourself as being surrounded by protecting pentagrams, and around you is a protecting canal filled with the waters of life. Now you look at your altar and see that you have arrived at the Island of Fire. You see that all the objects you have put on the altar have turned into living things. The red altar cloth and the candles have changed and are transformed into the angels of Geburah, the Seraphim: a burning purifying fire. You call upon the archangel Khamael and the purifying cleansing fires of Geburah. Stretch both your arms in the air, the palms of your hands turned outward.

Archangel Khamael,
I weigh my heart in the Hall of Judgment.
Let me grow in power by the might of the light.

Repeat this text until you see the appearance of the archangel before your inner eye. He stands opposite you and looks upon you as a flaming appearance radiating from the Island of Fire. He asks you what matter you have brought with you for which you want the Judgment of the Scales.

Now you put your letter with your personal query on the altar on the left side of the scales. The archangel takes a red feather from his red mantle and puts it on the other side of the scales. The archangel asks you if you are prepared to step into the flames of the Island of Fire, knowing that you are protected by the Forces of Light.

When you are prepared, hang the red shawl over your shoulders and light the charcoal. You put a little bit of the Dragon's blood incense on the charcoal. You visualize yourself surrounded by the fire. Concentrate on your question: feel the pain, the desire. Feel the emotions raised by your query, the passion, the desperation, and the love. You penetrate into all the emotions that are raised by this personal question.

Concentrate your mind on the flail as a spiritual symbol. Seeds need to be threshed to bake bread. You are a seed of creation. Try to feel what the spiritual reason is that you are tested so harshly over this issue. Your soul needs to rise to another level, to one of functioning above your present capabilities. What level is that? In which direction do you want to grow? What is causing you so much pain and struggle? Where is the light that helps you in this matter? What growth do you need to integrate this light force? Try to give words to your feelings. What kind of courage does it take?

Put the words and the images that are connected with these feelings on the scales. See if the scales balance. Or do they tip over to one side? If the balance is not yet completed, you need to work further—reformulate images, create new ones. Keep on going until the scales balance. If you do not succeed in balancing the scales, you leave the question lying on the scales and let the candles burn. You open yourself for a conversation with your holy guardian angel. In the days following, you will receive more information through realizations and dreams. In this case you leave the question on the altar and close the ritual down.

If you are capable of creating a balance during the ritual, you will feel lifted by waves of happiness. Try to create as many images as you can around this feeling. Then store these images within yourself. Gather the essence by making one sentence that summarizes the feeling of happiness. Repeat the sentence like a mantra. Then, let the images shrink, forming a red ball. This red ball you make into a jewel that you pin on your robe at your right shoulder.

Now it is time to conclude the ritual. You close the Pentagrams in the reverse order from which you called them up. When you have done this, you make the Kabbalistic Cross.

TIPHARETH, BEAUTY

The Sixth Path is called the Mediating Intelligence,
because in it are multiplied the influxes of the
Emanations: for it causes that influence to flow into all
the reservoirs of the blessings with which they themselves
are united.

SEPHER YETZIRAH

We have now arrived in the central Sephirah of the Tree of Life. Tiphareth is the harmonious center of all the divine emanations. The sphere is the

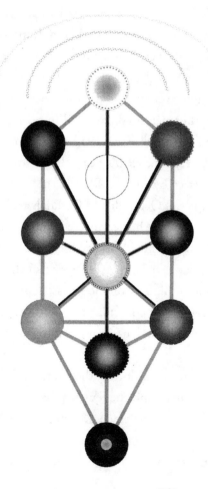

Tiphareth as the
central sphere of
the Tree of Life is
the meeting point
between the soul and
all the divine forces.

means by which the paths are directly connected with all the Sephirah, except for one. The only Sephirah that does not have a direct connection with Tiphareth is Malkuth. Because of his central position on the Tree, Tiphareth is called the Mediating Intelligence. Because all the emanations are gathered together here, Tiphareth balances all the energies and at the same time connects them.

Tiphareth has a very important function in the entire communications network that is the Tree of Life. I will describe some of the different relationships.

THE VISION OF THE HARMONY OF THINGS

Within the Ethical Triangle, Tiphareth is the sphere that balances mercy and severity; the opposing energies of expansion and limitation are brought into a subtle and exalted balance. The symbols are extremely old, because in Egypt this equilibrium was already expressed by the attributes of the pharaoh. Egyptian pharaohs were pictured with the crook and the flail in their hands. King Tutankhamen holds the flail in his right hand, at the position of Geburah, and the crook in his left hand, at the position of Gedulah. Then he crosses his hands over his heart. In this way, Mercy is limited by Severity, and Severity by Mercy. That is the harmonizing activity of Tiphareth. The energies of Geburah and Gedulah are balanced in the heart. Also, on the body, Tiphareth is connected with the heart.

Tiphareth connects Yesod and Da'ath. Yesod will be dealt with later in this book. Generally you can say that Yesod is the world of the subconscious mind. Da'ath is the world of higher consciousness. Tiphareth connects these two worlds by means of the conscious mind. In other words: all the riches from the depths of the mind are brought into consciousness in Tiphareth.

Tiphareth is located exactly in the middle of the Tree, on the middle of the Middle Pillar, between the male and the female pillar. Between the Black Pillar and the White Pillar all complementary energies are brought into balance.

All the polarized forces are balanced in Tiphareth. This harmonizing aspect of Tiphareth is summarized under the name of the Sephirah: Beauty. The Sephirah radiates a warm and fulfilling healing energy. Because of the fact that the sphere has a direct connection with Kether and mirrors Kether on a lower level, Tiphareth is also called the Lesser Countenance. This is in comparison with the title of Kether, who is called the Vast Countenance.

THE HEALER OF GOD

The godname with which you can connect yourself to the Sephiroth Tiphareth is Yehovah Eloah Va-Daath. This name means "the All-Knowing God." The archangel of the sphere is Raphael. He is the healer of God. He is helped by the angelic choir called the Malachim. These are the Messengers of God.

The entire Sephirah is panegyric on light, health, healing, and having a sense of fulfillment and significance. Healing in this sense is spiritual. You are healed in the world of the gods, not necessarily in the physical world. By raising yourself to this state of consciousness, you will get a different viewpoint of your life and your circumstances.

Tiphareth is the sphere of so-called peak experiences, which are exalted states of consciousness that render your life meaningful and significant. The event comes with a feeling of love and beauty. It is as if a layer is peeled off reality, and a deeper layer becomes accessible without any demonstrable cause. You get access to a beautiful, silent world wherein everything is exactly right. Peak experiences will increase in frequency and in length when you do the exercises belonging to this spiritual path. They are the signs of a more permanent state of Enlightenment. The exercises create the conditions for this type of experience.

DEVOTION TO THE GREAT WORK

When peak experiences last longer, they are accompanied by deep insights about the nature of reality. The beauty of this state of consciousness is breathtaking, and it is almost impossible to describe it. When you are together with people who know this experience, sharing the images and insights you have received from this state of Tiphareth consciousness can be enough to evoke this peak in someone else.

Generating and sharing these kinds of experiences is one of the workings of group rituals. Through telepathy, the images of the rituals of a group are more easily accessible for relative newcomers, and in this way they can get these Tiphareth encounters more quickly and easily. These experiences can create a personal understanding that magic really works. You feel it in your body, it becomes a part of your life, and you never want to lose it. In meditations, you will slowly start to experience a deeper mystical reality. This can cause an inner state that you can take with you in your daily life. Because of this, devotion and dedication to the path grows, and the practitioner becomes ready for initiation.

SCHEDULE OF TIPHARETH

WORLD	DIVINE ASPECT	TAROT ASSOCIATIONS
Atziluth	God-name, Elohim Gibor	Six of Wands: Lord of Victory
Briah	Archangel Raphael	Six of Swords: Lord of Earned Success
Yetzirah	Angelic Choir, Malachim, the Messengers	Six of Cups: Lord of Pleasure
Assiah	Planet, Shemesh, the Sun	Six of Pentagrams: Lord of Material Success

THE CROSS OF THE ELEMENTS— RITUAL

PREPARATION FOR THE RITUAL OF TIPHARETH

The souls are now on sea. Souls who do so are more secure
from many occasions of temptation, and the fire of Divine
Love is the more readily enkindled in them: for they
are so near that fire. However little when the blaze has
been fanned with the intellect, everything is set ablaze.
When no hindrance comes to it from outside, the soul
remains alone with its God and is thoroughly prepared to
understand the reflection.*

TERESA OF AVILA

Necessities:

Golden altar cloth
Golden scarf
Frankincense incense
Red rose
Rose petals
Small bowl with rose water
Glass filled with a little bit of wine
Piece of bread
Four tea lights
  Writing material

For the exercise of Tiphareth, you use a piece of golden fabric as your

---

*With this statement Teresa means that the souls have developed themselves and are past
the beginner's stage. They are now standing full on the path.

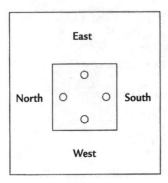

Meditation room with the altar in the middle and the tea lights on the four cardinal directions.

altar cloth. You also need four tea lights. You use frankincense incense, which is also called Olibanum. Take care that the incense is portable. Preferably you use a thurible. If you do not have one, you can use a solid terra-cotta bowl attached to lengths of chain so it can swing, and fill it with dry sand. Then you put the burning charcoal on the sand.

Further, you need a red rose, preferably one with a scent. There is a kind of rose called Ecstasy, and when you smell that rose, you will know what I mean. You can preorder them at a flower shop. Further, you need a chalice or a wine glass with a sip of wine in it, and a piece of bread on a platter, a bowl with rose water, and a small bowl with salt. You also need a gold scarf for the ritual. Put the scarf on the chair before you start. Take care that you can walk around the altar when you are working. Use a comfortable chair with armrests so that you are well supported during the meditation. Put your things on a small side table ready to use. As in all the rituals in this book, you will get more out of this when you repeat it. You will understand it better when you start to understand the symbols and their relationships.

THE MYSTERY OF THE CRUCIFIXION

Start with the Kabbalistic Cross and open the temple with the invoking pentagrams as you did in your last exercise. When you have opened the cardinal directions, take the bowl with rose water and sprinkle this around the altar. When you build up energy during a ritual, always walk clockwise. At the end of the ritual, when you close, walk counterclockwise to wind the energy down. Sprinkle the rose water clockwise around the altar and recite the following sentences like a mantra:

> **I purify my temple with the smell of the rose.**
> **I ask for insight into the Mystery of the Crucifixion**
> **To the amount that I am able to receive.**

Take your tea light and a lighter. Walk to the East of your meditation space. Light the candle and look in the direction of the rising sun. Lift the light upward in the direction of the pentagram, and vibrate:

> **In the name of Yehovah Eloah Va-Da'ath**
> **I honor the rising sun in the East.**

Then you put the tea light on the Eastern side of your altar. You walk to the Southern side of your meditation space, and taking your tea light with you, raise the burning candle in the direction of the noonday sun toward the pentagram. Put the pentagram down in the South and say:

> **In the name of Yehovah Eloah Va-Da'ath**
> **I honor the noonday sun in the South.**

Then put the tea light on the Southern side of your altar. Go to the Western side of your meditation space and, taking a tea light with you, raise the burning candle in the direction of the setting sun toward the pentagram you put down in the West, and say:

> **In the name of Yehovah Eloah Va-Da'ath**
> **I honor the evening sun in the West.**

Finally you put the tea light on the Western side of your altar. You now walk to the Northern side of your meditation space. You take the tea light with you, raise the burning candle in the direction of the night toward the pentagram that you put down in the North, and say:

> **In the name of Yehovah Eloah Va-Da'ath**
> **I bring honor to the birth of the Light in the North.**

Take the bowl with salt and sprinkle the salt around the four sides of the altar. Now you say:

In the name of Yehovah Eloah Va-Da'ath
I honor the realm of the earth.

Put the bowl with the salt down in the middle of the altar. Take the thurible and waft incense along the four sides of the altar. Here you say:

In the name of Yehovah Eloah Va-Da'ath
I honor the realm of the heavens. I fill this space with the
breath of the gods.

Now you walk to the Northern side of your meditation room and focus on the altar. Take the red rose and hold it against your heart as you repeat the following text. While you speak you visualize the text as clearly as possible:

Here I stand amidst the powers of the East, the South,
the West, and the North, the Above and the Below.
I connect my heart with the altar of Tiphareth,
the altar of the sun.

Now put the rose down on the middle of the altar of Tiphareth. You will do four short meditations in which you concentrate on the symbols that I give you. Put down your chair at the Northern side of the altar in such a way that you look in the direction of the altar. Take the rose petals and sprinkle a line from the rose in the middle of the altar toward the tea light on the North. Sit down, and take the golden scarf and put it over your head, then vibrate the first letter of the Tetragrammaton: Yod. Now you imagine that from the highest heavens a Yod, a spark of divine consciousness, comes down and implants itself into your third eye.

Meditation on the East

Now you go to the Eastern quarter. Put the golden scarf around your shoulders, and vibrate the second letter of the Tetragrammaton: Heh.

You imagine that from the highest heavens a Heh comes down, and this one connects itself with your arms and shoulders. Sit down again. Imagine that it is early in the morning, and you see the first rays of light appearing at the edge of the horizon behind you. You hear the sounds of birds waking up slowly and starting their songs to greet the rising sun. Then you notice that it is becoming warmer. You feel the sun rising and feel how the rays slowly warm your back. In your imagination, you see the rose that is on the middle of the altar unfolding. When the petals open, you see that inside the rose is an egg. It is the egg of a falcon. You hear the sound that the young bird makes when it pecks an opening in the eggshell. Then the egg breaks open, and you hear the whistling of the young falcon. A voice says to you: "This is the first gateway of the light."

Write down any thoughts you have at the end of your meditation.

Meditation on the South

Now you move your chair to the South. Look toward the altar, and pick up the basket with rose petals. Sprinkle a second line of petals between the rose in the middle of the altar and the tea light in the South. Let the golden scarf fall like a sash downward from over your shoulder, over your breast. Vibrate the third letter of the Tetragrammaton: Vav.

You imagine that, from the highest heavens, a Vav comes downward and connects the spark of consciousness in your third eye with your genitals. Sit down again. Now imagine that the sun behind you rises upward to its highest point. It becomes hot, and you feel how a warm glow suffuses you thoroughly. The golden glow surrounds you, and you smell the strong scent of the rose. The rays penetrate deep into your inner being and illuminate your aura with a deep golden glow. In your imagination your head is the sun, and rays shoot from this point in all directions. You appear to have the hair of a lion. You hear the sound of a roaring lion clearly in the background, and you hear the sound of a nail being hammered into a piece of wood. A voice speaks to you: "Meditate about the Mystery of the king."

At the end of your meditation write down your realizations.

Meditation on the West

Now change your place again and look from the West toward the altar. Sprinkle a line of rose petals from the rose in the middle of the altar toward the tea light in the

West. Put the golden scarf over your hips and legs, and vibrate the fourth letter of the Tetragrammaton: Heh.

Imagine that from the highest heaven a second Heh comes down and connects itself with your hips and legs. The sun now sinks behind you. You see that the sky changes its colors in all the pastels of evening red. Two stars appear in the heavens. In your imagination you see two sycamore trees at the Western horizon. The trees in the sinking sun create long shadows at both sides of you. An eagle appears in the evening sky. A voice tells you: "This is the second gate. It gives access to an even greater light. Feel how the goddess stretches her arms to you."

Write down your thoughts at the end of the meditation.

Meditation on the North

Now you move your chair, facing the Northern side of your altar again. You knot the golden scarf around your waist, which is a form of cord magic. By doing this, you connect the forces around you and tie yourself (literally) to them. In this way the golden scarf forms the ancient Egyptian hieroglyph Shen. This is the symbol that you find surrounding the names of pharaohs. The Shen is the symbol of the eternal ongoing circle of the cycle of the sun. Now you vibrate all the four letters of the Tetragrammaton at the moment you put the knot in the scarf: YHVH.

The sun now changes shape. You see a solar eclipse: the Winged Solar Disc. In the dark heaven the moon stands before the sun. The rays of the sun shine at all sides, and the rays of the solar corona form two wings. Around the winged Sun, the Milky Way appears in all her beauty. From this sun a vulture comes flying in your direction and encloses you in her wings. She lifts you up. Deep below you, you see an Egyptian sarcophagus drifting on a river. The voice tells you: "Meditate on the Mystery of the Sacrificed God."

At the end of your meditation, write down your thoughts.

Now you stand at the altar—the spiritual quarter—facing the East. Put your chalice with the wine on the altar and take the platter with the bread. Take the bowl with the salt. Walk once around the altar while you sprinkle the salt on the ground before you, and say:

"Holy is the ground on which I walk."

Waft incense over the altar again. Walk around the altar in a circle and say:

"The altar of my heart
Is enveloped by the divine breath."

Lift the rose upward and say:

"Holy is the perfumed rose
Which blossoms on the Cross of the Elements."

Lift the chalice and say:

"The chalice is filled with the blood of my heart."

Sprinkle a little bit of salt on the bread and say:

"Grain and salt are the fundamentals of my body.
The grain dies and by this it renews itself."

Now stretch out both of your hands over the bread and the wine. Then vibrate Yod-Heh-Shin-Vav-Heh* and let all the collected energy stream through the palms of your hands into the bread. Now drink from the wine and eat the bread.

Collect all these images into a golden sphere. The golden globe is located around your heart chakra. You can visualize it as a golden beating sphere. In this golden sphere you will store this and your future meditations and rituals about Tiphareth. The golden sphere shrinks and becomes a golden seed that melts into your heart, ready to unfold into a complete temple at the next opportunity.

It is now time to end the ritual. This you do by closing the Pentagrams. You start in the North and move counterclockwise to the East. Close down with the Kabbalistic Cross. Let the candles on the altar burn down.

---

*By adding the Shin in the middle between the letters of the Tetragrammaton, the name YHSH transforms into Yeheshua. Yeheshua is the Hebrew name of Jesus. In other words his name is a formula: through adding the Shin, the power of the Holy Spirit is inserted into the Tetragrammaton. The Four Elements are brought to life by the sun of Tiphareth—the redeemer god who is king and ruler over the Elements.

10
THE MAGICAL TRIANGLE

TRIANGLES AND
THE FALL INTO MATTER

Evocation is a Magical operation whereby the power
or the entity is called forth into a protected area. The
magician is protected in what is generally called a
"Magical circle," and the entity is called into the "Triangle
of Art." Such evoked forces are—for obvious reasons—
helpful demons and not Divine forces.

WIKIPEDIA ENCYCLOPEDIA

Above you read a summary of the current opinion about the magical triangle. However, this opinion is based on a misunderstanding and leads to
an incorrect use of the forces. I will provide another opinion of the magical
triangle, in the hope that this gives more clarity. The magical triangle is
also called the astral triangle. It consists of the Sephiroth Netzach, Hod,
Yesod, and Malkuth together. It is a three-dimensional triangle. It is built
up from the energies and the states of consciousness that are so crucial for
practical magic. At the same time, it is particularly this part of the Tree that
is understood incorrectly, and for this reason inaccurately applied.

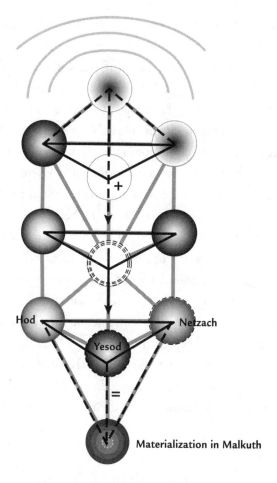

Materialization in Malkuth

Understand that Malkuth is a part of this triangle, and his presence is the end result of all the previously mentioned Sephiroth. If you see the Tree of Life as an arithmetical problem, then Malkuth would always be the solution or the end result. Let me explain again the essence of the triangles of the Tree of Life, so that you have the bigger picture in mind. The three upper Sephiroth (Kether, Chokmah, and Binah) together create the divine spark. They form the root of consciousness, and they are, and remain, an integral part of the All. Theirs is a transcending consciousness that will always be a part of the sacred at-one-ness. At the same time, this unity splits itself into a cascade of separate entities. These entities "fall" down from the unity and look for a way to express and experience themselves. This splitting from the one to the many is described in the esoteric lore as "the Fall." In magic we call it "the Descent."

The "sins" that come into being are the result of the limitations caused by the formation of Cosmic consciousness into structures. This limitation of form causes the energies to increase in power. Erosion of the original spiritual energies is the inevitable result of this process. Compare this process with erosion of mountains in nature. Spiritual erosion is the consequence of the process of creation, when Divine energy is encapsulated in form. This is the activity and the nature of the Sephirah Binah.

The ethical triangle comes into being because, on the way down, we "eat from the Tree of Good and Evil." During the trip into the world of matter, we gradually learn to know the effects of different types of consciousness and the friction they cause. You can compare this with white light that is viewed through a prism so that all the colors can be seen in their separate states. There are constructive forces and destructive forces working. Both types keep each other in a delicate balance. Both growth and pruning are necessary to keep the Tree of Life healthy. The heart makes the choice of what exactly needs to be trimmed and what doesn't. The consideration is based on the divine plan, which directs this entire process.

THE TRIANGLE OF ART

Within the magical triangle, these forces of consciousness are charged with emotions, thoughts, and images. Here, form emerges through all these different forces. These forms are charged with desires, dreams, and fantasies about how possibilities could become concrete realities. In the end, these images become so concrete that they will crystallize. The end result of this entire process is Malkuth: the physical manifestation of the creation process.

The magical triangle is the Triangle of Art. Some practitioners place the Triangle of Art outside the magical circle to evoke forces of consciousness to the level that they become visible appearances. Schemes like the mandala from the *Key of Solomon*—a medieval grimoire—which you see

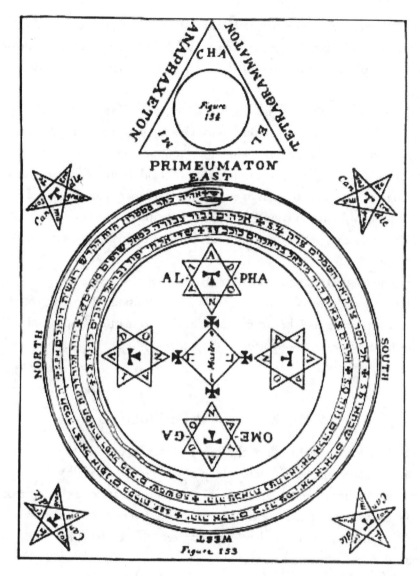

in the picture above, are sometimes interpreted on the wrong level of meaning. This is due to a lack of background knowledge.

The quote from *Wikipedia* at the beginning of this chapter shows us that misunderstandings about the art and nature of magical work are deeply rooted. These types of misunderstandings are responsible for the stumbling blocks of the over-adventurous magician. However, not only inexperienced magicians are subject to these obstacles, there are also some famous examples in the history of magic of people who should have known better. The misconceptions flowing forth from this type of manuscript make a number of the magical grimoires from the Middle Ages useless.

The significance of the magical triangle is its application to your everyday life. If you want to buy an ice-cream cone on a warm and sunny day, then you use at that moment—on a common level—all the forces of the magical triangle: fantasy, thought power, and desire. When you focus enough on the combination of these three powers of consciousness, you will probably start to count the pentagrams in your wallet and go to a shop where they sell ice cream. Your desire then manifests itself in the physical world.

The magical triangle consists of the four Sephiroth who generate concrete form and who capture us in the world of illusions. The forces of the magical triangle together form "conscious proto-matter." You could call this conceptions or thoughtforms. Low magic is based on working with these thoughtforms.

THE ROBES OF PERSONALITY

The four lowest Sephiroth of the Tree of Life also contain the collective forces that are involved in the buildup of someone's personality. In magic the personality is seen as astral clothing. It is the mantle of the self that you use to step into the world outside you. Here you also find the protective mechanisms a person develops to protect the self from threats from outside.

The ego is a part of that personality. Within magic, we start with the premise that, to survive in the modern Western society, you need an ego. You need to have a good and healthily developed personality to stay stable in your life and in your environment. Your ego is needed in your professional environment and to protect yourself and your family against threats from the outside world.

Your personality and your ego are protective mantles for your soul. By building a personality, you surround your soul and create a vessel for it.

You develop your ego and your personality during your entire life. Many people who are interested in spirituality think that they are not allowed to have an ego and a personality, because this would block their spiritual development.

BOW IN THE PRESENCE OF THE GODS

The core of the matter is that you are allowed to have an ego, but you must not be attached to it. You need to be able to take a step back, to excuse yourself when you have made a mistake. You have an ego, but you are not your ego. Before you can detach yourself from your ego, you first need to have one. Otherwise, to detach is no big deal. With these thoughts in the background, it is now time to explain the different Sephiroth of the magical triangle.

NETZACH, VICTORY

*The Seventh Path is called the Occult Intelligence, because
it is the refulgent splendor of the intellectual virtues
which are perceived by the eyes of the intellect and the
contemplations of faith.*

SEPHER YETZIRAH

Netzach is the first of the Sephiroth engaged in the buildup of the personality. The pitfalls of the personality are strongly connected with the "vices" of Netzach. Netzach's major pitfall develops out of the beauty of the physical body, the ego, and the personality when they overindulge in feelings of glamour and importance. This is a major point of attention. You must keep track of this pitfall during your entire magical development.

When performing magic, you build consciously on a number of subpersonalities in order to clearly separate your magical work from your everyday life. These subpersonalities are more vulnerable to glamour than your normal personalities, because they are built up astrally. This means that they are not subject to typical social restraints generated by everyday social interaction.

I will give you an example. Let us assume that your boss asks you to do something for him. You are rather annoyed because his manner is too dictatorial for your liking. At the moment you discover yourself thinking, "This weekend I was the vessel for the god Osiris. Who the hell do you think you are?" then it is clear that you have some work to do on your ego!

The four bottom Sephiroth can be connected to the Tetragrammaton. On the level of the personality, Netzach is Fire, Hod is Water, Yesod is Air, and Malkuth Earth. In this way, you can work on your personality by using the Four Elements.

In the buildup of the personality, Netzach represents the instincts and the emotions. On the Tree of Life, Netzach is the opposite of Hod. The relationship between Netzach and Hod needs to be understood: Netzach is a world of feelings, whereas Hod is an intellectual world. Feelings and reason must be balanced all the time in your life. There is a similar balance mechanism that works between Geburah and Gedulah, which one must seek continuously, and of Binah and Chokmah on the higher levels of the Tree of Life.

THE VISION OF TRIUMPHANT BEAUTY

Netzach is connected with the Vision of Triumphant Beauty and is the world of the creative imagination of the divine. The divine shows itself here as artistic creator of the universe. In Netzach, creative power takes up the paintbrush and paints breathtakingly beautiful formations of clouds, the most beautiful birds. It colors rainbows into the landscape. It takes up the flute of the winds and the birds to create heavenly music. Everything in the sphere of Netzach radiates a resplendent beauty and a pure artistic creative force. In the sphere of consciousness of Netzach, the greatest works of art in the history of humanity are created—the most beautiful musical compositions, the most elegant ballets. Also, the beauty of the physical body belongs to the virtues of Netzach.

Netzach is connected to endurance. Everyone who works in a creative profession knows that inspiration is not just a flash coming down from heaven. Before you can open your mind for this current whereon you can get inspired, you first need to wrestle with the resistance on the road. You can compare this process with a sportsman who must first warm up his muscles before he can give a good performance.

THE INFLUENCE OF NETZACH ON RITUAL

Working with beauty and creativity is important in the field of spiritual magic. Magic isn't called an art without reason. A beautiful ritual is a work of art. You see that in the text and the meaning. A beautiful ritual is comparable to a composition of music: it is a choreography of movements, a symphony of meaning. An altar is a still life whereon an inner reality is shaped in a creative way. A temple develops during a ritual as a three-dimensional mandala. A ritual is an interconnected composition of meaning, form, movement, sound, and imagery. A ritual does not only engender a feeling of inner silence and sacral devotion, it can also create ecstasy. During a ritual you work with emotions that applied arts can raise. This can be done with and without talent.

A ritual is a real art form, comparable to a theater production or a musical performance. In creating magic, energy whirls around, peaks, spirals, becomes silent, increases, and exalts in a way similar to music. One significant difference is that there is no audience during magical ritual. All the participants are involved in the end result. The magical currents move as the sum of the souls of the participants, while they raise themselves on the energies that are used during the ritual. This is the influence of Netzach in the rituals.

The word Netzach means "victory." This is because, in the creation mythology, Netzach is connected with the seventh day of creation. On this day the divine artist steps back to see the result of its creation and to get the overview—and sees that it is good.

LOVE

The sphere of Netzach is connected with love—divine love to be more precise. That is something different from sexuality and lust. Being unchaste is the vice of the Sephirah. The love that is meant here is the love for the divine. This develops by making a connection with the archetypal "best side" of yourself. A lot of people connect this feeling of love with another person, and are looking for a "soul mate." A soul mate is a person who is the object on which this ideal self is projected. According to people who search for one, a soul mate is the partner, the twin soul with whom they want to melt into a symbiotic unity.

Because there is no living human being who is a complete match for this archetypal ideal of the divine partner, this confusion causes a lot of sorrow. People look for loving fulfillment and think that they can find divine unity by projecting their image of an ideal partner onto a soul mate. They look for their lost twin soul, their alter ego, the yin that belongs to the yang. When this partner is found, the person needs to be "changed," because he or she does not fit the pattern of the ideal.

Mistaking the desire to unite with the highest part of yourself for the longing for a romantic partner causes an untenable pressure on a relationship. As long as the symbiosis does not hold, the relationship has not succeeded, and the redemption of the soul of the partner did not take and the partner is not saved. He or she needs to be "changed." A constructive way to go along with this theme is to look at what fantastic characteristics your partner displays. This can be the raw material for your own big change; an important part of the Great Work consists of making these outward projected qualities an active part of yourself.

VENUS

Netzach is located at the foot of the male pillar of the Tree of Life. It is typical that the goddess of love is the main archetype of this Sephirah. The planet belonging to this Sephirah is Venus; the Hebrew name for this planet is Nogah.

HANIEL

The archangel of Netzach is Haniel. His name means the "Grace of God." It is said that he is the archangel who took Enoch to the heavens. Enoch went into ecstasies about the beauty of Netzach, and raised himself in this way into a visionary heavenly state of enlightenment. Haniel is sometimes also called the green flame.

This title, the green flame, is also connected to the stone of Netzach, the emerald. Venus, the planet belonging to Netzach, has two manifestations. She can be seen as a morning star and as an evening star. As a morning star she comes up before the sun, and in this way announces the coming of light.

Under very special circumstances, the sunrise is preceded by a phenomenon called the green flash. It is a phenomenon that lasts less than a second. The horizon must be clear and the atmosphere dry. The air must be free of clouds. Under these circumstances you can sometimes see a clear green light on the top of the sun. You can find photographs on the Internet of this phenomenon. This is the son of Venus, the Son of the Morning. It is said of him that he is the light bringer. He wears a crown of emeralds on his head. I will go deeper into these Mysteries of Netzach during the ritual.

SCHEDULE OF NETZACH

WORLD	DIVINE ASPECT	TAROT ASSOCIATIONS
Atziluth	God-name, Yehovah Tzabaoth	Wands Seven: Lord of Valor
Briah	Archangel Haniel, Grace of God	Swords Seven: Lord of Unstable Effort
Yetzirah	Angelic Choir, Elohim, the Gods	Cups Seven: Lord of Illusionary Success
Assiah	Nogah, Venus	Pentagrams Seven: Lord of Unfulfilled Success

THE FACE OF THE GODDESS
OF LOVE—RITUAL

There is no true protection, except for the protection which
is granted by the accomplishment of the work of the Gods.
The only true servant is he who is a copper mirror for the
Unmanifested God.

EGYPTIAN WISDOM TEXT, TEMPLE OF DENDERAH

PREPARATIONS FOR THE RITUAL IN NETZACH

For this ritual you need to do a little bit of preliminary work. You will be making a Venus symbol to put on the altar. You need to buy a simple round mirror with a handle, and make a crossbar on the handle so that the mirror takes the form of the symbol for the planet Venus. With a little bit of paint from the hobby shop, paint the edges copper-colored. This will become the mirror of Hathor. If you are very skilled and want to do this perfectly, then replace the mirror glass with a polished copper disc. But this is not really necessary.

When you look at the equipment list below, you will see that you need to have colored oil lamps. They are also very easy to make yourself. Take the colored glasses and put olive oil in the bottom. Then take the wick and the iron base from a tea light and put them upright in the glasses with the oil. Then you have a very simple oil lamp. The olive oil is a symbol connected to Chokmah; the Sephirah Netzach also has a connection to Chokmah. The olive oil as a symbol is associated with wisdom, and this symbolism connects the ritual with the zodiac. As you will remember, Chokmah is connected to the Wisdom of the stars.

Necessities:

Green altar cloth
Green scarf
Mirror of Hathor
A taper

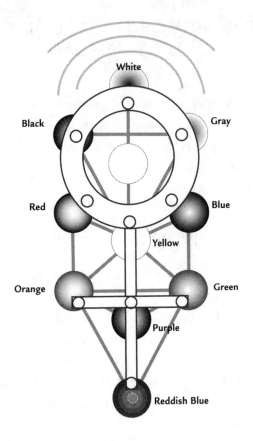

Seven oil lamps in colored glasses: white, blue, red, yellow,
    green, orange, and violet
Ten gemstones in the Briatic colors of the Sephiroth
Transparent quick-bonding glue
Incense benzoin
Thurible
Charcoal

HATHOR

Hathor is an Egyptian goddess whose place within the Egyptian pantheon
is comparable to that of the goddess Venus in the Roman pantheon. Her
name means "House of Horus." Horus is her husband, and this god is
the sun falcon. The sun falcon is a symbol for the soul. Hathor is heaven

itself. There is a very important temple dedicated to her that still exists, the Temple of Denderah. This temple is totally covered with astrological symbols. It is probable that the stars were observed from the roof of the temple and mapped by engraving them onto big copper mirrors.

In this ritual, you make yourself into the copper mirror, the mirror wherein the goddess of love looks to see herself. One of the highest mystical states in Chokmah is the meeting of the divine Face to Face. This can only happen when you make yourself into a mirror of the divine.

This is the work that is done with the mirror of Hathor. This is, of course, a lifetime's work, and not something that will be accomplished by a simple ritual, but by making the mirror of Hathor, you can start to use it as a magical tool. Every time you get into a situation in which life or circumstances hold a mirror in front of you, you can raise your heart toward the divine and ask for suggestions for how to deal with the situation.

THE MIRROR OF HATHOR

Prepare your ritual space. Place your altar in the middle of the space and cover it with a green altar cloth. Put your green scarf around your shoulders. Put the mirror in the middle of the altar. In the center of the mirror put the central altar light. This time you use the green light for a center light. Put the other lights in a circle around the mirror in the following order: white, blue, red, yellow, orange, and violet. Put the colored stones beside your mirror and divide them according to the Briatic colors of the Sephiroth. These colors you will find in the tables of correspondences in the appendix. In this ritual you will work with all the Sephiroth, including those that will be explained in the next chapters.

Start with the opening ceremony. Make the Kabbalistic Cross and call up the Pentagrams. Now walk to the middle of your temple. Fold both your hands before your heart, as if you hold your heart, and say:

"My heart is the rose on the cross of the Elements.

I connect this rose with the four roads to the heaven."

Walk from the middle to the East and put one hand on your heart. Stretch your other hand out and touch the core of the pentagram. Visualize being here at the moment when the sun rises. First you will see the planet Venus announcing the coming of the sun. Then you will see the green flash appearing on the top of the sun. Say:

> **"I connect my heart with the quarter of the sunrise.**
> **The green flame will lead me and exalt my heart,**
> **And lift me by beauty."**

Put both your hands on your heart. Walk back to the middle and connect yourself with the center of the altar. Now go to the South. The sun is here at its highest point, where it is at the top of its force. A gigantic bright light and a radiating power come toward you. Say:

> **"I connect my heart with the quarter of the highest light**
> **And the passion for life.**
> **I connect myself with the life force**
> **And with the highest joy.**
> **I connect my heart with the dazzling beauty**
> **Of the flame of the fire of life."**

Bring both hands to your heart and walk to the middle. Now go to the West. See how the sun sinks slowly below the horizon in a blaze of color. The planet Venus follows the sun here. Stretch your arms again and connect yourself with the pentagram of the West. Say:

> **"I connect my heart with the quarter of my ancestors**
> **And the spiritual knowledge**
> **That they left behind for us.**
> **The sinking sun leads me on this holy road."**

Return to the altar, and now walk to the North. Here you visualize the polestars, which turn slowly in the starry night. See how all the stars, constellations, and planets make an eternal dance around an invisible point. Here you stretch out your hand, touch the pentagram, and say:

> **"I ask for protection**

For performing the work of the gods.

Let me be a true servant

Who is a copper mirror for the unmanifested God."

Go back to the altar. Now put some grains of incense on the glowing charcoal, and encircle your temple slowly. Start and end in the East and walk clockwise. While you walk, imagine that the divine breath of divinity slowly fills the space. Say:

"I am a part of the source and the source is a part of me.

I am one with the at-one-ness of the All."

You have now walked within the room, and with words and gestures created an equal-armed cross within a circle in the space. Now connect yourself with the copper mirror symbolizing the ankh. The ankh is an Egyptian hieroglyph that has the same form as the mirror of Hathor. The hieroglyph means "life" and was also a symbol indicating copper. By calling the ankh into yourself, you connect yourself to the meaning of this symbol.

Stand at the altar looking toward the East. Connect yourself with the planet Venus, which rises before the sun. Use both your arms. Stretch them parallel toward your feet, and in one movement bring them straight before you to the level of your heart. Now let your arms make a circle around your head. The left arm swings to the left, the right arm to the right. Your hands cross above your head and meet each other again at the heart. From here, make a horizontal movement by stretching your arms over the horizon. You have made the sign of the ankh.

"I connect myself with my spiritual ancestors.
The ankh is the sign of life.
I am life, I honor life,
And I honor the heritage they have left for us."

Now enter into the temple and light the altar light. Use a taper to do this. Keep it upright in the direction of the East, and visualize lighting it from the flame of the planet Venus herself. Say:

"I light my light to your star: lady of the morning light, light my temple with your flame of love."

Now take the green altar light in your hand. Light this light with the taper, which now sparkles with starlight. Go into meditation. Hear the voice that speaks to you in your mind. Every time the voice speaks to you, close your eyes and follow the instructions. Let the message of what you are being told penetrate deeply into your subconscious mind.

Watch, here is the eternal burning lamp of the temple
The lamp is filled with olive oil.
The olive tree is the symbol of the initiates of all times.
This lamp will never be put out.
It burns from the time of our ancestors until the present.
The lamp is filled with oil
Of the tree whereof the doors of the temple are made.
The oil is the product of this tree.
It is the symbol of the Wisdom gained in Chokmah.
This oil is the fuel of this eternal burning lamp.
I look toward the wick of the Lamp of Wisdom.
When the wick of the lamp is refreshed,
Then the new wick will be lit from the old one.
In this way the tradition is passed on from generation to generation.
I watch the flame of the Lamp of Wisdom.
I see that the flame has the same form as a Yod,

The flame has the form of a spark of the soul.

The eternal soul comes from the stars,

He connects himself with the wick and feeds from the oil.

This is the lamp that burns deep in our hearts.

He burns in a transparent glass that has the color of emerald.

Like the lamp the task of the soul is to light the environment.

Now stand upright, make the gesture of the ankh, and then raise the green light in front of you. Say:

"The lamp of the goddess of love is the high light that transforms the darkness.

It brings grace and enlightenment.

Hold in your hand this light, which represents the light of love.

It enlightens that whereon the light is focused."

Put the green altar light back into the middle. Now take fire from the green light with your taper. Before you light one of the lamps, you first make a sign of the ankh with the taper above the green light. This means that you give life to the symbols that are lying before you. In other words: you will live them. With your taper, take a flame from the green light and light the white light. Move your chair and sit down before this lamp. Say:

"The white light is the lamp of life itself.

Bright and clear it comes forth directly from the unseen source itself.

This lamp carries within itself all possibilities."

The next lamp is the blue one. Again, light it from the green light and make the gesture of the ankh with your taper. Say:

"The next light is the light of the blue lamp.

This is the most exalted light.

This light can only be lit from the green lamp of the most beautiful love,

Because in this lamp burns the light of obedience

To the highest laws of the cosmos."

Replace your chair. You are now sitting before the red lamp. Light your taper again from the green light. Make the gesture of the ankh with your taper. Now light the red light and say:

"This is the lamp of the sacrifice.

This light is lit by love.

It burns in remembrance of the sacrifices that were brought by the initiates,

So that the light of the tradition could be passed on.

This lamp burns in honor of those who took care

That this light of the tradition was passed on until this present time."

What sacrifices are asked of you? Remember that sacrificing means that you transform energy to a higher quality.

The next lamp is the yellow one. Again, light it from the green light. With your taper, make the gesture of the ankh. Say:

"Now I light the golden lamp.

In the golden lamp burns the light of truth.

This light can only be endured when it is lit from the light of love.

Then this light opens the way for me

To my highest potential."

Move your chair. Light the next light with the taper from the green lamp, after you have made the ankh. Now sit for the orange lamp and say:

"This is the lamp of power.

It balances the lights of severity and mercy.

That I may use my power with insight from the heart, which is lit by love."

Go to the violet lamp. This light is also lit from the green light. With your taper, first make the gesture of the ankh. Say:

"This is the lamp of the memory.

Lit with the light of love

This light connects me with the knowledge of my ancestors

Into the depths of the past."

Now concentrate fully on the green lamp. You are back at the East. Look toward the symbol of Venus. Now you start to work with the stones and connect them with the Tree of Life in yourself.

Take the white crystal in your hand. In your thoughts, connect it with the crown of your head, and say:

"As Above, so Below.

The god in me connects with the God that surrounds me."

When you have made this energetic connection, glue the stone onto the mirror. Now take the gray stone. Hold it on the left side of your head and speak with the voice of Wisdom of Chokmah:

"As Above, so Below.

Inexhaustible is the Wisdom of the Zodiac."

When you have made this energetic connection, glue the stone onto the mirror. Now take the black stone in your hand. Hold it on the right side of your head and speak with the voice of compassion of Binah:

"As Above, so Below.

The compassion of the goddess is without end."

When you have made this energetic connection, glue the stone onto the mirror. Now take the blue stone in your left hand. Connect the energy with your left arm and shoulder, and speak with the voice of the richness of Chesed:

"As Above, so Below.

My hand is the source of the Fountains of Mercy."

When you have made this energetic connection, glue the stone onto the mirror. Now take the red stone in your right hand. Connect it with the energy of your right arm and shoulder and speak from the power of Geburah:

"As Above, so Below.

My hand is armed with the Lightning Flash of Severity."

When you have made this energetic connection, glue the stone onto the mirror.

Take the yellow stone. Connect the energy with your heart and speak from the Mystery of Tiphareth:

"As Above, so Below.

The Sun Falcon lives in my heart."

When you have made this energetic connection, glue the stone onto the mirror. Now take the purple stone. Connect the energy with your genital center and speak from the life-giving forces of Yesod. Speak:

"As Above, so Below.

I connect myself with the cosmic pendulum of the Tides of life."

When you have made this energetic connection, glue the stone onto the mirror. Take the russet stone. Connect the energy with the soles of your feet. Honor the Kingdom of Malkuth, and say:

"As Above, so Below.

The Lord of the World walks on holy ground."

When you have made this energetic connection, glue the stone onto the mirror. Take the orange stone. Connect the energy with your right hip and with the clear mind of Hod, and say:

"As Above, so Below.

The House of the Gods is supported by the Pillars of Splendor."

When you have made this energetic connection, glue the stone onto the mirror. Take the green stone. Connect the energy with your left hip and with the love of Netzach, and say:

"As Above, so Below.

The House of the Gods is supported by the Pillar of Victory."

Make the gesture of the ankh over yourself to connect all these energies with the symbol of the goddess of love.

Take up the green lamp, which burns in the middle. Sit in meditation, your focus on the East. Now imagine the following scenes: You see the first light appearing above the horizon of the morning. The planet Venus announces the sun. Then you see the colors that accompany the sunrise shift. The clouds are colored in the most beautiful shades. The birds start to sing. The temperature rises. You see the sun coming up over the horizon and next the green flash. From the green flash an emerald tumbles downward. It falls into your lap. The stone is so big that you need two hands to hold it. You look at the shape and you see that it is shaped like a chalice. You hear a voice:

> *Hear, hear, and see here the gift of the morning star,*
> *This is the stone from the crown of the light bearer:*
> *It is the Holy Grail.*
> *It is made of emerald.*
> *The grail is the womb of the goddess of love:*
> *And her name is Nature.*

Now write down the insights that you had during the ritual. Then rise and connect all these images with the mirror of Hathor. Make the gesture of the ankh one last time to connect all the insights. Then close the ritual by closing the pentagram.

Leave the mirror to dry, and let the lamps burn out. The mirror should remain in the temple for a minimum of twenty-four hours so that all the energies can penetrate and the glue can dry. Then wrap the Mirror of Hathor in your green scarf. When it is necessary, you use the mirror to connect yourself with the divinity within. You can communicate with it. When you look into it, you can make a connection with the most beautiful, wise, and most loving part of yourself. You start that work with the affirmation:

I ask for protection to do the work of the gods. Let be me a true servant who is a copper mirror for the unmanifested God.

Then you concentrate on one of the lamps. Light the lamp that is most closely connected with the aspect of divinity that you want to contact. Draw all these experiences together into a green ball. The ball gets the form of a green, corroded copper lamp, which you hang on the belt that you wear. The lamp hangs on your left hip.

HOD, SPLENDOR

The Eighth Path is called the Absolute or Perfect
Intelligence because it is the mean of the Primordial,
which has no root by which it can cleave or rest, save in
the hidden places of Gedulah, from which emanates its
proper essence.

SEPHER YETZIRAH

The Sephirah Hod is connected to the intellect. On the Tree of Life you find Hod opposite Netzach. Hod is the lowest Sephirah of the Pillar of Form, whereas Netzach represents perfect creativity. Hod as the opposite Sephirah is the sphere of the perfect intellect. In Netzach you feel the influence of divine inspiration, in Hod the so-called thoughtforms are created.

Thoughtforms are images of abstract forces created by fantasy. Thoughtforms are made by I-magi-nation. The arts were, in former days, a means of making these invisible forces visible. That resulted in religious paintings illustrating visions and in statues representing the gods, angels, and saints. The magical images of the Sephiroth are thoughtforms as well.

THOUGHTFORMS

Why are thoughtforms necessary? In some religions—Islam for example—it is forbidden to create images of sacred forces. Within the Roman Catholic faith, on the other hand, there is an extensive culture of imagery. The sphere of Hod is connected with the planetary forces of Mercury, and Mercury is connected with the ability to communicate. Communication with divine energies gets easier when we give them a form; otherwise they remain abstract and intangible. For example, I myself was never capable of building any relationship with abstract concepts of physics, such as mass, because I am not capable of building a useful and relevant thoughtform about it. God-forms and angelic powers are abstract forces as well, which is why they are relevant to my physics example. Most images of gods and angles look like human beings, but this imagery doesn't necessarily mean that gods and angels truly resemble humans. It means that they have a frequency on which they resonate within human beings, and we can tune into this wavelength of consciousness.

You can see a god or an angel as a mass of energy patterns on this same wavelength of consciousness. This is the idea behind the geometrical patterns in religious symbolism.

ELOHIM TZABAOTH

The godname of Hod is Elohim Tzabaoth. This means "Lord of Hosts." The godname indicates the abundance of forms that serve to clothe all these forces. Hod is connected with the creation of these thoughtforms. By making these thoughtforms, you can develop relationships with the divine, and you can communicate with it. Otherwise, it is very difficult to develop a relationship with, for example, archangels. They exalt above everything and are all-penetrating. They work on the smallest cell level as well as on a cosmic scale.

In rituals and during meditations, you consciously create a human form for these forces and connect them with symbols. You connect these images with the appropriate human characteristics. You also connect your images with appropriate clothes and attributes. You create all kinds of association chains. In this way, you can approach these forces with your feelings and your imagination. You build up the thoughtform around you, in you, before you. When you create such a thoughtform outside yourself, this is called evocation. When you build the thought-form inside yourself, this is called invocation.

COMMUNICATION

In spiritual magic, you try to develop a relationship with divine forces in order to activate the part within yourself that is connected with those forces. At the moment you can do this, you can tune in to these frequencies. In chapter 4 I explained to you the Law of Hermes Trismegistus: This law tells us:

> That which is Below corresponds to that which is Above, and that which is Above corresponds to that which is Below, to accomplish the miracles of the One Thing.

Within the Mysteries, we work with the Sephirah Hod to give form to divine forces. Then you become capable of tuning in to the "Above." You yourself are the "Below" from the Hermetic law. By attuning yourself with the right forces, you become an open channel between Above and Below *to accomplish the miracles of the One Thing,* as formulated in the Law of Hermes. Hod is the sphere wherein you can make yourself into a channel that can fine-tune into the frequencies of divinity.

FREQUENCIES OF DIVINE ENERGY

Compare Hod with a radio that is tuned to a certain broadcasting station. In Hod, all the keys to the different frequencies are systematically stored. These keys are the instruments that you use to search for the right wavelength. You use your mind as an instrument to broadcast a certain frequency, and to receive the messages of this wavelength.

When you have a certain interest or hobby, you put out feelers for anything that is connected to your passion. If you are a fan of a certain rock band, then you are interested in what news surrounds this group. This often leads to meeting certain people and forming relationships with them. The more important a certain passion in your life is, the more people you will have in your life connected to that interest. Because of this interest, all kinds of events will start to happen in your life, and in this way you create your karma and your life. The synchronization of certain cosmic channels takes place in the Sephirah Hod.

Let us assume that your passion is healing. Probably you work in a profession in health care, or you are an alternative healer. In both cases you can tune into the divine frequency, the broadcasting company of archangel Raphael. You will generate many experiences that are connected with healing. You can communicate with Raphael, and this means that you will be informed when new healing techniques are released from the Inner Planes. You will receive healing energy. You will slowly get inspiration from unknown sources and, by coincidence, meet the right people who teach you more about healing. Because of your experience connected to healing, you will, by consequence, attract people who are unhealthy. In this way, you will share sorrow with the people to whom you relate: you attract and cause karma.

Tuning into the frequency of "Radio Raphael" will become easier if you know on what frequency you can receive him, and you will be better able to hear his messages if you know on what range he emanates and how his voice sounds. The thoughtforms of gods and angels that have been made in history have already proven their effectiveness.

THOUGHTFORCE

The principle of frequencies of divinity has far-reaching consequences. Thoughts are powers to which you have access and that you can use to attune yourself to these frequencies. On the other hand, haven't we all experienced a bombardment of thoughts in our minds? You decide to which thoughts you give energy. Which thoughts do you take seriously? Which thoughts do you use to work with? These choices have a big influence on what you will witness and how you feel. You will realize the far-reaching consequences of thought power when you start to observe this mechanism. When you develop positive thoughts about yourself, you will feel good. You will attract good things in your life. If you think negatively about yourself, then this will work against you. When you influence your thoughts consciously in a positive way, things will start to happen more easily in your life.

"Energy follows thought," a magical law tells us. This means that, when you think intently in a certain way, and create images accompanying these thoughts, then you will generate events in your life. Advertisers make use of this mechanism. The "Adventurous World of Peter Stuyvesant" connected smoking cigarettes with the tough image of an explorer—but not with lung cancer. By associating a product with a positive self-image, the suggestion is created that using a product creates this desired self-image.

Spiritual magic anchors positive images and characteristics of yourself by means of imagination and the power of thought. Methods that we use are, among others, evocation and invocation. The stream of thoughts is anchored in the subconscious mind by means of concentration and imagination. Everything that is regulated by the subconscious mind does not need to be regulated by your conscious mind. You do not need to give the contents of your subconcious much energy. Breathing is one of the things your subconscious mind regulates for you. It is an automatic process. Thoughtforms are anchored in a deep layer of your subconscious mind, and this causes a stream of events in your environment.

IMAGINATION AS A RESOURCE

When you want to tune in to a divine frequency, you make use of a god or an angel to connect. This you can do by giving the god or the angel a human form and attributes. When the divine frequency has this human form, you can talk with it. You can create a relationship, and he or she will generate events and experiences and karma in your life.

Within the Mystery schools, we build thoughtforms consciously and precisely, to help our minds to resonate on the different frequencies. We decide in advance which channels we want to open, and we fixate these thoughtforms in our minds. We also decide consciously on what frequencies we do *not* want to resonate. In this way, you have influence on what coincidences happen in your life; they become phenomena that accompany your magical work. You determine what thoughts you want to give energy. The consequence is that you become responsible for how you feel, what choices you make, and on what potential future you concentrate. Thoughts are unbelievably powerful forces—they are instruments with which you color your life. Thoughforms and creating Thoughforms are powerful instruments for an initiated magician.

If Netzach is the Sephirah of beauty and power, then Hod is the sphere of the Vision of Splendor. Without this vision we can still experience splendor, but we need the Thoughtform to work with it. Without an all-encompassing image, the forces leak away in all directions, the concepts stay too fluid and will never become so solid that we can work with them. Because Hod creates form from abstraction, it is the Sephirah of magic par excellence.

ARCHANGEL MICHAEL AND THE BENI ELOHIM

Archangel Michael is the ruling archangel of Hod. This archangel is placed in the Southern quarter of the magical circle. He is the angel who is connected with the defense of light and truth. Michael is the angel who conquers Satan during the War in Heavens. He is also called the Prince of the Light. He was the commanding officer of the angels of light in the battle against the angels of darkness. He is the angel who spoke to Moses from the Burning Bush, and who announced the coming of the Shekinah. Michael leads the souls of the justified ones to the eternal light. His major qualities are protection, perfection, and power.

The angelic choir of Hod is called the Beni Elohim. They are the "Sons of God." There are different stories about the nature of the Beni Elohim. Tradition tells us that the Beni Elohim are the sons and daughters of the gods who came to earth to develop relationships with humanity. From these relationships a race of wise men came into being. In later times this race became discredited and was gradually eliminated.

In the ancient temples, the priesthood practiced the so-called Holy Marriage. A priest or a priestess connected himself with the energy of a god or a goddess. This entity had intercourse with a human being. The children that were born from these unions were called the Sons of God. In Greek mythology we find a number of examples of these demigods who came forth from such a union. "Son of God" was also a title that Christ used to present himself to humanity.

Another view of the Beni Elohim is that they are spiritual children. New inventions, thoughts, and inspiration are received because divine energies make contact with humanity. In this way, humanity can make big jumps in its development. According to this view, the Beni Elohim are energy frequencies: polarized human consciousness that reaches toward humanity to develop the human intelligence. They form a circuit of force between humanity and divinity. In this perspective, the Beni Elohim are lower divine thoughtforms that can make contact with the growing spirit of humanity. They are our first conscious contact with that part of divinity that tries to lift us Above the material human world. They are the god-gene that is embedded in our bodies, in our DNA. The human being is seen as a potential god. This viewpoint has the risk of blowing our egos out of proportion, and this can be the reason why the Sons of God sometimes receive such bad press.

THE MAGICAL IMAGE

The magical image belonging to Hod is the hermaphrodite. A hermaphrodite is an organism that is both male and female. The spiritual viewpoint belonging to this magical image is: when you are touched by the Beni Elohim your mind is exalted by a divine frequency of the opposite sex. Through this you develop yourself further to the point where you have interiorized your opposite anima or animus and have united it with your consciousness.

HERMES, HERMES TRISMEGISTUS, AND THOTH

The Greek god Hermes is the Messenger of the gods. He wears a winged helmet and winged sandals, which enables him to travel in two worlds. The expression of being "born with the helmet" originates from Hermes' helmet. Because of his ability to travel, he is connected on the lower levels with traveling and merchandising and, by association, with tricks and cheating. In this way, Hermes was downgraded to a god connected with the vices of lying and falsehood, and he became the god of traders and thieves.

Hermes belongs to the most ancient gods. In diverse pantheons he appears under different names, such as Hermes Trismegistus and the Three-Times Great Hermes. He is also known as the Egyptian god Thoth. Thoth is a creator god. He is the creator of the first image, the giver of writing and of the Word.

The Egyptian hieroglyphs consist of small drawings, and this holy script was drawn on the walls of the temples. Here the texts of important rituals were engraved. In this way, Thoth became the god of magical ceremonies. The Sephirah Hod is comparable with a big library where the world memory of humanity is stored in the form of images. In Hod we consciously work with the images and words that were given by the god Thoth.

By the precision with which Thoth measures, he is connected with the development of alchemy and, with that, of the sciences in general. The Sephirah Hod is connected with magic as a science. Magic is the science of the sacred. It studies the behavior of unseen currents of consciousness and researches how matter is influenced by the spirit. Until the Renaissance, magic was taught at universities. Thoth is the leading force behind these wavelengths of consciousness and, as Hermes Trismegistus, he is the leading entity behind the hermetic tradition as a Wisdom tradition.

SCHEDULE OF HOD

WORLD	DIVINE ASPECT	TAROT ASSOCIATIONS
Atziluth	God-name, Elohim Tzabaoth—Lord of the Hosts	Wands Eight: Lord of Swiftness
Briah	Archangel Michael	Swords Eight: Lord of Shortened Force
Yetzirah	Angelic Choir, Beni Elohim	Cups Eight: Lord of Abandoned Success
Assiah	Kochab, Mercury	Pentagrams Eight: Lord of Prudence

THE LANGUAGE OF MYTHS—
MEDITATIVE TRAINING IN HOD

The tarot is called the Book of Thoth or Tahuti, the
Egyptian Mercury. . . . The Atu of Tahuti, who is the
Lord of Wisdom, are also called Keys. They are guides
to conduct. They give you the map of the Kingdom
of Heaven, and also the best way to take it by force.
A complete understanding of any Magical problem is
necessary before it can be solved. Study from outside, and
actions from outside are always abortive.

ALEISTER CROWLEY, *THE BOOK OF THOTH*

The tarot is also called the Book of Thoth. This is a very appropriate title for the tarot, because the entire series of cards is drawn in the language of Thoth—symbolic language. The Book of Thoth is much more extensive than the sequence of the cards. The true Book of Thoth is equal to the entire world of appearances.

We are no longer used to symbolic language. In antiquity, symbolic language was a very common form of communication. In a time when many people were unable to read and write, it was a very effective way to transfer information. Also, memory was much more important than in our day and age, and it was used to connect important information. By association, connections were made in the subconscious mind that revealed insights about related subjects. These insights manifested themselves through symbolic language.

Old symbols are directly related to phenomena that are interconnected in nature, the climate, and the language. This makes symbolic language less accessible in our days. We no longer live as closely to nature as our ancestors, and we do not feel nature's influence as intensely with respect to our lives and our survival. This makes it more difficult to apply the symbols.

Within the Mystery tradition, working with symbolic language is essential. It is the method we use to make a direct connection with information stored on the subconscious level, or with currents of consciousness to which we are attuned. When we gain access to these currents, we can also change them.

THE LANGUAGE OF THE SUBCONSCIOUS MIND

Think about the stuff of your dreams. Dreams are created in the world of the subconscious mind. In dreams we are in all kinds of situations, we see images, and we experience emotions. Some say that dreams are a deception. In the Mysteries, we do not share this viewpoint. Dreams are real experiences that we encounter in a parallel reality: it is the reality of our mythical mind. They give us a lot of information about how we are doing. They determine the quality of our sleep, and they are very important in influencing how we feel during the day.

Meditating on symbols, and learning to understand the archaic symbol language, generates experiences that are comparable to dreams, but there are a few important differences. First of all, in your meditations you yourself determine which inner realities you tune in to. In addition, you learn to understand the language, and in this way, you will understand the content of your experiences. By learning symbolic language, you create a bridge between your conscious mind and your subconscious mind. In this way, you gradually build a direct communication line with divine frequencies: with "Radio Raphael" and the other broadcasting companies.

The evocations and invocations are formulas to open these lines of communication. To master these, you need to use your imagination, symbols, and language. The tables of correspondences that you find in books about magic are based on associations of *inner experiences* generated by these symbols at the moment you really contact them. Also, these correspondences are hidden in mythological stories and fairy tales: myths are how our ancestors passed on important Knowledge of the Mysteries.

THE LANGUAGE OF MYTHOLOGY

Myths were constructed very precisely in antiquity, because within the core of the mythical stories were hidden the keys to the Mysteries. When in a mythical story details such as a narcissus flower are mentioned, this is important information. The flower is not a lily, a rose, or some other plant. At that moment, the flower relates to a state of consciousness. In the case of a narcissus, the flower indicates the search for self-knowledge.

These inner experiences of symbolic language can be generated within yourself by means of meditation, contemplation, and study. First of all, you will need to build a vocabulary, because without "words" you cannot learn a language, and you cannot understand what is communicated. This is a slow process. Gradually you need to make a connection between your intellect and your intuition, and this connection can be made through meditations over a long period of time. This means several years of daily systematic meditation. These meditations are not spectacular in the beginning. They simply ask for a daily discipline.

LEARNING THE LANGUAGE OF SYMBOLS

In doing the exercise for Hod, you will notice that there are no shortcuts to attaining magical skill. Meditation work sometimes is like homework. Here are the finger exercises to learn to play the keyboard of the Kabbalistic grand piano. When you start to learn symbolic language, you spend several days on each symbol. Before you begin, do some research in good books to give yourself a background. The easiest method is to follow the sequence below and also use all your senses: seeing, hearing, feeling, tasting, and smelling.

1. *First of all you pick an object. As an example I'll use the pen, because the pen belongs to the Sephirah Hod.*

2. *Enter into a meditative state. By doing the Middle Pillar exercise, you*

generate magical energy. In this way you also create some distance between the exercise and the thoughts coming from your daily life. You do not want to be disturbed by these everyday thoughts.

3. When you are sufficiently relaxed, visualize the pen before your inner eye. When you have fixed it, enter into a receptive state of mind and ask the Inner Planes to give you additional information about the pen. First of all, natural associations will come up, because you encounter them daily. You might see paper as an association, for example. Then a few other modern associations might arise, such as computers, keyboards, and printers. Follow these associations until you feel you have examined them all.

4. The next step is to ask for older information. Concentrate on your pen so that it stabilizes before you. Now you may recieve associations of a feather and ink; with parchment and papyrus; of a piece of wood and clay; or a finger writing in the sand. The quantity of these symbols is connected with your previous knowledge of the history of writing. But what if you suddenly see a tongue and a sword?

5. From the moment other symbols that you do not recognize from your direct experience start to appear, your subconscious mind is joining. Now you need to ask yourself whether these symbols are still connected with the pen, or if you have started to get distracted. Do you go further on the links of this association chain? Or do you stop it here and refocus on the image of the pen? Can you connect the things you see, smell, hear, and taste to the pen?

6. Each subject takes a few days to research and to gather the associations. Then the period comes where your mind is dry and is not capable of thinking of something new. Nonetheless, stay in a state of expectation and receptiveness.

7. Take a good encyclopedia of mythical symbols and go on with the associations you find there. It will take you to the next step.

You will find that you can easily meditate for a week on one symbol. During the meditation you will get dry periods until your realizations bring you to a deeper layer of meaning.

The pen is, of course, just one of the symbols connected to Hod. But there are more objects connected to this sphere. You can choose an endless series of symbols and follow the association chains in your mind. At a certain point, you will discover that the symbols are starting to explain each other. In this process, the logical mind will gradually make room for the subconscious mind to play a part in the dialogue, and your understanding of symbolic language will grow.

DECIPHERING ICONOGRAPHY

Slowly you will start to apply this knowledge to the iconography of magical and alchemical pictures. Gradually you will discover that these mysterious pictures are a kind of mandala. As you work longer with the pictures, the meanings slowly unfold. This work is not finished. When you think you have unraveled a symbol to the bottom, it reappears unexpectedly in a totally different context, and then you get a full layer of meaning and associations that unfold on top of the knowledge you already had.

At first this is a very dry exercise. But after a while it will pay you back more than the effort. Compare this exercise with practicing musical scales while learning to play an instrument. They are necessary exercises. At a certain moment, you have enough keys in your hands, and then the process will unwind before your inner eye like a movie. The symbols develop into a real language, which gives you access to the deepest layers of your self. The meditation on symbols will develop into deep mystical experiences.

Nature's symbols haven't lost any of their inner meaning. Nature still contains the symbols of the ancient cultures. In spite of the time that has passed, in spite of the differences in culture and circumstances of life, their legacy is still accessible to us. Around us the landscape still holds the key to the language of the gods.

Gather the knowledge and insights you acquired by doing these exercises into an orange ball. Make a buckle of it and hang it on your cincture at your right hip.

YESOD, THE FOUNDATION

The Ninth Path is called the Pure Intelligence because it purifies the Emanations. It proves and corrects the designing of their representations, and disposes the unity with which they are designed without diminution or division.

SEPHER YETZIRAH

Yesod is also called the Treasure House of Images. In Hod I also talked about images. What is the difference between the images of Hod and those of Yesod? Hod is a Sephirah of the mind and Yesod a Sephirah of basic matrixes. When spiritual energy condenses in matrixes, it can crystallize on those matrixes in different patterns.

As a metaphor, you can imagine this process like the dew that condenses on a spider's web. The threads of the web are at first invisible, but the pattern is there. The spiritual energy condenses on the matrix, and then the web becomes tangible and visible.

There are countless patterns whereon things can manifest themselves. There is a matrix for every plant, every animal, and every chemical substance. Every material has a basic pattern that underlies the form. This matrix determines in what form matter crystallizes when it manifests in Malkuth. In this way, the patterns of every manifested thing are stored in Yesod.

This is why Yesod is called the Foundation. The vision of Yesod is given the image of the Vision of the Machinery of the Universe.

TIDES

Another way of viewing Yesod is to visualize it as a great ocean with tides. The moon's influence on the tides is connected to Yesod, and the Hebrew name of the moon is Levanah. The Cosmic Waters of spiritual energy condense on the web of matrixes, and these are subject to tidal fluctuations. There are fruitful times when the tide is "in," during which everything comes to its fullest manifestation, and there are times when the tide is "out"—during which everything withdraws itself and is made undone. In between ebb and flow there is dead tide. The Cosmic Tides work in the same way as the motion of the ocean caused by the moon.

With Yesod, we are talking about the third important Sephirah of the magical triangle. In Netzach, the most important energy is desire. Desire, however, creates a vacuum. Because the universe craves balance, it will start to fill the emptiness. In Hod, this emptiness is translated into images and thoughts. In Yesod, these images and desires condense upon the framework of the matrixes.

THE ASTRAL WORLD

Yesod forms the entrance to the astral world. The word *astral* refers to the stars. It has become a generic term for a range of different types of consciousness and indicates that the mind is active on layers other than that of daily consciousness. The psyche picks up images and creates from other states of consciousness, such as the dream world.

In the Mystery Tradition, we divide consciousness into different intensities. It is a gradual scale starting from full consciousness, which leads us through daydreams, trance, and meditation, to sleep. The most peculiar viewpoint of this concept is that death is also seen as a state of consciousness.

In the Mystery Tradition, we see these levels of consciousness as parallel worlds, each with its own natural laws. Within each layer consciousness acts according to certain patterns. It is very important not to mix up the levels of consciousness. In other words: when you are having a dream, you have experiences in the dream reality. They do not have the same meaning in the world of daily consciousness—a translation must be made. Experiences encountered in trance are realties within the world of trance-consciousness. Yesod is, in this way, connected to the subconscious.

Everything you experience in trance, in your dreams, in your meditations is true . . . on its own level of reality!

The subconscious mind contains a gigantic potential of power. Not only is it the place where all suppressed parts of consciousness are stored, it is, at the same time, the place where as yet undeveloped talents are waiting to be discovered. Enormous reservoirs of life energy are available when the time is ripe and the channels to use them have developed.

VITAL LIFE FORCE

The God-name belonging to Yesod is Shaddai El Chai, which means "almighty living God." This title is connected with the divine force of fertility. The location of Yesod is the genital center, where all the organs connected with procreation are found. In Yesod, the energies of the higher Sephiroth are received and collected. They are woven into a pattern and born from Yesod. The magical image of Yesod is a beautiful, strong naked man. This could as easily be a beautiful, receptive fertile woman. This is again a reference to the reservoir of vital life force belonging to Yesod. The life force stored in Yesod is, in Eastern systems, connected to Kundalini Shakti, the snake who is rolled up in the genital center and rises through all the centers along the spine.

ARCHANGEL GABRIEL AND THE ASHIM

The name Gabriel means the "mighty one of God." He is the archangel who is associated with the coming of the redeemer. In his hands he holds up a horn. This instrument can be used in two ways. You can turn a horn into a trumpet, which then acts as a sound amplifier, and you can also see it as the horn of plenty, a symbol for fertility. Like the angel himself, the horn is ambiguous. As a horn it is a phallic symbol. As the horn of plenty it is female. It turns into a chalice. Gabriel is seen as the divine Messenger, bringing the Word. Gabriel is associated with the moon; he is the archangel of the tides of life and fertility. Gabriel is also the archangel connected to resurrection from death. You can see him on the tarot card the Judgment, together with his horn.

The angelic choir of Yesod is called the Ashim, which means "the fire soul." The essence of humans is seen as a divine spark, a fire soul. The Ashim are the spirits of the ancestors, the souls of humanity who passed the test of justice after their physical death.

LEVANAH—THE MOON

Levanah, the Hebrew name for the moon flame, refers to the spiritual sphere of the moon. This is the unseen energy of the moon that causes change, growing, and shrinking. It is the active moon sphere. The lunar sphere is described in antiquity in terms of the twenty-eight mansions of the moon. Every mansion represents one day of the cycle of the moon, during which it waxes or wanes. Often, gods are connected to the houses. The waxing moon is connected to growing vitality, the waning moon to shrinking.

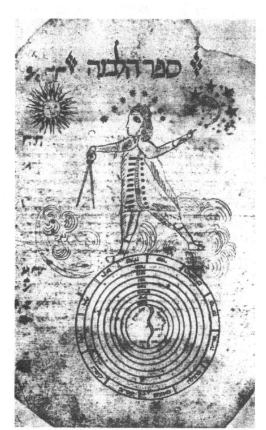

Sepher ha-Levanah. At the front of this sixteenth-century manuscript is pictured an astrologer who balances the sun and the moon. He holds a compass. He is standing on a globe in which the seven spheres of heaven are pictured. In the outer ring you see the zodiac.

The moon is the very first instrument used by our ancestors to measure time. The entire agricultural calendar was based on its cycle and was in use long before the solar year was. The waxing and waning moon are also seen as indicators of the Astral Tides. Compare this with the oceans on the earth. The ebb and flow of the tides are by the influence of the moon. On the Astral Plane, the moon is the clock of the time of the great Cosmic Ocean. She indicates the times of divine consciousness. You can study these Astral Tides, and as a magician, influence the outcomes of these powers. Also, you can use the mythology of the starry heaven and of the cosmos magically. This phenomenology belongs to stellar magic, the secrets of the Sea Mysteries of antiquity. These Mysteries belong to the oldest streams of magic. Even in the oldest Egyptian pyramid texts this magic is mentioned.

The study of the Astral Tides was the task of the priest-astrologers from antiquity, and influencing the effects caused by the astral tide was the job of the priest-magician. The priest-magician also interpreted the spiritual meaning of these phenomena. In magic, this work is extremely specialized: you can say that many are called for the job but few are chosen.

Under the influence of the waxing moon, new things will come to life easily and will blossom. With a waning moon it is easy to cause things to disappear from your life. Classically, the appearances of the moon are connected to all kinds of applications of so-called low magic. This is the form of magic that was often used by farmers to gauge the rhythm of planting and sowing.

Within the Mystery tradition, we also work with the Astral Tides, but here we use them as an indicator of times when it is easier to communicate with divinity. The same knowledge is used in planning great religious feasts connected with the lunar calendar. The appearances of the moon are also used as omens.

SCHEDULE OF YESOD

WORLD	DIVINE ASPECT	TAROT ASSOCIATIONS
Atziluth	God-name, Shaddai el Chai— The Almighty Living One	Wands Nine: Lord of Great Strength
Briah	Archangel, Gabriel	Swords Nine: Lord of Despair and Cruelty
Yetzirah	Angelic Choir, Cherubim	Cups Nine: Lord of Material Happiness
Assiah	Planet, Levanah, the Moon	Pentagrams Nine: Lord of Material Gain

THE JOURNEY OF
THE MOON GOD—RITUAL

*It is justly that the Moon is regarded as the Star of the
Spirit. It fulfills the Earth and fertilizes bodies when he
approaches. He empties them when he leaves. Even the
human blood increases and decreases on the Moonlight.
Leaves and herbs also react on this. It is the same force
penetrating in everything.*

PLINIUS THE OLDER (23–79 CE)

PREPARATIONS FOR THE RITUAL IN YESOD

This ritual meditation is meant to align you with the different aspects
of the moon. During a month, the moon shows her different faces. She
has mansions in the different constellations. Some of these constellations are part of the zodiac, but not all. Against the background of the
stars, the moon has her own—different—course than that of the sun.
The mansions of the moon are not similar to the houses of the horoscope. They are areas of the night sky through which the moon appears
to travel. The moon mansions are pictured on Cylinder B of Gudea,
dating from 2600 BCE.

If you look at the plan of the mansions of the moon, you will see that
the moon visits seven mansions in each cardinal direction. The exotic
names within the circle are the Arabic names of the stars in which the
moon has her residences.

In this way, the moon travels through the night sky and visits all
twenty-eight palaces. The time of a mooncycle from new moon to new
moon is twenty-nine days. This means that every month the full moon
appears in the next mansion. The full moon then radiates with a different
astral energy in the background and, because of this, the naturre of the
powers of the moon change every month. The Astral Tide slowly changes
between ebb and flow. The twenty-eight palaces are easy to place in the

Shamash de Sun, Sin de Moon, and Isthar Venus. Louvre, Paris.

temple of the Mysteries. In every cardinal direction the moon has seven residences.

Nanna is the name of the Sumerian moon god. The Sumerian civilization is among the oldest in the world, and from this culture derives the most ancient written text from human history.

Necessities:

> Background music: the waves of the sea
> Silver altar cloth
> Silver shawl
> Silver candle
> A silver disc standing upright in a bracket
> Black bowl filled with water
> Jasmine oil
> Salt
> 14 tea lights, white
> 14 tea lights, violet

I advise you to do this entire ritual first with a full moon. Then you wait for two weeks before starting to work on each cardinal direction in a separate ritual. In one week you do a quarter of this ritual, completing the entire ritual in four weeks: at the new moon, the half waxing moon, the full moon, the half waning moon, and the new moon. If you then want to deepen your realizations even more, you can take each of the mansions* of the moon for a meditation subject.

Prepare your ritual room. Put the altar in the middle of the room, and this time you cover it with the silver altar cloth. Put the silver scarf over your shoulders. Put the silver disc upright in the middle of the altar. Next to it you place the central altar light. This time you use a silver candle as your taper. Place a black bowl filled with water in the middle of your altar in such a way that the silver disc is reflected in the water. The white tea lights are placed in a half circle from the East to the South. The violet tea lights complete the circle and are divided between West and North. The moon palaces and the signs of the zodiac are divided over the cardinal directions in the temple according to this plan.

This ritual has been arranged so that the signs of the zodiac are written clockwise. Assume that the constellations are pictured above you—on the ceiling of the temple.

THE JOURNEY OF THE MOON GOD

Choose a time when it is dark, and the full moon is visible in the heavens. When you have prepared everything, wash your hands and your face with water to which you have added a little bit of salt and a drop of jasmine oil.

You can do this ritual outside if you are lucky and have a pool nearby. In that case, the pool takes the place of the black bowl with water. The full moon then radiates into the water instead of the silver disc.

---

*The names of the moon mansions are the names as written down by the Sufimaster Muhyiddin Ibn 'Arabi (1165–1240 CE).

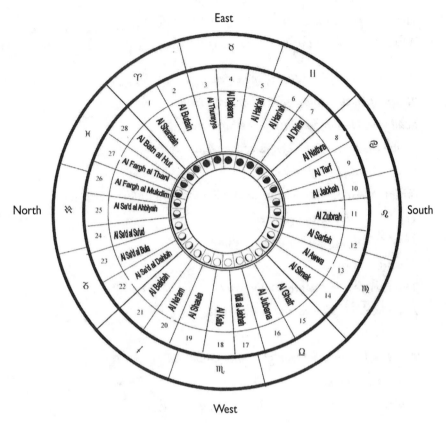

East

West

North

South

The mansions of the Moon

Again, start with the opening ceremony. Make the Kabbalistic Cross and call up the Pentagrams. Stand in the middle of your temple, and fold both your hands before your heart as if you're holding it. Start by saying the Prayer to the Gods of the Night:*

"I appear before your eyes to learn,
Teach me the old profession of the tupsharru-priest.†
I pray to the Gods of the Night,
To Thee who are asleep and dwell in the Cosmic Ocean.

---

*The text of the Prayer to the Gods of the Night is inspired by several texts from Old Babylonia from 2000 BCE.
†The tupsharru-priest was a Babylonian priest who specialized in the interpretation of the signs and omens that appeared in the night sky.

The human flock is quiet
And I open the portals to the heavens."

Here you make the gesture of the Opening of the Veils.
"I call upon the Moon god, I call upon Nanna.
I call you, Nanna, who aren't asleep now,
I open the bolts of the Doors of Heaven:
I ask you and I pray to you
Initiate me in the knowledge of the Enuma Anu Enlil. *
The Gods sleep in the Heaven.
They do not judge, they do not decide.
The night is veiled,
The Temple and the most holy places
Are covered in silence and in darkness.
I am the traveler on his quest,
And I call upon the Moon god while Shamash†
has withdrawn himself in his room,
I call upon the Great Ones, the Gods of the Night."

Here you sprinkle salt in the bowl of water and say:
"As Above, so Below,
The Cosmic Ocean reflects.
He mirrors himself in the oceans of the Earth."

Now you sprinkle some drops of jasmine oil on the surface of the water, and a drop of jasmine oil on every candle you have prepared.
"A sacrifice for Nanna, a scent that will delight him:
Nanna, appear in the night sky

---

*The Enuma Anu Enlil is a text in cuneiform writing that was found in the library of the Akkadian king Ashurbanipal (669–626 BCE). The text consists of a collection of omens related to astrological phenomena. The tablets are based on the rising and descending of planets and the appearances of the moon.
†Shamash is the Akkadian sun god.

And mirror yourself in the waters of the oceans below."

Now you sprinkle the water from the bowl around you on the floor of the meditation space to purify the place and make it more attractive for Nanna.

"I call upon the stars,

Who light the nightly Mansions of the Moon:

O, great Gods of the Night.

He who names all the stars,

Knows for sure that he gets what he desires!

I call upon all of you, the pure Heaven, the pure Earth,

The pure stars of the High Heavens,

The pure stars of the Low Heavens.

Pure Gods, pure Goddesses.

My lips are pure, my hands are washed.

I call upon you:

The stars of the North, the South, the East, and the West.

The famous stars and the smaller stars

Which are not visible with the bare eye,

Who cannot be seen by the superficial observer.

I call upon the stars of the Paths of Anu, Enlil, and Ea. *

Surround me, all of you, gather yourselves around me.

I have prepared a pure sacrifice for you.

I sacrifice pure incense.

Appear to me and enlighten me with the knowledge for which I am searching."

Light the silver altar candle and speak the following text:

"I open the mansions of the moon and the first heavenly palace opens
the way that starts at the dark moon. The path of the dark moon leads

---

*The Path of Anu is an area with a width of seventeen degrees at both sides of the heavenly equator. The Path of Enlil is the Northern half of the heaven, and the Path of Ea is the Southern part of the heaven.

to Al Batn al Hut. It is the belly of the heavenly Whale where the initiate rests for three days and nights between the stars."

Walk to the East and light a white candle every time you seek access to a moon place in the Eastern quarter. When you open the moon mansion, you enter into meditation for a short moment. You connect yourself to the answer of the moon god, and try to feel which images come toward you on the energy.

From the waxing moon until the full moon, you work with the rising astral tide. During this tide, new insights of the cosmos stream toward you as well as new events, opportunities, and chances. After the full moon and during the waning moon, the tides withdraw. That which you want to release can be taken back on these tides; they return to the Primordial Ocean.

Start your work in the East with the gesture of the Opening of the Veils:
"I open the seven palaces of the Moon
At the Eastern side of the firmament.
I call up the Lights that illuminate these Mansions,
I ask access to the waves of the Cosmic Ocean."

1. *Nanna, open to me the path of flood leading to Al Sharatian, the mansion of the two faces. Tell me about this palace of the divine essence.*

"Here the great journey starts, the search and the quest. Open your heart as I bring you the knowledge of the first intellect, which is symbolized by the pen."

2. *Nanna, open to me the path of flood leading to Al Butain. Tell me about the belly of Aries, and about the mansion of the one who calls.*

"I am the one who calls! I lead you to the light of the universal soul, which is symbolized by the prepared clay tablet: ready to become engraved with experiences."

3. *Nanna, open to me the path of flood leading to Al Thurayya, the many little lights of the Pleiades. Bring me the many little insights and realizations, the knowledge from within.*

"Every light opens like a flower and carries the image leading to redemption. This is why the symbol of this palace is the interior."

4. **Nanna, open to me the path of flood leading to Al Dabaran, the disciple. Tell me about the palace that lightens up the eye of the Heavenly Bull.**

"In this mansion, the first material is created that you can use to build solid houses for your ideals. The symbol for this palace is the position of the last one, because you follow the road of those who lit this road before you."

5. **Nanna, open to me the path of flood leading to Al Hak'ah. Tell me about the palace of the white spot of the Heavenly Bull.**

"The body of the bull creates a fertile soil where new life can root and grow. That is why the keyword of the mansion is manifestation."

6. **Nanna, open to me the path of flood leading to Al Han'ah. Tell me about the mansion of the little star with the great light in the sign of Gemini.**

"This light is also called the insignia of the wise. This moon palace shows you that Wisdom is created from embracing two opposites."

7. **Nanna, open to me the path of flood leading to Al Dhira. Tell me about the mansion of the Throne, located in the embrace of the Twins.**

"This palace teaches you that you are carried by your warm relationships with the people who surround you."

Now you have gained access to the seven moon mansions of the Eastern Heaven. All these palaces have a clear relationship with the first quarter of the moon. You will now create access to the Southern palaces.

Walk to the South, again light the white candles one by one. When opening the moon mansion you go into a short meditation and connect yourself with the answer of the moon god. Feel the energy rise. It is still rising tide here.

Make the gesture of the Opening of the Veils:

"I open the seven Mansions of the Moon
At the Southern Heaven of the firmament.
I call upon the lights that enlighten these palaces.
I ask access to the waves of the Cosmic Ocean
Which color the spirituality of these forces."

8. *Nanna, open to me the path of flood leading to Al Nathra. Tell me about the mansion located between the pincers of Cancer, the palace that is connected with friendship and gratefulness.*

"The symbol of the palace is the footstool, a sign that there also is a place to rest and to enjoy yourself during the quest."

9. *Nanna, open to me the path of flood leading to Al Tarf. Tell me about the mansion that is called the splendor of Cancer.*

"The Heavenly Waters surrounding this palace cause waves and movements bringing independence and wealth because of the attractive powers of the moon. The night does not wear many stars on her robes here."

10. *Nanna, open to me the path of flood leading to Al Jabhah. Tell me about the mansion located in the forehead of Cancer.*

"This is the palace of the mighty ones. These Waters offer access to the highest heavens and the deepest depths of the soul. In this palace the Opener of the Ways prepares the road for the redeemer."

11. *Nanna, open to me the path of flood leading to Al Zubra. Tell me about the mansion located in the hair of the Lion.*

"In this mansion lives the highest light, the Redeemer of the World. This palace is also called the lotus of the final border. It is the heavenly flower that spreads the scent of sanctity."

12. *Nanna, open to me the path of flood leading to Al Sarfah, the changer. Tell me about the mansion located in the tail of the Lion.*

"In this palace are stored the ability and the power to divide the Heavenly Waters and the oceans of the earth. He Who Knows uses the snake wand to accomplish this."

13. **Nanna, open to me the path of flood leading to Al Awwa. Tell me about the mansion located in the wings of the Heavenly Virgin.**

"The barking dog at her feet is the announcer of the swelling of the heavenly rivers. This is the source. Here the Descent begins—the watershed."

14. **The moon is full. Her light radiates in the darkness and exalts all the spiritual forces. Nanna, open for me the path of light leading to Al Simak. Tell me about the mansion located in the ear of corn of the Virgin.**

"She is the unprotected purest light. This is the palace where the wise and the gods arrive when they Ascend to Heaven."

Walk to the West. Now the moon starts to wane, and you are dealing with the withdrawing tide. The creative forces recede in the primordial ocean. You now work with the violet candles. As the forces of the moon withdraw, the Cosmic Tide ebbs, and the Waters flow back to the source. It is now time to give back the items that were unfruitful: let them float back on the currents and return to the nothingness.

Make the gesture of the Opening of the Veils:
**"I open the seven Mansions of the Moon
At the Western Heaven of the Firmament.
I call upon the Lights who light these Palaces."**

15. **Nanna, open to me the path of ebb leading to Al Gafr. Tell me about the heavenly palace located in the sign of the Scales.**

"Here you balance your life. What is balanced in your life? When a lid is lifted, everything that was hidden is exposed to the light. It is time to change directions."

16. *Nanna, open to me the path of ebb leading to Al Jubana. Tell me about the heavenly palace located in the Southern Claw of the Scales.*

"In this palace the stars cause pressure, revealing the truth of your life, and you have to take responsibility for all the sins you have committed."

17. *Nanna, open to me the path of ebb leading to Iklil al Jabhah. Tell me about the heavenly palace located in the crown of the constellation Scorpio.*

"It is called the house of illustrations. In this mansion the moon exalts your powers. You know where you can find your resources."

18. *Nanna, open to me the path of ebb to Al Kalb. Tell me about the heavenly palace located in the red heart of the constellation Scorpio.*

"The waters surrounding this palace consist of meteorites and fire. When the moon travels through this area, all the inessentials are taken away by the fiery forces of purification."

19. *Nanna, open to me the path of ebb to Al Shaula, the sting of the Scorpio. Tell me about this heavenly palace.*

"Here all illnesses and unbalanced forces are discharged to the heavenly source. The light that shines in this palace is called the living one."

20. *Nanna, open to me the path of ebb to Al Na'am. Tell me about the moon palace that is located in the arrow of Sagittarius.*

"This palace is surrounded by heavenly water. Here you find the great water well. Over it are two wooden beams on which hang pulley blocks to pull up the Heavenly Waters. Over these beams, ostriches and camels cross the heavenly river. In these Astral Waters the thoughtforms are pulled up from all the animals that will be born in the new spring."

21. *Nanna, open for me the path of ebb to Al Baldah. Tell me about the mansion of the moon located above the horns of the Sea Goat in the sign of Sagittarius.*

"In this palace lives the giver of death. In this mansion you find an entire city in which the souls of the deceased live. It is also called the Ostrich Nest."

Walk to the North. Make the gesture of the Opening of the Veils:

"I open the seven Mansions of the Moon

At the Northern Heaven of the Firmament.

I call upon the Lights that enlighten these palaces."

22. *Nanna, open to me the path of ebb to Al Sa'd al Dhabih.*

"In this palace lives the shepherd of souls. He is the jewel that is carried on the horns of Capricorn."

23. *Nanna, open for me the path of ebb to Al Sa'd al Bula. Tell me about the mansion that is located in Capricorn.*

"This palace contains the gate of the gods; the royal road of the descent of life. It is the path over which a procession of lights descends into matter, preceded by the greatest light, the newborn redeemer."

24. *Nanna, open to me the path of ebb to Al Sa'd al Su'ud. Tell me about the light that is lit in this mansion.*

"This mansion determines the luck and fate of the king. Aquarius pours out his gifts over the earth. From this moon palace, manna falls from the heavens. The season of new growth is prepared. The bellies of the animals grow bigger, caused by their pregnancies."

25. *Nanna, open to me the path of ebb to Al Sa'd al Ahbiya. Tell me about the mansion of the moon that hides the fortune of the concealed.*

"This palace is located in the bowl of the Water Bearer. A flight of angels is poured out to prepare the life when the daylight grows in this season."

26. *Nanna, open to me the path of ebb to Al Fargh al Mukdim. Tell me about the moon mansion that causes the new sprouts to surface.*

"This palace awakens the Djinns, who become active again. They imprint the thoughtforms of the new life into the prepared matrixes on the Astral Plane."

27. *Nanna, open to me the path of ebb to Al Fargh al Thani. Tell me about the mansion that is located in the constellation Pisces.*

"This palace is woven from flax thread. Here the astral cord is woven of everything that will be born. It keeps every living being connected to the roots in heaven."

28. *Nanna, open to me the first heavenly palace of the moon. Tell me about the mansion of the dark moon.*

"The path of the dark moon leads to Al Batn al Hut. It is the belly of the heavenly Whale, the place where the initiate rests for three days and three nights between the stars."

Now all the candles are burning, and you have visited the entire circle of the moon mansions once. Meditate about their connections. Write down your realizations. Be aware that realizations will pop up over time after having finished this ritual. When you have concluded, you close the veils starting from the North and moving counter- clockwise. You thank Nanna for the realizations he gives you. Then you close your magical circle. You leave the candles to burn down, because this is your sacrifice to Nanna in exchange for his knowledge.

Collect all the insights and experiences belonging to the Sephirah Yesod into a violet ball and store it in your genital center. When you return to Yesod in the future, you can unfold the ball into cosmic proportions. It will still contain the pow- ers that you have stored there now, and you can add new experiences and realiza- tions of Yesod.

11

MALKUTH, THE MYSTERIES OF THE EARTH

MALKUTH, THE KINGDOM

The Tenth Path is called the Resplendent Intelligence, because it is exalted above every head and sits upon the throne of Binah. It illuminates the splendors of all the Lights, and causes an influence to emanate from the Prince of Countenances, the Angel of Kether.

SEPHER YETZIRAH

We have arrived at the Sephirah forming the bottom of the Tree of Life. The Sephirah Malkuth is drawn under the feet of Adam Kadmon. The Sephirah is devoted to the earth and all the forces of manifestation and growth.

From a spiritual viewpoint, Malkuth is the most important Sephiroth. However beautiful and exalted the higher Sephiroth may be, when their powers are not earthed, the beautiful visions and realizations keep hanging

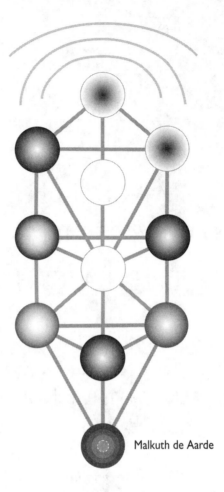

Malkuth de Aarde

in thin air. People with an especially mystical makeup sometimes have great difficulties with the earth, and appear to fly away from it.

On the other hand, the opposite is equally true. When the gifts of the earth are not spiritualized, then your life on this globe remains flat, meaningless, mechanical, and functional. That is often the feeling of modern people within Western civilization. It is accompanied by a feeling of desperation and instability. Life is no longer lived in a transcendental way, and there is no connection with a source of significance. This lack of inner values and vision is often acted out in aggression and materialism.

Malkuth is the end result of all the divine forces who, in their richness, come down from the source. Malkuth, the earth, is sacred. Seen from this point of view, escaping from the trials of the earth in asceticism and visions are the blasphemy of the mystic. Denying the sacredness of the earth by denying all the divinity of matter is the blasphemy of science.

THE MARRIAGE BETWEEN HEAVEN AND EARTH

Within the field of magic, all matter is seen as ensouled. All matter is built up on a divine matrix. The divine matrix contains a spiritual frequency where upon it manifests in perfect harmony with the less manifested frequencies of consciousness. The material world is the crystallization of all the spiritual forces streaming downward from the source in Kether. This happens under the influence of the archangel Metatron. The magician Gareth Knight describes Kether and Malkuth as two terminals of a great cosmic battery. One end in Kether is the pole of spirit, the other end in Malkuth is the pole of matter. Spirit and matter are two sides of the same coin.

This principle of the undividable interconnectedness between the highest spiritual regions and the earth is an important starting point in the most ancient cultures.

On page 332 you see a picture of the palette of Narmer. Narmer was an Egyptian pharaoh who probably lived around 3030 BCE. In general it is assumed that this palette represents the foundation of the state of Egypt. One side of the palette is connected to Upper Egypt, and the other side to Lower Egypt.

The palette has a second meaning that is not as well known. Upper Egypt is a metaphor for heaven. Lower Egypt is a metaphor for earth. At the moment that the two lands are connected, this pharaoh gives us a vision of the mission statement of the entire Egyptian culture: connecting the two lands. In the ancient Mesopotamian culture this was expressed as the *Hieros Gamos,* the Sacred Marriage between Heaven and Earth.

The ability to experience your spirituality within your daily life, on the mundane level, is the goal of spiritual magic. As William Blake said: "To see a world in a grain of sand, and a heaven in a wild flower. . . ."

*Palette of Narmer,
Northern side*

SYNCHRONICITY

Carl Jung described this as integrating consciousness and named one of the effects it has on the human mind "synchronicity." Synchronicity comes forth from an experience of mystical at-oneness. Synchronicity occurs when the phenomena of the mundane intersects with the inner meaningful world. The outer signs and the inner experiences appear at the same time or within a short time frame, creating a meaningful coincidence. The material phenomena feel like an undividable part of the inner experience.

Synchronicity can appear on a small scale and on a very big scale. At the moment that the inner and the outer phenomena coincide, intense peak experiences take place. The appearance of these phenomena is one of the signs of magic in full motion. Within the Mystery school this is called the earthly check.

Synchronicity in magic is a phenomenon that is interpreted slightly differently from other traditions. The word *synchronicity* is often used to explain the mechanism behind divination methods such as, for example, tarot cards. But the phenomenon is much bigger. It is an ongoing phenomenon, and you can resonate upon the currents. If you are able to find the right pitch, you can use it to create. The art of the training in the Mysteries is to fine-tune to these phenomena, and then you can work with these forces: as Below, so Above. When you are capable of doing that, your magic really starts to work. I will give you a short example to show you what I mean.

An important event needed to be blessed and marked by means of a ritual. Using magical techniques, I looked for a favorable day for this ritual. That date was set several months before the event, and then the preparations began.

A ritual is always written based on the instructions of the Inner Plane Master. Then a series of events is put into motion that will have an effect both on the Inner Planes and outer planes. On the day of the ritual, people came from all sides of the Netherlands and from abroad. Some people gathered together in my house, and it became very clear that each traveler had been accompanied on his or her journey to my house by a series of rainbows. When I stepped out of my door myself, I immediately faced a double rainbow in the morning sky.

During the trip to the location for the ritual more rainbows appeared, and on arriving at the meeting place the series of rainbows were the topic of conversation. The rainbow is a symbol of the bridge between heaven and earth. The gods showed us that the connecting road was open.

The day was intense, and the ritual went very well. The program lasted all day, and it was already night when I came home. Then I got a phone call to check the news on the Internet, and after doing so, immediately got in my car to drive to a dark place. The northern lights were visible on that night in the Netherlands! The day started with the light of the gods and was crowned by them in the end.

THE GRAIN MYSTERIES

*Sleeping Melissae and Priest kings, resting in the Belly
of the Earth Goddess: her sacred Omphalos. Wake up
from the subterranean beehives of the Earth! Priest kings,
resting under a golden heaven of woven honeycomb, wake
up! I feed you with honey. Follow the call of the queen
bee, she is awake and challenges you to continue the Great
Work. Together we will feed the Bee folk with milk and
honey.*

FOR THE SLEEPING PRIEST KINGS

The Sephirah Malkuth is connected to the Grain Mysteries. The god-name
that belongs to Malkuth is Adonai Ha Aretz. The name means "Lord of
the Land" or "Lord of the Earth." The gods associated with Malkuth are
the so-called Corn Gods. Examples of Corn Gods are Ninlil, Demeter,
Osiris, Baal, Tammuz, Adonis, and Attis. But Christ also belongs to the
Corn Gods. Corn Gods can be both male and female. Also, Underworld
gods such as Hades, Pluto, and Persephone are connected with Malkuth.

What are Grain Mysteries and what is a Corn God? The Grain
Mysteries are connected to the agricultural cycle. During the cycle of the
year, the land is "wounded" by the plow. Then the seed is sown into the
ground. It disappears and dwells in the Underworld. Then it starts to
grow again. It sprouts and grows into an ear of corn, bearing fruit again.
The sheaves of corn are harvested with a scythe. The land is plowed, and
a new grain cycle starts.

ELEUSIS AND ELYSIUM

The Mysteries of Eleusis are an example of Grain Mysteries. Demeter is
the mother of the land. She is the fertile force taking care that everything grows and bears fruit. Demeter's daughter is called Kore. Kore
is a young girl who dances through the meadows. She plucks narcissi.

Kore is abducted by Hades; the ground splits open, and the Lord of the Underworld steals the virgin and makes her his wife. Kore is not only the daughter of the Earth Mother, she is also the seed of the grain. These mysteries are made into an astral image: Virgo, holding the Ear of Corn, is seen as a constellation in heaven.

After her daughter is abducted, Demeter searches the land to find her. Demeter grieves intensely about the fate of her daughter who disappeared, and she is no longer capable of taking care of the land as the earth goddess. The land changes into a desert and all the plants wither.

Meanwhile, in the Underworld, Kore has become an adult. As the Bride of the Lord of the Underworld, she has changed her name to Persephone, the Queen of the Underworld. She is married to Hades. Demeter agrees to continue her task as the goddess and mother of the earth, on the condition that Persephone gets permission to visit her one part of the year. During Pesephone's visit with Demeter, the land starts to blossom again. The Mysteries of Eleusis were about the grain cycle. This is also the red thread behind the Descent of the goddess Inanna into the Underworld in the Sumerian Mysteries, and the Mysteries of the god Osiris in ancient Egypt, to give just a few examples.

Wounding and healing, death and resurrection are, on a mythical level, connected with the death of plant life in the winter and the renewal of vegetation in spring. The sacraments of bread and wine in different religions are derived from the Corn God myth. The wine is his or her blood and the bread is his or her body.

THE FISHER KING AND THE WOUNDED LAND

The Wounded Land in the Arthurian legends is the mythical landscape of the Corn God. The Fisher King—the grail king—gets wounded, and this causes the land to be wounded as well. It is no longer capable of bearing fruit and changes into a barren wasteland. When the king is cured, the land can be cured as well. When the grail knight visits the castle of the Fisher King and asks the grail questions, the king will be cured. The grail questions are: What is the grail? What purpose does it serve?

In a metaphorical sense, the land is your life. The four cardinal points of the land are the East, the South, the West, and the North. You are, in the kingdom of your life, the Element of Spirit. The four cardinal directions are metaphors for the psychic qualities that need to be transformed to a higher plane of consciousness.

The Mysteries of the Eearth are connected with gaining mastership over the Four Elements to cure the land. Looking into the mirror that your life provides you is a part of the process of healing your land.

THE MIRROR IMAGE OF NARCISSUS

Before the girl Kore was abducted by the god of the Underworld, she was gathering flowers in the meadow. She was plucking narcissi, the flower of the Greek hero who fell in love with his own mirror image. The narcissus is the symbol for the search for knowledge of the Self.

To heal the land, you need self-knowledge. You need to be prepared to make the Descent into the Underworld of your own mind to face yourself. There, the marriage between the god of the Underworld and the grain maiden is celebrated. Here the dark Hades turns out to be one of the few faithful gods of the Greek pantheon; he is not a bastard at all. His kingdom is the subconscious mind, where treasures are hidden under the surface.

The Mysteries of Death are closely connected to Malkuth. In the end, we all die, and our bodies are reabsorbed and fall apart in the Four Elements. The Underworld and Malkuth are connected with the Mysteries of Initiation and of the death and resurrection. The death of the Corn God forms a matrix for the initiations of some Mystery schools and shamanic traditions. The myths serve to raise the practitioner's consciousness toward a higher spiritual level.

EARTH, THE BRIDE OF THE COSMOS

The Kabbalists call Malkuth the Bride. Her name is Kallah. They say that the Bride is a young woman. She is crowned and seated on the Throne of

Binah. Binah is the great mother of life and death. In this last aspect, she was known in Eleusis under the name of Hecate: the Goddess of the Crossroads. The great mother—Demeter—is the ruler of birth and life. With this life comes her second gift, the inevitable consequence of death. When the girl Kore descends into the Underworld, she also walks into the realm of death.

Initiates distinguish seven degrees of death. The mythical meaning of the word *death* is to "enter into another reality." The seven degrees of death vary between a light trance and stone dead in the normal meaning of the word. An initiation is a death compared with the former phase of life, and it is a birth into a next life. This is the reason why an initiate is called Twice Born. To make it even more complex, death is the portal into a new life, a part of the cycle of life and death. What was born into earthly life dies only to live again in heaven—what dies on earth is born into the heaven. The great mother of life and death is a channel on which boats move in two directions. These are the Crossroads.

In the lives of humans, a child develops in the womb of its mother until he or she is ripe to be born. In the eternal life, a soul develops further after death. The sarcophagus is sown into the earth as a seed. The soul grows further into the womb of the great mother until the time that it is ready to ascend into the heavens and eternal life. The Mysteries here show the two roads that are possible after death. Reincarnation is the most common form of afterlife.

SANDALPHON AND THE CHERUBIM

Cherubim means "the winged ones." They are the angelic choir guarding the portals of paradise. The name comes from the Akkadian word *Karibu.* This word means "someone who prays." They were statues that were placed at the entrances of temples as spiritual guardians.

Cherubim are also described as the four fixed signs of the zodiac: the Bull, the Lion, the Eagle, and the Human. The difference with the choir of Kether is that the angels are winged and reside on a much higher level of the mind. The map of paradise is an equal-armed cross in a circle. The four cherubs are the guardians of the Four Elements at the portals of paradise. You can enter into paradise when you master the Four Elements. The cherubim are the angels who are pictured on the Ark of the Covenant. The attention of the viewer is drawn into the point between the angels' wings. This is the place of the "presence," where it is said that the Shekinah manifests. The Shekinah is the female face of God.

Ark of the Covenant

Sandalphon is seen as another form of Metatron. Do you remember the archangel of Kether? Here also it is repeated that the earth and the most high are part of one unity. Sandalphon is described as an immense archangel. He is so enormously big that as he stands upon the earth, he reaches the throne of God. This means that Sandalphon is as big as the entire Middle Pillar of the Kabbalistic Tree of Life. Sandalphon's presence can be perceived when you hear the soft sound of sandals. You feel someone coming toward you, and when you look up the presence is just outside your range of vision.

SCHEDULE OF MALKUTH

WORLD	DIVINE ASPECT	TAROT ASSOCIATIONS
Atziluth	God-name, Adonai Ha Aretz—Adonai Malekh	Wands Ten: Lord of Oppression
Briah	Archangel Sandalphon	Swords Ten: Lord of Destruction
Yetzirah	Angelic Choir Ashim—Souls of Fire	Cups Ten: Lord of Perfected Success
Assiah	Planet, Aretz, Earth	Ten of Pentagrams: Lord of Wealth

A SUN RAY IN A CAVE—
RITUAL

PREPARATIONS FOR
THE RITUAL IN MALKUTH

Necessities:

A pomegranate and a yellow altar cloth at the East

A russet candle and a russet altar cloth at the South

A glass of wine and an olive altar cloth at the West

A piece of bread and a black altar cloth at the North

A scarf of a black and white spotted fabric for over your head

A black altar cloth in the middle, with a white top cloth

Music, drumbeat to the rhythm of the heart

A black, a white, and a golden candle on the altar

Prepare yourself for a meditative ritual. In the necessities you see that the entire ritual space is decorated in the colors of Malkuth. If you want to perform this ritual perfectly, choose the day of the winter solstice, in the Northern Hemisphere this is December 21, to perform it. The space must be as dark as possible when you start. You begin this ritual with the Opening of the Veils, the Kabbalistic Cross, and the exercise of the Middle Pillar. Doing the Middle Pillar exercise, you pay close attention to the cir-

340

culation exercises, because they will make the connection between heaven and earth in you. When you have done this, you sit in meditation and build the following images.

THE FERTILIZATION OF THE EARTH

The images of your temple melt into visions that form before your inner eye. You close your eyes and concentrate upon the scenes you envision. A man comes walking in. He is dressed strangely. He wears a leather tunic that is closed around his waist with a leather lace. He wears simple sandals made of rough leather. In his hands he holds a wooden wand carved in the form of a snake. He wears a mantle made of white eagle feathers. He wears a headdress made from the head of an eagle. In his eyes you see a concentrated, attentive look. You are touched by this look. It appears to hold something unearthly, as if there is another presence behind the eyes of this man. The shaman asks you if you are ready to travel with him.

At the moment you agree, the rhythm of the drums increases in intensity. Your perception becomes stronger and sharper. The shaman tells you that you do not need to panic. You are completely safe under his guidance.

Together you walk to the Northern wall of your meditation space. The shaman knocks with his snake wand ten times on the wall, and the wall becomes fluid: a vortex opens a road into a black tunnel. Then you walk through it.

"We now walk back in time," the shaman tells you. It feels strange when you pass through the tunnel. As you walk, all kinds of images whirl around you. They appear to be projected onto the walls.

"These are the memories from the earth itself," the shaman explains. "The people who you see as shadows on the wall are the Ashim, your ancestors. Through the Justified Death, every initiate has access to their knowledge of the earth. And this is an extensive knowledge that comes forth directly from the Book of Nature. This book contains the keys to all the secrets of life and death."

At the end of the corridor, you find a rocky coast by the sea. It is night. What you notice immediately is the difference in temperature. Further away, you see that the landscape is clothed in snow. The white blanket is specked with black spots, the holes of rabbits and other animals that show the blackness of the surface of the earth. The shaman points at an animal that quickly disappears, an ermine that hid himself in a hole in the ground. It is cold, and nature has withdrawn all its forces. The shaman points over the water. The sea splashes roughly against the cliffs and forms fountains of salty water. Below, at the end of a staircase carved out of the rocks, you see a primitive rowboat. The shaman descends the stairs, and you follow carefully. You need to pay attention to prevent yourself from slipping on these extremely slick rocks. You step into the boat.

A ferryman takes the oars, and the three of you embark in the direction of the open sea. You ask yourself if this is safe. The north polestars are clearly visible. They shine as the sole lights in a pitch-black night. There is no moon visible. In a moment, you are completely surrounded by water and no land can be seen. Now you really start to worry, and ask the shaman where you are going.

"We are going to the First Land," he answers. "The primeval island that comes out of the ocean as the First Land. You can see it in the distance if you really pay attention." Indeed, a horizon appears. As you come closer, you see that this land is also covered in snow. The black spots give the entire land the appearance of the ermine. You row until you touch the coastline. Here also a slippery staircase gives access to the island. After climbing upward, you stand in the roaring wind. You notice that the island is very small. A group of people gathers on the island. They come from all times and all cultures. They walk up the only hill the island has. The shaman tells you that this is the Primal Hill of the First Land. It is a sacred place.

In the darkness, you all walk uphill in a procession. An old woman walks alongside you, and asks you if you can help her carry the offerings. Of course you want to help. You take the great basket that she carries. You ask what is in the basket. She says that it contains pomegranates, a wedding gift for the goddess of the earth, and amadou, and a very expensive piece of rock crystal. Furthermore, the basket con-

tains wine, bread, charcoal, and a leather bucket to carry fire, filled with sand.

The little procession has now reached a point where two wooden doors close a gap. The shaman walks to the doors and opens the bolts. The doors swing open and reveal a corridor that leads to a dark underground space. The entrance to the space is low. You need to bow before you enter into the sanctuary of the gods. You now walk through a long straight corridor into a small underground room. In the middle of the room is a stone that functions as an altar.

The crowd develops an intense activity. The old woman starts to unpack her basket. She puts the amadou on the altar stone, together with the rock crystal and the charcoal. Other people create seats. They fill sacks with straw and put animal skins on top of them. The food is put on the altar. Then a strange noise comes from outside. Everyone who is inside looks with concentration at the procession of priestesses who walk inside. They all wear white animal hides. Accompanying the procession is a rattling sound—the jewelry worn by the priestesses. Around their ankles they wear bracelets of cowry shells. One priestess is dressed differently. She wears the head of a black wolf upon her head, and the rest of the pelt is draped around her body. She also carries a snake wand in her hand. The shaman bends respectfully to the woman as she passes. He whispers to you: "She is the oracle of the goddess."

The entire group has gathered around the altar, and slowly everybody becomes silent. It is pitchdark in the cave. Everyone looks in expectation toward the exit of the cave. Then the shaman rises and addresses the company.

"The moment of the winter solstice approaches. We are in expectation of the appearance of the winter sun. With the first ray of light, our father the sun will penetrate our mother the earth deeply. In this way Father Sun and Mother Earth will perform the Sacred Marriage. With this marriage comes the birth of the new light. After the light has been born, it will grow. It will spread itself. It will spread itself over the entire land. The plants will grow under this light, and the animals will give birth to young, and the people will have children. When we cause the creation of the new light by means of our ritual, the land will come alive and Mother Earth will bear fruit. We now expect the moment of the penetration. . . ."

Slowly it becomes lighter on the horizon, a sign that the sun approaches. Suddenly, a ray of light shoots through the cave, illuminating the interior. The light of Father Sun penetrates deep into the vulva of Mother Earth, into her womb. The light falls through the rock crystal and in this way enflames the amadou. It creates a small fire, which is immediately taken care of by the old woman. The charcoal is put around it, and in a short time a fire is burning in the cave. Now you can actually see your environment.

In the middle of the space you see the altar stone. Around it there are big megaliths, which are painted with red ochre. You see that a great honeycomb is painted on the ceiling. On the megaliths forming the walls are pictured snakes in the form of spirals and ears of corn. The shaman points toward the megaliths and says: "Count them. There are exactly twenty-nine, the sacred number of the moon!" He points to the pictures and says: "Look at the holy symbols that are given to us by the gods: the symbol of the honey bee, the ear of corn, and the red thread that will lead us through the labyrinth. And, of course, the secret that you have witnessed: the Mystery of Fire. It is time to pay attention, because the ritual has not finished yet."

The oracle with the wolf mask stands upright and raises a pomegranate. With a stone flint, she opens the fruit and lifts it for everyone to see.

"The belly of the Great Mother is filled with her blood. In the warm darkness of her womb she carries the fruits inside her. She carries many seeds in one womb, and shows us in this way how one body can make a community into a whole. We will all eat from the seeds of the pomegranate, so that everyone is aware of this again."

The pomegranate is handed around the circle, and everyone takes a bite from the seeds. The oracle takes a goblet filled with wine and pours it into one of the terra-cotta bowls. She breaks off a piece of the bread. She holds up both the wine and the bread so that everyone in the company can see what she does.

"Look here, the Mother," she says as she raises the wine. "Look here, the Father," she says while lifting the bread. "When the Father unifies with the Mother, new life is created," she says, as she drops the bread into the wine. "Drink all of this wine, it is consecrated to this holy union." The oracle passes around the bowl, and everyone present takes a sip of the wine.

Suddenly she turns around and looks at you. She says, "Here we have someone in our company who will plant these symbols in a far future. We will crown this person as our king."

She invites you to sit on a dais that is dressed with animal skins. One of the priestesses comes walking toward you, and she holds a pomegranate in her hand.

"Look at this pomegranate. It is the symbol of the marriage with the land. It is the sign that you are connected with the tradition. You yourself are one of the seeds of the Corn God." She kneels and, with a ceremonial gesture, she puts the pomegranate into your hand.

Another priestess steps forward with the snake wand and gives it to you. "Look here, the sign of power over the land. May you become king in your life and of your environment, ruler over the four cardinal directions of the Inner Landscape."

A third priestess steps forward and gives you the leather bucket. She fills it with sand and with burning charcoal and says, "Look here, the light of the tradition. May your spirit be enlightened with this light, and crown you with its beauty."

Then the last priestess approaches. She puts a skin of ermine around your shoulders and says, "Know that you are dressed in light and darkness. Both carry the seed of each other's presence in their essence. The spotted pelt is a symbol of the unification of heaven and earth. Who is capable of wearing this mantle becomes king of his land."

The oracle with the wolf mask continues: "But for now, this is a gift for the future. I will guide you, together with the shaman, into your time and space, and help you to give these holy signs a place in your sacred space."

She helps you to rise, and the three of you walk out of the cave: the oracle, the shaman, and yourself. Outside it has become light. It is the day of the winter solstice. The shaman and the priestess stand you between them and, with their snake wands, they knock on the floor ten times. Before you, in the direction of the sun, a vortex opens. The vortex is colored gold, and the three of you travel through it in the direction of the light, back through time. The journey ends in your meditation room.

The shaman and the oracle take places in two corners at the Eastern side of your temple. The shaman tells you, "Put the fur of ermine on the floor." At the moment you do this, the black and white spotted fur changes into black and white tiles. "The wise man walks over a road of light and darkness," he says.

The oracle instructs you to lift the burning charcoal out of the fire bucket, and use it to light the altar candle. "The temple is lit by the light of the tradition that has been transferred since primordial times from initiate to initiate. This is called passing on the torch."

The shaman instructs you now to take the pomegranate. At the moment you take it out of your leather knapsack, it multiplies. The shaman and the oracle both take a pomegranate and put it on their heads. Then the colors of the temple shift, and the shaman and the oracle change into the Black and White Pillar.

You stand and look at what happened, still holding the snake wand in your hand. Your mind forms one big question mark while you look at it. Then you clearly hear a voice in your mind telling you: "You yourself are the Middle Pillar. Now perform the Marriage between Heaven and Earth . . ."

Come slowly out of your meditation. Turn on the music. Stand upright and first light the golden candle. Visualize yourself being the Middle Pillar.

Next you light the black and white candle and visualize the two Pillars of Equilibrium. You realize the meaning of them. Go to the East, and raise the pomegranate here. Visualize and realize the meaning of this symbol: the seeds in the womb. Eat consciously of the seeds.

Go to the South. Light the russet candle from the gold one. Here you meditate on the flame of the light itself.

Go to the West. Visualize and realize the meaning of the chalice, the symbol of the womb of the goddess. Put the chalice on the altar.

Go to the North. Visualize and realize the meaning of the bread as the symbol of the Corn God, being a metaphor of death and rebirth. Put the bread on the altar.

Go to the main altar and focus on the East. You connect with the new light, which spreads and multiplies. Then you put the bread in the chalice of wine and drink it down. Kneel before the altar and leave the ritual space with the candles still burning. Let the music play until the candles are burned down.

12

THE RITUAL OF THE EXALTATION OF THE SUN

The Way Back

The Way Back is the phrase used in the Mystery tradition to indicate the search for the reunion with the divine. Our search starts when we are born on earth in a physical body. What is called "the Fall from Paradise," we call within our tradition "the Descent into Matter." These terms indicate a totally different attitude toward the same phenomenon. By descending, the divine experiences itself. Together, and each of us separately, we are a part of the All who divides itself into a cascade of sparks. We are all one of those sparks. The All wants to experience itself, and does this by manifesting on the physical plane. In the Egyptian Mysteries, this is expressed beautifully by the rising sun—named Khephera*—which comes forth from the primordial darkness:

Khepher means "to be, to exist, to be created, to happen." In the old Egyptian text, instead of the word *creation,* all forms of the word *Kheper* were used.

I am the Creator of what comes into being,
I come into being in the forms of Khephera
Coming into being in primeval time.
I come into being in the forms of Khephera.
I am the creator of what comes into being,
That is to say: I produce myself from the primeval
matter
Which I create . . .
. . . and I, even I, came into being
in the form of things which came into being,
and I came into being in the forms of Khephera.
I came into being from the primeval matter,
Coming into being in multitudes of forms from the
beginning.

FROM *THE HISTORY OF THE CREATION*
OF THE GODS AND THE WORLD
(EGYPTIAN PAPYRUS)

The Way Back takes us right through the earth and the dust of matter. The Way Back is a focus of the Mystery tradition because you connect yourself with the divine, which surrounds you everywhere. The old magicians said: "There is no thing that is not of the gods." On this statement, the entire Mystery tradition has been built. The robes of the magician are the expression in cloth of the divine weaving itself into being.

White is my under robe,
Because it symbolizes the purity of my soul.
Black is my outer robe,
Because it symbolizes the richness of the earth,
And veils and protects the purity
With which I devote myself to the knowledge of the
divine
In myself and around me.

The temple is a metaphor for the holiness of the universe, with which every magician connects himself or herself. In his sacred circle the sun rises, travels through the heavenly vault, sinks in the West, and subsequently journeys through the Underworld to rise again by day. The moon travels in all her appearances through the heavenly mansions. Together they form the eyes of the creator.

The temple is called the House of Life and is built on the Double Horizon, between the day and the night. The temple stands between the Mountains of Sunrise and Sunset. In this sacred building the magician lives, prays, and works. He purifies himself with the Waters falling down from heaven. The Waters are the tears of the gods themselves—manna, also called the nectar of the gods.

The magical circle is the land of milk and honey. To come here, you must divide the Waters with the Wand of Power. This staff is in the possession of Adam Kadmon, the Heavenly Human. This wand symbolizes knowledge of the Tree of Life. On this tree, in the Garden of Creation, apples grow.

In other words, according to Greek mythology, in the country Hesperia there grows a tree in which lives a snake. This snake guards the Golden Fleece. This Golden Fleece is the daylight, the sunlight that covers the landscape of life with a mysterious, meaningful, golden glow.

These sentences are the last sentences of this book, but this does not mean that everything has been said about this subject. On the contrary. With this book I have just dusted off the surface of an immemorial tradition. After these pages, one could write hundreds of books, all about the spiritual experiences of an unprecedented worldwide sacred culture.

In pre-Christian times, the language of the Mystery was alive, and it was an international language. There was just one language describing this tradition. That language was and is nature. The true Mysteries are revealed when you learn to understand the language of the stones, plants, animals, and stars. The voices of the gods sound on the noise of the wind and in the waves of the oceans. They are to be heard in the crackling of fires and the heartbeat of the earth itself: the continuous drum that sounds, caused by the beating heart of all that lives.

What do we of modern times and tempos have to gain from this old Wisdom? How does this fit into our lives? Is this not just history and declined glory? With the practice of magic come incredible feelings of meaningfulness, encounters with beauty, and peak experiences. You will develop a relationship with the living nature surrounding you. You will learn to resonate on the matrix of harmony. You will clear away blockages and will access greater quantities of energy. By learning to think intuitively, you will be in touch with your creative energy. When this energy is freed, you can rely on it to find the way back through the dust of the earth, to the Temple of the Double Horizon. Then you take this fulfillment with you in your daily life when you walk out of the temple. You are fed with spiritual food. This book is a first step, and challenges you to plant the Tree of Life in your own life.

When, years ago in Afghanistan, the fundamentalists destroyed the ancient statues of the gods, the entire world revolted. That was the destruction of a very important cultural inheritance. What happened with the Mystery tradition is an even bigger and more radical loss.

This book is a first step toward restoring the monuments that are standing upright in the astral and archetypal world. Sometimes monuments are found under the surface of the earth, as in the bronze statue Sit-shamshi, which you can visit in the Louvre Museum in Paris. This bronze statue depicts two people who perform an offering ceremony. They purify themselves with water in a magical location. The two mountains in the background are ziggurats, constructed to serve as stairways to heaven. Together they form the two Mountains of Sunrise and Sunset. The two people are bald; this is the classic style of the priesthood. The two people sit opposite one another, face to face, and mirror each other as the godhead mirrors itself in nature. The ziggurats and the priests together represent the Double Horizon.

The two ziggurats point toward the horizon of the night. Steps made of lapis lazuli tiles form the road toward the gods. The priests create the horizon by day, the golden horizon. They cause the exaltation of the sun, which is exalted by the intensity of the experience of the rising light.

Behind the priests you see the Tree of Life and the water jar from

Sunrise Sit-shamshi

which manna from heaven is poured out by the gods. The statue itself is probably an old divination board. The little holes tell us that this could have been an oracle game.

When we have knowledge of the cosmic order, we can adjust ourselves to be in harmony with it. We can put our hearts on the offering table of transformation, and let our prayers go out toward the gods. The gods have retired to unseen areas. Now it is time for their lights to start to shine again and for humans to learn from them again, and grow through their wisdom. Let us look upon our world with awe and wonder. Within this world, the sunrise is a mythical and magical moment. Let us learn from the wise of old how they experienced this moment—the text below is the inscription in the bronze statue:

> *My name is Shilhak-Inshushinak. I am the son of*
> *Shutruk-Nahhunte and the beloved servant of the God*
> *Inshushinak. I am king of Anzan and Susa and the*
> *protector and King of the land of Elam: I have performed*
> *the Ritual of the Exaltation of the Sun (Sit-shamshi) of*
> *Susa in bronze, so that this rite may be preserved for ever.*
>
> INSCRIPTION IN CUNEIFORM WRITING
> IN THE LOUVRE, PARIS

GLOSSARY

Adam Kadmon: Metaphor for a human being who has developed to his or her highest potential; also called Heavenly Man or Heavenly Human.

Adept: One who has received initiations into the higher levels of a tradition by a living Master of the tradition.

Arcanum: A series of symbols that disclose a magical, mental, psychic, and moral energy area of a human at one time.

Artificial Elemental: A thoughtform made of magical energy for a specific goal and for a limited amount of time.

Ashim: Fire spirits; the angelic choir of Malkuth.

Azoth: The name used by the ancient alchemist to indicate the One Thing. The A and the Z point toward the Greek Alpha and Omega, the beginning and the end. The Azoth is symbolized by a seven-pointed star.

Cartouche: Old Egyptian symbol indicating the Throne name of a pharaoh. The symbol is a form of cord magic, which protects the name.

Chaldea: The eleventh dynasty of the kings of Babylon (sixth century BCE) is called the Chaldean Dynasty. Chaldea is the plain in the South between the Euphrates and the Tigris.

Consecration: The ceremony of blessing objects, persons, statues, or space to transform them into sacred objects.

Contacted Mystery School: A school that is under the guidance of a master from the Inner Planes.

Corona Borealis: Constellation of stars in the Northern heavens. The name means "Northern Crown." The constellation is also called Corona Ariadne, and is associated with the goddess Ariadne of Crete.

Creation myths: The myths that explain the creation of the universe.

Earthly check: You can ask for an earthly check when you want to have confirmation of an inner plane exchange of knowledge (such as inner visions, clairaudiently received information or inspiration). The inner planes will send you this confirmation within twenty-four hours in the form of meaningful events in the outer world.

Elementals: Consciousness at its most basic level: Sylphs of Air, Salamanders of Fire, Undines of Water, and Gnomes of Earth.

Elements (of the Wise): Consciousness on its basic level. They are divided into four different types: Air, Fire, Water, Earth. Together they create the fifth element: Spirit.

Eleusian Fields: Term from the Mysteries of Eleusis indicating a state of consciousness in which one is in the "First Time." One regains this realm of consciousness after death.

Elohim: The Bible begins with the sentence "Bereshit bara Elohim et hashamayim ve'et ha'arets." This is translated as: "In the beginning God created heaven and earth." But this translation is inaccurate. *Elohim* is a word that means the "Sons of God." The final ending of the word is female. *Elohim* is the unification of the male and female aspect of divinity.

Evocation: A ritual technique in which a god or an angel is called to appear outside of the practitioner.

Gnosis: Knowledge and insight coming forth from personal experiences of a divine reality. Gnosis is based on experience and not on fate.

Gnothi Seauton: A phrase that was written over the Temple of Delphi. It means "Know Thyself."

God-form assumption: A series of techniques used to personify divine or angelic forces during rituals.

Hekau: An old Egyptian term for "words of power," magical words that fell under the residence of the god Heka.

Hermes Trismegistus: The Greek name for Thoth, the Egyptian god of writing and sciences. The name means "Three Times Great Hermes."

Hierophant: High Priest.

Inner Planes: An expression to indicate the spiritual layers of consciousness.

Invocation: A ritual technique whereby you call up a god force or an angelic force into yourself.

Khabs Am Pekht, Konx om Pax, Light in Extension: A ritual phrase meaning "may you receive the blessings of the light and the mystical experience, the goal of all your work."

Khaemwaset: The fourth son of Ramses II. He was the High Priest of Ptah in Memphis. His name is mentioned in inscriptions of the old and middle kingdom in connection with renovations of ancient monuments.

Kundalini yoga: A form of yoga in which you work with Kundalini Shakti, the snake power that is raised by means of spiritual exercises. It causes energy to rise through the spine and the chakras. The power leads to the purification of the Elements of the body.

Lamen: Piece of jewelry worn over the heart that channels the force of the heart energy and shapes it into symbolic form.

Magical personality: An artificially created personality that is built up systematically for magical work.

Mandala: A design, map, or geometrical pattern that represents the cosmos in a metaphysical or symbolical way.

Mantra: A religious word-sound combination that is used to develop singly pointed concentration.

Melissae: Priestesses working in the service of the bee goddess Melissa. The Melissae fed themselves with honey and were inspired oracles.

Mesopotamic tradition: A generic term indicating successive pre-Christian cultures active in the tradition of the "fertile crescent of the moon" and who used cuneiform writing.

Minoan tradition: The Mystery religion of Crete from antiquity. The name of the tradition is based on the legendary king Minos.

Mitras tradition: A Mystery religion originally deriving from Persia that was practiced in the first century CE in Rome.

Mundane chakra: Points of manifestation on the material level where divine forces come together.

Nemhys: An Egyptian headdress.

Novice: An apprentice in the Mysteries.

Obsidian: A black stone of volcanic glass.

Omphalos: A religious artifact made of stone. *Omphalos* in Greek means "navelstone." The stone would indicate the location of the navel of the world. It has the shape of a beehive. The most famous omphalos is in the sanctuary of Delphi, in Greece. Under this stone Python, the earth dragon of Delphi, would be buried. Omphalos was also the name for a tomb built in the shape of a beehive.

Orphic tradition: A Greek Mystery religion from antiquity, based on the descent and resurrection of Orpheus from the Underworld.

Ouroboros snake: A snake biting himself in the tail. It is a symbol for the unity and interconnectedness of everything.

Regalia: The generic term for ritually consecrated artifacts, clothing, and jewelry.

Sepher Yetzirah: The Book of Creation. The oldest known written Kabbalistic text.

Sephirah (plural Sephiroth): The name for the different divine emanations of which the Kabbalistic Tree is built.

Sigil: A magical symbol that connects a series of meanings.

Synchronicity: The phenomenon of the appearance of related psychic phenomena and material circumstances.

Tabard: A short toga, with or without sleeves, which is worn over a robe.

Telesmatic images: Images of divinity that have been given a human form.

Tetragrammaton: The unspeakable name of God represented by the letters YHVH. The letters represent the Four Elements. They are alternating male and female. In a vertical line they represent the Heavenly Man.

Thoth: Egyptian god of writing and of science.

Ushabtis: Little statues often made of terra-cotta and enameled in a blue color, representing magical helpers. They were given to the dead to work for them in their life after death.

Vortex: An energy form that behaves as a whirlpool having an inducing fluid.

Zep Tepi: The literal meaning of the word is "First Time." It is an old Egyptian word indicating the time of the creation, the mythical time when the gods lived upon the earth, and when everything happened for the first time. Zep Tepi is a timeless space with which we connect ourselves preceding magical work. It is a state of consciousness in which there is no notion of time. It is always Zep Tepi.

Zoroastric Avesta: The tradition named after the Persian prophet Zoroaster, also called Zarathushtra. The Avesta is the collection of sacred writings of this tradition.

TABLE OF CORRESPONDENCES

On the following pages you will find the Tables of Correspondences. They are a handy tool to quickly look up chains of symbols that are traditionally connected. However, do not make the mistake of learning these symbols by heart or by rationally analyzing them. By working with them in a purely rational way you will block the meditative mind instead of gaining access to it. Symbols and numbers contain very subtle aspects, and it is exactly these hidden aspects that will allow you to access the deeper levels of the mind.

SEPHIRAH	KETHER	CHOKMAH	BINAH	DA'ATH	CHESED
Meaning	Crown	Wisdom	Under-standing	Knowledge	Mercy
Titles	Arich Anpin/ The Vast Countenance	Abba = Father	Ama = Mother	The Empty Room/The Invisible Sephirah	Love/ Majesty/ Splendor
Meaning Titles	Divine Unity	The Will to Create	The Receiving Form-power		The Giving Principle
God-name	Eheieh Asher Eheieh	Yehovah/Yah	YHVH Elohim	YHVH Elohim	El
Meaning God-name	I am that I am	The first two letters of the Holy Name/ Polarity	The Male and Female Union		The Strong God
Archangel	Metatron	Ratziel/Raziel	Tzaphkiel	Uriel/ Raphael/ Michael/ Gabriel	Tzadkiel
Meaning Archangel	Lord of the Countenance	The Will of God/The Mystery of God	Attention of God	The Four Archangels of the Cardinal Directions	The Righteous God
Angelic Choir	Chaioth Ha Qadesh	Auphanim	Aralim	Serpents	Chasmalim
Meaning of the Name	Holy Living Creatures	Wheels	Thrones	Winged Serpents	The Shining Ones
Firmament	First Swirlings, Rashit-ha Gilgalim	Zodiac/Mazlot	Saturn, Shabbatai	Sirius	Jupiter/ Tzedek

GEBURAH	TIPHARETH	NETZACH	HOD	YESOD	MALKUTH
Severity	Beauty	Victory	Glory	Foundation	Kingdom
Justice/Awe	Mercy/ The Lesser Countenace	Firmness/ Valor	The Perfect Intelligence	The Honest One	Kallah/ the Bride
The Principle of Boundaries	Equilibrium	Response to Creativity	Appreciation of Boundaries/ Reason/ Logic	The Subcon- sciousness	Matter/ Manifestation
Elohim Gibor	YHVH Eloah va Da'ath	YHVH Tzabaoth	Elohim Tzabaoth	Shaddai el Chai	Adonai ha Aretz
The Mighty God	The All- knowing God	Lord of the Hosts	God of the Hosts	Almighty Living God	Lord of the Earth
Khamael/ Chamael/ Samael	Raphael	Haniel	Michael	Gabriel	Sandalphon
The Glowing Wrath of God	Healer of God	Grace of God	Who Is as God	Mighty One of God	Lord of the Earth
Seraphim	Malachim	Elohim	Beni Elohim	Ashim	Cherubim
Burning Ones	Messengers	Gods	Sons of Gods	Fire Spirits	Winged Ones
Mars, Madim	Sun, Shamash	Venus, Nogah	Mercury, Kochab	Moon, Levanah	Earth, Aretz

SEPHIRAH	KETHER	CHOKMAH	BINAH	DA'ATH	CHESED
Tarot	Four Aces	The Twos	The Threes		The Fours
Color Atziluth King Scale	Brilliant	Soft Blue	Bloodred	Lavender	Deep Violet
Color Briah Queen Scale	White Brilliant	Gray	Black	Silver Gray	Royal Blue
Color Yetzirah Emperor Scale	White Brilliant	Bluish Pearl Gray	Dark Brown	Pure Violet	Deep Blue
Color Assiah Empress Scale	White flecked with Gold	White flecked with Red, Blue, and Yellow	Gray flecked with Purple	Gray flecked with Gold	Azure Blue flecked with Yellow
Quality	Spirituality/ Mysticism	Will/ Wisdom	Realization/ Rest/ Discipline	Transform-ation	Bene-volence/ Growth/ Order
Virtue	Bliss/ Completion of the Great Work	Devotion	Silence	Perfection of Justice/ Detachment	Obedience
Vice			Greediness	Doubt/ Apathy/ Cowardice	Hypocrisy/ Tyranny/ Zealotry / Gluttony
Body Association	The Top of the Skull	Left Side of the Head/ The Third Eye	Right Side of the Head/ Third Eye	Throat Center/The Ventricles of the Brain and Pons	Right Shoulder and Arm

GEBURAH	TIPHARETH	NETZACH	HOD	YESOD	MALKUTH
The Fives	The Sixes	The Sevens	The Eights	The Nines	The Tens
Orange	Clear Pink	Amber	Violet Purple	Indigo Blue	Yellow
Bloodred	Golden Yellow	Emerald Green	Orange	Violet	Yellow/Olive Green/Russet Brown/Black
Deep Bloodred	Salmon	Clear Yellowish Green	Russet Brown	Dark Purple	Yellow/Olive Green/Russet Brown/Black sparked with Gold
Red flecked with Black	Golden Amber	Olive Green sparked with Yellow	Yellow-ish Brown sparked with Gold	Citrine Yellow sparked with Blue	Black with rays of Olive Green and Citrine Yellow
Power/Strug-gle/Justice	Healing/Equilibrium	Love/Relation-ships/Art	Thinking/Speech/Intellect	Dreams/Sexuality/Intuition	Matter/Money/Earthly Business
Energy/Courage	Devotion to the Great Work	Unselfishness	Truthfulness	Independence	Discrimination
Cruelty/Destruction	Pride	Unchasity/Lust	Falseness/Dishonesty	Idleness	Avarice/Inertia
Left Shoulder and Arm	The Heart	The Left Hip and Leg	The Right Hip and Leg	Genitals	Feet

SEPHIRAH	KETHER	CHOKMAH	BINAH	DA'ATH	CHESED
Spiritual Experience	Union with God	The Vision of God Face to Face	Vision of Sorrow	Vision across the Abyss	Vision of Love
Magical Image	A Bearded King Seen in Profile	A Bearded Male Figure	A Matron	A Face Looking in Two Directions	A Mighty Crowned King on a Throne
Symbols	The Point/the Swastika/the Crown	The Lingam/the Yod/the Phallus/the Inner Robe of Glory/the Standing Stone/the Upright Wand of Power/the Straight Line	The Yoni/the Kteis the Vesca Pisces/the Chalice/the Outer Robe of Concealment	The Monastery Cell/the Prism/the Empty Space	Pyramid/Equal-Armed Cross/Pomeroy/Staff/Scepter/Shepherd's Crook
Gods	Atum-Ra/Uranos	Thoth/Anu/Athene	Tefnut/Tiamat	Janus/Horus-Seth/Anubis	Zeus/Marduk/Jupiter
Animals		Male	Female		Unicorn/Deer
Plants	Blue Lotus	Olive	Cypress		Olive
Stones	Diamond	Star Ruby	Pearl	Star Sapphire	Sapphire
Metals			Lead		Tin

GEBURAH	TIPHARETH	NETZACH	HOD	YESOD	MALKUTH
Vision of Power	Vision of the Harmony of Things/ Mysteries of the Crucifixion	Vision of Beauty Triumphant	Vision of Splendor	Vision of the Machinery of the Universe	Vision and conversation with the Holy Guardian Angel
A Mighty Warrior in a Chariot	A King, a Child, and a Sacrificed God	A Beautiful Naked Woman	A Herma-phrodite	A Beautiful Naked Man	A young Woman, Crowned and Throned
The Pentagram/ The Five-Petaled Tudor Rose/ The Sword/ The Spear/ The Scourge/ The Chain	Lamen/ Rosecross/ Calvary Cross/ Cube	Lamp/ Girdle/ Rose	Names/ the Apron	Parfums/ Winged Sandals	Altar/Double Cube/ Equal-Armed Cross/ Magical Circle
Mars/ Aries/ Sekhmet	Osiris/ Ra/ Dionysus/ Apollo/Christ	Venus/ Hathor/ Isthar	Mercury/ Hermes/ Herm-Anubis/ Thoth	Osiris/ Isis/ Thoth/ Diana/ Artemis	Demeter/ Hades/Pluto/ Ninlil/Osiris
Basilisk	Lion	Lynx	Hermaphro-dite	Elephant	Sphinx
Oak	Acacia/ Grape	Rose	Moly	Jasmine	Lily/Ivy/ Oregano
Ruby	Topaz	Emerald	Fire Opal	Amethyst	Rock Crystal
Iron	Gold	Copper	Mercury	Silver	Mica

BIBLIOGRAPHY

Agrippa, Henry Cornelius. *Three Books of Occult Philosophy*. Edited and annotated by Donald Tyson. St. Paul, Minn.: Llewellyn, 2000.

Allen, Richard Hinckley. *Star Names: Their Lore and Meaning*. New York: Dover, 1963.

Ashcroft-Nowicki, Dolores. *The Shining Paths: An Experimental Journey through the Tree of Life*. London: Aquarian Press, 1983.

———. *The Ritual Magical Workbook: A Practical Course of Self-Initiation*. London: Aquarian Press, 1986.

———. *Illuminations: Mystical Meditations of the Hebrew Alphabet, The Healing of the Soul*. St. Paul, Minn.: Llewellyn, 2003.

Ashcroft-Nowicki, Dolores, and J. H. Brennan. *Magical Use of Thoughtforms: A Proven System of Mental & Spiritual Empowerment*. St. Paul, Minn.: Llewellyn, 2001.

Barrett, Francis. "The Magus." *Sacred Texts*. Online: www.sacred-texts.com/grim/magus/.

Butler, W. E. *The Magician: His Training and Work*. Hollywood: Wilshire Book Company, 1969.

———. *Apprenticed to Magic and Magic & the Qabalah*. Introduction by Dolores Ashcroft-Nowicki. London: Aquarian Press, 1981.

———. *Magic: Its Ritual, Power and Purpose*. Loughborough, U.K.: Thoth, 2001.

———. *Practical Magic and the Western Mystery Tradition*. Loughborough, U.K.: Thoth, 2002.

"The Book of the Secrets of Enoch." *The Reluctant Messenger*. Online: http://reluctant-messenger.com/2enoch01-68.htm.

Cicero, Chic Cicero, and Sandra Tabatha Cicero. *The Middle Pillar: The Balance Between Mind and Magic*. St. Paul, Minn.: Llewellyn, 1998.

———. *A Garden of Pomegranates: Skrying on the Tree of Life*. St. Paul, Minn.: Llewellyn, 1999.

Davidson, Gustav. *A Dictionary of Angels: Including the Fallen Angels*. New York: Free Press, 1971.

Everard, Dr., trans. *The Divine Pymander of Hermes* (1650). San Diego: Wizards Bookshelf, 2000.

Faulkner, R. O. *The Egyptian Book of the Dead: The Book of Going Forth by Day*. San Francisco: Chronicle, 1998.

———. *The Ancient Egyptian Coffin Texts*. 3 vols. Warminster, U.K.: Aris & Phillips, 1977–96.

———. *The Ancient Egyptian Pyramid Texts*. U.K.: Oxford University Press, 1998.

Fortune, Dion. *De Mystieke Kabbala: Een sleutel tot de kennis der wetten van geest, ziel en lichaam*. Amsterdam: Uitgeverij Schors, 1992.

———. *The Sea Priestess*. York Beach, Maine: Weiser, 1993.

———. *Moon Magic*. York Beach, Maine: Weiser, 1994.

———. *The Cosmic Doctrine*. York Beach, Maine: Weiser, 2000.

Gray, William G. *The Ladder of Lights: A Step-by-Step Guide to the Tree of Life and the Four Worlds of the Qabalists Including the Angelic and Archangelic Realms*. York Beach, Maine: Weiser, 1968.

Hanegraff, Wouter J. *Dictionary of Gnosis & Western Esotericism*. 2 vols. Leiden: Koninklijke Brill NV, 2005.

Hauck, Dennis William. *The Emerald Tablet: Alchemy for Personal Transformation*. New York: Penguin Compass, 1999.

Iamblichus. *Theurgia, or On the Mysteries of Egypt*. Online: www.esotericarchives.com/oracle/iambl_th.htm.

Jacobsen, Thorkild. *The Treasures of Darkness: A History of Mesopotamian Religion*. New Haven: Yale University Press, 1976.

Kaplan, Aryeh. *Sefer Yetzirah: The Book of Creation In Theory and Practice*. Boston: Red Wheel/Weiser, 1997.

Kinder, Hermann, and Werner Hilgemann. *The Penguin Atlas of World History. vol. 1, From Prehistory to the Eve of the French Revolution.* London: Penguin, 1978.

King, L. W., ed. *Enuma Elish: The Seven Tablets of Creation: Or the Babylonian and Assyrian Legends Concerning the Creation of the World and of Mankind.* 2 vols. London: Luzac and Co., 1902.

Knight, Gareth. *A Practical Guide to Qabalistic Symbolism. Vol. 1, On the Spheres of the Tree of Life. Vol. 2: On the Paths and the Tarot.* London: Kahn & Averill, 1991, 1993.

Levi, Eliphas. "The Magical Ritual of the Sanctum Regnum." *Blackmask.* Online: www.blackmask.com, 2001.

Matthews, Caitlín, and John Matthews. *The Western Way: A Practical Guide to the Western Mystery Tradition.* London: Penguin Arkana, 1994.

Meador, Betty De Shong. *Inanna, Lady of Largest Heart: Poems of the Sumerian High Priestess Enheduanna.* Austin: University of Texas Press, 2002.

Philo, Alexandria. *The Works of Philo.* Peabody, Mass.: Hendrickson, 2000.

Pinche, Geraldine. *Magic in Ancient Egypt.* Texas: First University of Texas Press, 1995.

Pseudo-Magriti. *"Picatrix": das Ziel des Weisen.* London: Warburg Institute, 1962.

Quispel, G., trans. *Asclepius: De volkomen openbaring van Hermes Trismegistus* [*Asclepius: The Complete Revelation of Hermes Trismegistus*]. Amsterdam: In de Pelikaan, 1996.

Regardie, Israel. *The Golden Dawn: A Complete Course in Practical Ceremonial Magic.* St. Paul, Minn.: Llewellyn, 1995.

———. *De Boom des Levens: Een studie in de magie.* Amsterdam: Uitgeverij Schors, 1992.

Rhodes, Michael D. *The Hor Book of Breathings: A Translation and Commentary.* Provo, Utah: The Foundation for Ancient Research and Mormon Studies (Brigham Young University), 2002.

Roulin, Gilles. *Le Livre de la Nuit: Une composition égyptienne de l'au-delà.* Göttingen: Vandenhoeck & Ruprecht, 1995.

Schwaller de Lubicz, Ischa. *Her-Bak: The Living Face of Ancient Egypt.* 2 vols. Rochester, Vt: Inner Traditions, 1998.

Schwaller de Lubicz, R. A. *Temple of Man. 2 vols.* Rochester, Vt: Inner Traditions, 1998.

van den Broek, R., and G. Quispel, trans. *Corpus Hermeticum.* Amsterdam: In de Pelikaan, 1996.

Wang, Robert. *The Qabalisitc Tarot: A Textbook of Mystical Philosophy.* York Beach, Maine: Weiser, 1983.

ABOUT THE AUTHOR

Ina Cüsters-van Bergen was born in 1957 in the town of Roermond in the Netherlands. A former artist, she devoted herself from a very young age to her spiritual development. She started her search with yoga and Zen Buddhism, worked with the material of Fritz Perls and Eva Pierakos, and practiced the bioenergetics of Alexander Lowen.

Her search took her through a range of Eastern and Western traditions, until she came into contact with the books of Dolores Ashcroft-Nowicki, who wrote about the Western Mystery Tradition and Ceremonial Magic. This tradition touched her so deeply that she decided to immerse herself in it, and has not stopped since.

After she signed on for the study course of the Servants of the Light School for Occult Sciences, she first progressed to supervisor, then to European co-coordinator, and, as a third-degree adept, founded her own school, the *Ordo Templi Lucis Asterum,* a.k.a. *The Hermetic Order of the Temple of Starlight.* This school became a full-fledged initiating school in the direct line of the Golden Dawn, via Dion Fortune, Ernest Butler, and Dolores Ashcroft-Nowicki.

Ina gives workshops and lectures about the Western Mystery Tradition in several European countries. Her mission is the "Unification of the Two Lands"—connecting the spiritual world with the everyday world around us. She wants the old Mystery texts and techniques to be made accessible to modern people who are interested in practical esotericism. In addition, she wants to give the original temple magic its rightful place within the broad scale of spiritual techniques.

You can find more information about Ina Cüsters-van Bergen and the Hermetic Order of the Temple of Starlight Foundation on the website

www.templeofstarlight.eu
info@templeofstarlight.eu

INDEX